About the Book and Author

Based on formal content analysis of the writings of Admiral Sergei G. Gorshkov and past Soviet ministers of defense and heads of the Politburo, James J. Tritten interprets what the Soviets say they will do in the event of nuclear war. He then constructs a hardware and exercise analysis of the strategic employment of the Soviet Navy in a nuclear war, offering three possible cases--the "bolt from the blue," with existing forces on patrol; full mobilization; and a plausible case of partial mobilization. In addition, Dr. Tritten examines, from a Soviet perspective, concepts of deterrence, the strategic goals and missions of the fleet, nuclear targeting policy, the Sea Lines of Communication (SLOC) disruption mission, and the potential for tactical nuclear warfare limited to the sea. The author concludes by assessing the implications of Soviet politico-military planning for Western defense strategy and arms control.

Commander James J. Tritten is currently assigned as Assistant Director, Net Assessment, in the Office of the U.S. Secretary of Defense.

Soviet Naval Forces and Nuclear Warfare

Weapons, Employment, and Policy

James J. Tritten

Westview Press / Boulder and London

Westview Special Studies in Military Affairs

This Westview softcover edition was manufactured on our own premises using equipment and methods that allow us to keep even specialized books in stock. It is printed on acid-free paper and bound in softcovers that carry the highest rating of the National Association of State Textbook Administrators, in consultation with the Association of American Publishers and the Book Manufacturers' Institute.

All rights reserved. No part of this publication may be reproduced or transmitted in any form or by any means, electronic or mechanical, including photocopy, recording, or any information storage and retrieval system, without permission in writing from the publisher.

Copyright © 1986 by Westview Press, Inc.

Published in 1986 in the United States of America by Westview Press, Inc.; Frederick A. Praeger, Publisher; 5500 Central Avenue, Boulder, Colorado 80301

Library of Congress Cataloging-in-Publication Data
Tritten, James John.
  Soviet naval forces and nuclear warfare.
  (Westview special studies in military affairs)
  Includes index.
  1. Soviet Union--Military policy. 2. Soviet Union.
Voenno-morskoi flot. 3. Nuclear weapons--Soviet Union.
I. Title. II. Series.
VA573.T75 1986   359'.03-0947   86-4037
ISBN 0-8133-7206-2

Composition for this book was provided by the author.
This book was produced without formal editing by the publisher.

Printed and bound in the United States of America

 The paper used in this publication meets the requirements of the American National Standard for Permanence of Paper for Printed Library Materials Z39.48-1984.

6   5   4   3   2   1

Contents

List of Tables xi
Acknowledgments xiii

PART I CONTENT ANALYSIS

    CHAPTER 1   INTRODUCTION 3

    CHAPTER 2   METHODOLOGY 11
                    Previous Investigations 12
                    Data to Be Analyzed 13
                    Hypothesis Testing 17
                    Analysis Mechanics 19

    CHAPTER 3   NAVAL INFLUENCE ON WAR 25
                    Victory in War 26
                    Influence on Outcome of War 27
                    Influence on Course of War 30
                    Means to Influence Outcome and
                        Course of War 31
                    Strategic Missions and Goals 32
                    Strikes 34
                    Findings 34

    CHAPTER 4   FLEET VERSUS SHORE 41
                    Missions 42
                    Soviet Submarine Strikes 43
                    Targets of Soviet Submarine
                      Strikes 43
                    Sea Lines of Communication (SLOCs) . . 48
                    Findings 49

CHAPTER 5	FLEET VERSUS FLEET 53
	Threats from the Sea 54
	Prevention of Attacks on USSR 57
	Protection of the Soviet Fleet 59
	Naval Aviation 60
	Surface Ships 60
	Submarines 61
	The "Blue Belt of Defense" 64
	Findings 65
CHAPTER 6	SOVIET MILITARY STRATEGY 69
	General, Limited Nuclear
	and Conventional War 69
	Deterrence 71
	Withholding 73
	Advantages of Naval Forces 74
	Command and Control 75
	Naval Art Versus Military
	Strategy 76
	Naval Operational Art and Tactics 78
	Latent Lessons of History 79
	Czarist History 80
	World War I 81
	Inter-War Years 82
	World War II 85
	Post-War Era 88
	Value of Historical Analysis 90
	Arms Control Impact 91
CHAPTER 7	FINDINGS OF DECLARATORY POLICY 97
	Bastions 97
	Withholding SSBNs 98
	Targeting 99
	Sea Lines of Communication (SLOC) . . . 100
	Tactical Nuclear War at Sea 101

PART II HARDWARE ANALYSIS

CHAPTER 8	METHODOLOGY 105
CHAPTER 9	STRATEGIC NUCLEAR FORCES 113
	Static Measurements 113
	Dynamic Measurements 125

CHAPTER 10 NUCLEAR THREAT ASSESSMENT 133
            Bolt from the Blue 133
            Mobilization 136
            Surge 139
            Assessment of Counterforce
               Damage to U.S. 142
                  C3 Disruption 142
                  ICBM Pin-Down 143
                  Attacks on Bombers/Naval
                     Bases 144
                  Counterforce Assessment 146
            Assessement of Countervalue
               Damage to U.S. 146

CHAPTER 11 NAVY STRATEGIC NUCLEAR FORCE ISSUES . . . 153
            Withholding 153
            Exercises 156
            Yankee Obsolescence 157
            Ballistic Missiles Versus Fleets 159
            SSBN Air Defense 160

CHAPTER 12 SENSITIVITY ANALYSIS OF NAVY
            STRATEGIC NUCLEAR FORCES 163
            Strategic Missile MIRVing 164
            SLBM Reliability 167
            MIRV and Reliability 169
            SSBN Deployment Areas 170

CHAPTER 13 GENERAL PURPOSE FORCES 175
            Data Base 175
            Task Group Baseline 179
            General Purpose Force Issues 183
            SLOC Mission 189

PART III FINDINGS AND CONCLUSIONS

CHAPTER 14 FINDINGS 197
            Navy Strategic Nuclear Forces 197
               Forward-Based Systems 199
               Long-Range Systems in Soviet
                  Waters 200
               Theater Systems 203

	Miscellaneous Nuclear Issues	204
	Ballistic Missiles Versus Fleets at Sea	204
	Limited Nuclear War/Tactical Nuclear War at Sea	205
	General Purpose Forces	207
	Bastion Defense	207
	Anti-Carrier Warfare	208
	Strategic ASW	209
	SLOCs	210
	Soviet Military Strategy for Deterrence	211
CHAPTER 15	<u>CONCLUSIONS AND IMPLICATIONS</u>	215
	Soviet Political-Military Doctrine	215
	Soviet Military Strategy	222
	Implications for the West	228
	Methodology	233
	Content Analysis	233
	Hardware Analysis	236
	General Comments	237
APPENDIX	Material Used for Content Analysis	239
I.	Pre-Study Period (1956-1964)	239
II.	Research Period (1964-1983)	244
III.	Post-Study Period (1984-1985)	271
INDEX		275

Tables

2.1 The USSR Is a Maritime Power 20

3.1 Strategic Missions/Targeting Associated with Influencing the Course and Outcome of War 35

4.1 Gorshkov's Specified Targets for Soviet Fleet Versus Shore 44

9.1 Soviet Navy Ballistic Missile Submarines (1985) 114

9.2 Strategic Soviet SLBM Launchers (1985) 115

9.3 Possible Static Soviet SLBM Warheads (1985) 117

9.4 Assumed Static Soviet SLBM Warheads (1985) 118

9.5 Static Soviet SLBM Warhead Raw Megatonnage (1985) 119

9.6 Static Soviet SLBM Warhead EMT (1985) 121

9.7 Soviet SLBM Warhead CEP (Meters) (1985) 122

9.8 Soviet SLBM Warhead CMP (1985) 124

9.9   Soviet SSBN/SSB Fleet Assignments
      (1985) 126

9.10 Soviet SSBN/SSB Threat Tabulation
      (1985) 128

10.1 Analytic Probabilities Assumed 133

10.2 Bolt from the Blue (1985) 135

10.3 Mobilization - Yankees Forward
      Deploy (1985) 137

10.4 Mobilization - Yankees Withheld
      (1985) 138

10.5 Surge - Yankees Withheld (1985) 140

10.6 Surge - Yankees Forward Deploy (1985) . . . 141

13.1 General Purpose Active Navy Forces
      (1985) 176

13.2 Northern Fleet Surge/Mobilization
      Threat (1985) 177

13.3 Pacific Fleet Surge/Mobilization
      Threat (1985) 178

13.4 Typical Task Groups 181

13.5 Northern/Pacific Fleet Task Group
      Baseline (1985) 182

Acknowledgments

The author undertook this project initially to satisfy his requirements for a dissertation at the School of International Relations at the University of Southern California. This initial version of the book appeared in December 1984 as "The Strategic Employment of the Soviet Navy in a Nuclear War." The author acknowledged those who assisted in the preparation of that dissertation and once again would like to thank: Dr. Robert Herrick, Michael MccGwire, Captain Wayne Hughes, Dr. Don Walsh, Dr. Robert Friedheim, and Dr. William Van Cleave.

The author also spent two years at the Rand Corporation where he worked on the Rand Strategy Assessment Center. Rand published the content analysis portion of this book as: "Declaratory Policy for the Strategic Employment of the Soviet Navy," P-7005. The author once again thanks Dr. Paul Davis, Dr. Bruce Bennett, Dr. Rose Gottemoeller, Nancy Nimitz, Rear Admiral James Winnefeld, Captain Charles Pease, Mike Kurtz, and especially Marge Behrens for their assistance in the work he conducted at Rand that appears in this book. The International Studies Association is likewise thanked for allowing the author to present the content analysis section of this book at the 1985 Annual Convention. Thanks is given to Michael MccGwire and Dr. Sergei A. Karaganov for their comments at this presentation.

Finally, thanks is given to Ensign Michael Green for acting as the independent auditor for the content analysis and to Cathy Munson for her typing. Opinions or assertions contained herein should not be viewed as official or the views of the Department of the Navy.

James J. Tritten

PART ONE

Content Analysis

1

Introduction

The growth of the Soviet Navy from a coastal defense force, whose participation in World War II was heroic but whose contribution was marginal, to a major fleet has been the subject of an overwhelming amount of analysis and reporting in the past twenty-five years. 1/ A great deal of the literature in the West has been primarily descriptive. Much has involved speculation as to why, how, and when past decisions were made in the Soviet Union regarding their growing navy.

All of the studies eventually tackle the question of the intended use of the fleet in war. At one extreme we have a body of analysts who view the Soviet Navy primarily as the loyal helper of the army, with a primary role of homeland defense and second-strike deterrence. Most of these analysts credit the Soviet Navy with expanded defensive perimeters beyond mere coastal waters, but still see defense as the primary motivating factor for fleet construction. 2/

Some have argued that the USSR has been "forced" to build a blue water fleet in order to react to the offensive strike potential of U.S. and NATO. 3/ Action-reaction obviously implies that U.S. actions can influence Soviet reactions, but it fails to account for inaction-action, action-inaction and other potential combinations. This action-reaction theory has, in turn, been challenged by others who acknowledge the need for homeland defense but stress the actual use of the Soviet fleet in support of peacetime Soviet foreign policy objectives. 4/

Another group argues that the fleet will be used in a future war with the West or in naval diplomacy conflicts over raw materials and resources. 5/ Finally, there are a few analysts who think the fleet may have simply grown by inertia i.e., allocation decisions were made some time ago and have been adhered to regardless of need. 6/

Decision-makers in the West have no lack of well written, logically presented studies which purport to explain what the Russian bear is doing at sea. There appears to be a common thread to all: the predominance of the employment of the Soviet Navy in a nuclear war with the U.S.

Virtually all existing studies account for nuclear war with the U.S. first, since these requirements appear to have priority over all others. If predominance is in fact, given to such nuclear missions, then the USSR is limited in using its navy to whatever fleet capability exists above and beyond that reserved to support nuclear deterrence, participate in Soviet nuclear strikes, and terminate in a nuclear war on terms favorable to the USSR.

This book is primarily concerned with what appears to be the primary role of the Soviet Navy: preparation for or fighting of a nuclear war involving the USSR and the U.S. in which the homeland of each of these nation's is threatened with or subjected to destruction by long-range strategic nuclear systems (as *strategic* is generally used in the West).

The Soviet use of the word strategic is *not* the same as how the West views the term. The Soviet concept of strategic goals, strategic missions, and strategic nuclear forces will be developed fully in the text. Briefly, the author's plan was to begin his investigation with only two major notions: that of (1) war and (2) of deterrence of war. These were the subjects to be researched as they involved the U.S. and USSR and naval forces.

The author used the evidence provided by the Soviets themselves to map his research, i.e., what was it that the Soviets said could influence the outcome of a war, and/or what types of forces did they say they had and actually did have for missions capable of such influence. In the West, such missions and forces are termed as "strategic." In the USSR, long-range nuclear forces are considered strategic, but that other missions and some conventional forces are also "strategic." Part I establishes the logic of what naval forces are to be considered herein and what target base is associated with them before addressing issues of military strategy and employment.

The interaction between Soviet strategic nuclear forces and general-purpose forces is such that the two cannot be considered separate. Although the primary subject of this study is Soviet Navy strategic nuclear forces, questions on the employment of certain general purpose forces in support of these strategic nuclear will also be addressed.

Current studies of the Soviet Navy are primarily based upon (1) limited content analysis or selective extraction of Soviet military/naval writings, (2) micro-hardware analysis, which emphasizes individual ship/aircraft capability, and (3) consideration of deployments and exercises. Each of these methods offers advantages, but each is limited. Some of the best analyses to date blend all three methods. It is the opinion of the author that the present methods employed to analyze the Soviet Navy have not taken advantage of newer techniques that could enhance the analysis. This book will develop a better methodology for future assessments.

Current Western analysts of the Soviet Navy are similar to the general traditional area specialist in the field of international relations. Most analysts of the Soviet Navy are well versed in naval operations and warfare. Most speak Russian, and many have served in Moscow with their national military missions.

In reviewing the work of these traditionalists, one is immediately struck by the absence of international relations quantitative and behaviorist techniques. For example, despite numerous analyses of Soviet literature, none qualify as academic or <u>formal</u> content analysis, i.e. analysis over time, by author, with an accounting for the medium and audience.

The author has been struck by the difference in what various different Soviet authors had to say about the fleet. Army officers do not write the same way about the Soviet Navy as do navy officers. Nor does the Minister of Defense, who is senior in the chain of command to the Soviet Navy Chief. Some analysts have noted these differences in selected periods of high interest, but no one has viewed the literature as a whole over time. The existing analyses of the Soviet Navy literature could be enhanced by an improvement in techniques.

Hardware analysis has been deficient in its failure to quantify the nuclear threat or to aggregate general-purpose forces. The lack of nuclear warfare data is surprising due to the centrality of this issue and the routine use of such techniques by analysts in the strategic nuclear field. The author was not able to find an unclassified aggregation of the general purpose forces of the Soviet Navy into major war-fighting task groups. Existing hardware analysis has only rarely accounted for the potential for mobilization, and has rarely been subjected to sensitivity analysis.

The author is <u>not</u> advocating a wholesale replacement of existing traditional analysis with empirical methods. The sterility of the results of an outside analyst who does not know his subject matter is a major problem in other disciplines where the quantitative specialist attempts to replace the traditional expert.

Problems with gathering and processing raw data to be analyzed are almost insurmountable for a researcher outside of government. In this project, the author had the advantage of utilizing unclassified material and resources generally only available to personnel inside government. In general, this type of data involves the translation of materials for which there are copyright restrictions. These materials are totally unclassified but are unavailable to the general public. 7/

A primary consideration in research is whether to approach data with a theory in mind in order to search for evidence, or whether data can or should be approached without a preconceived theory and findings allowed to simply appear. True inductive reasoning is probably impossible by the analyst who understands the field already. One solution is to test all probable theories and present findings, and to select conclusions, given the weight of evidence and the intuitive knowledge of the area specialist. The author generally presented in the hardware analysis the maximum threat, the minimal threat, and one case in between these extremes.

This book is concerned with two major issues. The first is to consider the strategic employment of the Soviet fleet in nuclear war and deterrence involving the Soviet and American homelands. Second, an important by-product is the creation of a better methodology for analyzing the Soviet Navy. The new methodology will be tested by consideration of these deterrence and war roles.

The existing body of widely held conventional opinions will be challenged directly either to validate official Washington's and other widely held views or to suggest alternatives. Findings will present the range of evidence and the author's selection of the case most likely to match declaratory policy and hardware capability.

The use of the Soviet Navy for peacetime coercive or other naval diplomacy is not the subject of this research, nor should a reader feel that findings or conclusions from this study would be valid in those areas. The methodology to be used to analyze the naval diplomacy problem, however, should be essentially the same as that applied here.

Part I will begin with an detailed explanation of the variety of content analysis used herein. Soviet writings, speeches, etc. are then analyzed to ascertain the Soviet declaratory policy for employment of its fleet in deterrence of or a major nuclear war with the U.S. Where possible, multiple approaches to investigation of the same question will be undertaken to verify evidence. During the content analysis, only passing reference will be made to hardware since the point is to determine what the Soviets say they will do, not what they can or cannot do. It will not be necessary to verify historical facts, only to determine messages conveyed by the use of history (if any). The correctness of historical data is a side issue which is not addressed here.

Once declaratory policy has been established, only then will a cross check be made against hardware capability, deployment, and exercise behavior. This phase (Part II) of the research was done independent of the content analysis and serves as a primary cross check. As an internal verification of hardware capability, sensitivity and contingency analysis will be employed. In doing so, major assumptions with regard to hardware capability and deployment patterns will be varied to see the effect (how sensitive the findings are to variations in assumptions).

Finally, Part III, the evidence will be compared to see if there is an ability to do what they say or if they can do more or less. The search for a doctrine/force mismatch will be integral in the final findings chapter. The findings chapter in Part III will summarize the individual findings that have been more extensively presented at the end of each major section in the analyses chapters. Findings do not introduce any new concepts or ideas, and are tied directly to the evidence presented by the analysis.

In the conclusions chapter, larger issues than those subjected to analysis will be addressed in order to provide implications for the West and policy recommendations. These will include the issues of Soviet military and political-military doctrine and strategy and their concepts of deterrence. Western concepts such as mutual assured destruction (MAD) and various arms control impacts will also be a part of the final chapter.

A definitive answer to the topic is not likely since we cannot know actual Soviet war plans, hence probabilistic answers are given. Since the Soviets openly state they can and will use force for political gain and war is a continuation of politics, it will be assumed that they will choose to do so. The questions of why or when are not addressed herein.

The author also assumed that the Soviets will employ their military forces as they say they will in declaratory policy. Declaratory policy can be ascertained from the writings and statements of key political-military officals in the Soviet Union. The public statements of the senior official of an organization represents the official view of that group. For the purposes of this book, democratic centralism as a Soviet political concept was taken at its stated face value.

The author felt that the campaigns and scenarios likely to be involved in a strategic nuclear war can be identified from the content analysis, hardware and deployment limitations, and exercise behavior. In other words, if the Soviets say they will do something, have the hardware to do it, and practice it, then we should feel entitled to draw conclusions. The most likely employment of multi-purpose naval forces can be determined from their hardware, exercise behavior, and deployment patterns.

The probability of successful outcomes in warfare is beyond the scope of this research. Formal modeling of a strategic nuclear war itself would be a separate research topic, and could be based in part on data and findings contained herein. There is a need for comparison between stated intent and actual capability, which is a prime goal of this study.

NOTES

1. Due to the wide variety of existing bibliographies of secondary sources already in existence, the author has not included one herein. See for example: Myron Smith, <u>The Soviet Navy, 1941-78: A Guide to Sources in English</u>, (Santa Barbara: ABC-Clio, 1980); and William Green, <u>Soviet Nuclear Weapons Policy: A Research Guide</u> (Boulder: Westview, 1986).

2. Robert Herrick, Soviet Naval Strategy: Fifty Years of Theory and Practice (Annapolis: Naval Institute, 1968) remains the best example of this school of thought. The same conclusion is argued more recently. See for example, James Westwood, "Soviet Naval Strategy, 1968-1978: A Reexamination," U.S. Naval Institute Proceeedings/Naval Review 1978, May 1978, pp. 114-127.

3. Michael MccGwire was the leading advocate of this school for many years. Later, MccGwire acknowledged that Soviet Navy forces on forward deployment could also be available for naval diplomacy. See "The Evolution of Soviet Navy Policy: 1960-74," Soviet Naval Policy: Objectives and Constraints, Michael MccGwire, Ken Booth, and John McDonnell, Eds. (New York: Praeger, 1975), p. 520.

4. Soviet Naval Diplomacy, Bradford Dismukes and James McConnell, Eds. (New York: Pergamon, 1979) is the best example of this school. In their conclusions, they argue that the naval diplomacy mission has a higher priority than strategic defense (p. 294) and was the primary motivation for development of the fleet, but then backpedal (p. 295) and admit that they cannot rule out warfighting as the motivating factor. This extremely worthwhile study devotes little attention to the long and short-term effects of naval diplomacy.

5. Robert Hanks, The Unnoticed Challenge: Soviet Maritime Strategy and the Global Choke Points (Cambridge: Institute for Foreign Policy Analysis, 1980); Richard Nixon, The Real War (New York: Warner, 1981), pp. 25-36; Thomas Moorer, "The Worldwide Resources Conflict," Wings of Gold, Fall 1983, pp. 4-5.

6. Bryan Ranft and Geoffrey Till, The Sea in Soviet Strategy (Annapolis: Naval Institute, 1983), p. 11.

7. An example of this type of material is the U.S. Navy translations of Morskoy Sbornik, the main journal of the Soviet Navy. There are other translations like this that are not available to those outside government or contracting organizations.

2

Methodology

The first major goal of this book was to determine the Soviet Union's declaratory policy for the use of naval and other military forces in oceanic theaters in the event of a major (including nuclear) war that involves the superpower homeland, or for the threat of such use. Without access to Soviet war plans, we must rely on unclassified statements by the Soviets that are found in their speeches, articles, books, radio and TV addresses, etc. Using a methodology termed thematic content analysis, the author elucidated the Soviet Union's declaratory policy for the use of naval forces in a "strategic" nuclear war. Declaratory policy is that policy made public so that others may know it.

Primary emphasis is on those naval missions that the author discovered that the Soviets themselves associate with "strategic" nuclear warfare or with succeeding in the attainment of war aims.

Content analysis is a research "technique for making inferences by systematically and objectively identifying specified characteristics of messages." 1/ Simply put, it is a method of observation and measurement of who said what, to whom, and how, in order to infer why it was said and with what effect.

The author selected academic formal content analysis due to the frequent and often valid criticism that many analysts of the Soviet Union have selectively searched for citations to support preconceived conclusions. Instead of being selective and arbitrary, this method allows comprehensive and definitive work without access to official Soviet planning documents.

Themes were selected as the most appropriate unit of analysis. Prior analysis has made extensive use of individual words. Words as a unit of measure is inadequate to measure major military concepts, since context is often overlooked as well as the intended audience.

Analysis based upon words (translated into English) such as "main," "prime," "important," "basic," etc. to describe importance of missions and forces has resulted in much controversy with no real resolution. Word understanding is important in correctly coding themes and will be discussed again later but themes allow us to sidestep problems associated with focusing only on words.

Previous Investigations

In March 1975, Lieutenant Michael Cramer attempted to apply thematic content analysis to the statements of Admiral of the Fleet of the Soviet Union Sergei Gorshkov. 2/ Cramer analyzed some 113 documents and used 50 major themes to investigate Soviet naval and military matters.

C.A.C.I. Inc., completed a study in the fall of 1975 3/ that utilized, among other techniques, content analysis to identify varying Soviet perceptions of U.S. policies. C.A.C.I. used thematic coding and measured importance by frequency of appearance. They concluded content analysis was a highly productive methodology for identifying Soviet perceptions.

C.A.C.I. obtained their data from the U.S. government PASKEY computerized translation files. PASKEY is a data bank of Foreign Broadcast Information Service (FBIS), Foreign Press Digest (FPD) and Joint Publications Research System (JPRS) translations which can be accessed by author or subject and date. PASKEY provided C.A.C.I. with English translations of Soviet statements on desired subjects. This method of obtaining and verifying primary data was also used for this book.

C.A.C.I. also used bureaucratic analysis to distinguish themes presented by Soviet personnel in the varying different levels of the ruling hierarchy. They were able to show that certain classes of speakers appear to have proprietary rights on certain themes.

In some previous analyses of the Soviet Navy, the assumption has been made that Admiral Gorshkov, as Commander-in-Chief (C-in-C) of the Soviet Navy, was articulating approved military policies. Cross checks of similar statements of policy by officials senior to Admiral Gorshkov has generally not been done.

John McDonnell completed a content analysis of the Soviet Navy themes for the Center for Advanced Research at the Naval War College in July 1977. 4/ Unfortunately, the data base was only Morskoy Sbornik, the primary Soviet Naval journal. The primary worth of his research is its procedures to code Soviet source data.

Ketron, Inc. completed an exhaustive study of "Soviet Perceptions of U.S. Antisubmarine Warfare Capabilities," in September 1980. 5/ The Ketron study is useful since one of its themes tracked over time since 1960 was the Soviet perception of their ballistic missile submarine fleet's ability to carry out its wartime missions. Ketron also included appendices extracting key statements that related to their major themes. Their bibliography demonstrated that Ketron recognized the requirement to consider more than just what Admiral Gorshkov has to say in order to analyze naval matters properly.

Two extremely well-written critical examinations have been focused on previous secondary source analyses of the Noviet Navy. 6/ In the first, Frank Stech questions the lack of rigor of current analysts' methodologies. Stech's 1981 technical paper prepared for the Office of Naval Research is required reading for anyone attempting to enter the field and make new contributions.

The second examination was done by Stephen Walt and deals directly with the substance of poor content analysis. 7/ Walt's analysis, prepared for the Center for Naval Analyses, indicates that he shared this author's opinion that existing methodologies are wanting. Walt advocates comparing speakers and tracking themes over time, considering all potential interpretations with examination of the evidence for each.

Data to Be Analyzed

One might question using Soviet open-source statements regarding a future war, since invariably the Soviet context is a war unleashed by the forces of imperialism. In other words, if we take the Soviets at face value, there is no contingency plan for a war that they would start. The author rejects this assertion and views all such statements as attempts to ensure ideological conformity.

According to Marxism-Leninism, if the USSR engages in a war, it must be a just war. 8/ Just wars always involve defense of socialism against imperialism or struggles by oppressed peoples against imperialism or the bourgeoisie. From a doctrinaire standpoint, the Soviet Union cannot initiate a predatory war, and all warfare will be in response to actions taken by an aggressor.

Soviet statements that they would be involved in a war should imperialism unleash one does not mean that we cannot use their declaratory statements, since they can be expected to justify _any_ future war as being brought on by imperialism. Whether or not the first strike by military forces is carried out by either side is not the question; it will be the political conditions that the Soviets will use to justify the war was forced upon them.

This section will present navy roles and missions as articulated by the head of the Politburo, the Minister of Defense, and C-in-C of the Soviet Navy. Under democratic centralism, statements by the head of each organization should be taken as the official position of that group. This is true both while a subject is under discussion and when final decisions are announced.

Debate over policies does exist in the Soviet Union. Lower ranking personnel often advance concepts and advocate varying positions. Once the debate within a particular organization is closed, however, a statement of final policy is generally issued. By tracking the policy positions of the heads of the three prime bureaucratic actors in the chain of command, the author was able to cut through the tons of extraneous material and focus on those items that each leader was willing to identify his name with.

The specific data to be analyzed will be the statements, articles, books, speeches, etc. of the Soviet Navy C-in-C, the serving Ministers of Defense, and the senior member(s) of the Politburo. The time frame will be 1965, subsequent to the removal of Secretary Nikita Khrushchev, until the end of 1983, the approximate date of the death of Yuri Andropov, the subsequent 1984 death of Dmitry Ustinov, the Minister of Defense, and the 1985 retirement of Gorshkov. A post-study validity test was conducted for 1984-1985 and is found in the conclusions chapter in Section III. The study begins in 1965 since the Soviets have told us that a fundamental change in military doctrine occurred following the October 1964 planning session of the Communist Party of the Soviet Union Central Committee. 9/

The statements of each of these leaders at the three levels of the hierarchy provide the views of the Politburo, the Ministry of Defense, and the navy. Within each group, especially the military, there is a vast source of primary data written by other personnel. This data was read by the author but was _not_ formally tracked via thematic content analysis. Where appropriate, comparisons will be drawn between the data used in this book and some of these works of other more junior Soviet authors.

Although these other writings represent an interesting source of information, the object of this section was to identify approved bureaucratic positions and not items of internal debate within groups. This author feels that analysis of Soviet military writings that indiscriminately mixes materials from lower and senior levels is flawed. Due to Soviet democratic centralism, we must separate debate, trial balloons, and minority views from approved positions of policy. This has not been done in many prior studies.

Two different approaches were used to determine the size of the sample to be analyzed. For Admiral Gorshkov, the author attempted to obtain every document authorized by Gorshkov that exists in English. The final Gorshkov total for the specified time-period was 182 primary documents, the largest unclassified collection utilized in any one study that the author is aware of. A full list of all documents is included in the appendix. Rather than footnote all citations, dates will be presented in the text, and the reader can then draw on the appendix to get the full citation. This book generally uses the signed-to-press date for books rather than the publication date itself.

Document authenticity and reliability appears to be without question. Some materials used were taken from Soviet-provided English language sources such as TASS or Embassy press releases, journals published by the Soviets, or publications authorized by the Soviets in the West. For materials that appear in their original version in Russian, the author utilized official U.S. government translations, and, where available, translations commissioned by private sources. Where more than one translation of a document existed, all were read to compare the material. Additionally, 10% of all translations were randomly checked against the Russian originals to verify that they did in fact exist and were attributed to the individual alleged to be the author.

For documents by the Minister of Defense, PASKEY was tasked to provide a printout of all documents that had been coded as containing any navy-related theme. The Ketron study provided similiar citations. The author also did a manual search of party and government meeting speeches, FBIS Daily Reports of Soviet Armed Forces Day, Navy Day, and similar annual materials. A search was made of JPRS indexes and relevent secondary source citations. A total of 66 documents authorized by Ministers of Defense Marshals of the Soviet Union Rodion Malinovskiy, Andrey Grechko, or Dmitry Ustinov were identified as having relevent themes and used for this study. Only documents authorized while these individuals were serving as Minister of Defense and containing navy-related themes were utilized.

Finally the Politburo leader's statements were obtained using the Ketron bibliography, secondary source citations, and a PASKEY search containing passages coded for any navy themes. Some 17 documents by Leonid Brezhnev, Aleksey Kosygin, and Yuri Andropov were used in this study. Documents authored while the individuals were not in the Politburo were not used.

It is not possible to ascertain the completeness of the data base since all materials in the USSR were not available. The final compilation of documents to be analyzed represents, in the author's view, the most comprehensive ever attempted on the questions to be considered.

Some final areas of controversy deserve mention. It is recognized that many or even most of the documents analyzed were not in fact authored by the individual whose name appears as author. For example, Admiral Gorshkov publicly acknowledges those officers who have "assisted" him in the preparation of his book The Sea Power of the State. In fact, they probably wrote the bulk of it. It is the author's view that such "ghost-written" documents represent ideas or concepts that had to be approved by the principal individual or for some reason were issued under the leader's name. It is a common bureaucratic procedure for staffs to prepare rough drafts of speeches or position papers for a principal's approval.

Some types of content analysis that investigate writing style would be useful in identifying the actual author of some documents, but this task is outside the scope of this book. Tracking actual authors would be of interest to other authors since one could then read further materials signed by the ghost writer himself and note differences. This was not done in this book. Only official approved positions were analyzed, not trial balloons or bureaucratic positions to which the principal would not append his name. No matter who actually wrote an article, etc., once the principal's name is on the document, it is his public position.

Another potentially troublesome point was that the research was done using English translations. The author admits that the potential exists for manipulation by translators. 10/ Translations were obtained from a wide variety of government and private sources, including official Soviet translations of materials into English. Where key phrases appeared crucial to the understanding of a point, the author consulted extensively with Russian linguists familiar with defense terminology.

Examples of key words that cause problems in English are: "deterrence," which has no direct Russian counterpart, and "defense." Defense can be taken from the Russian "oborona" or "zashchita." The former implies active military defense, while the latter has been described as a more pacific "shield" or as "protection." 11/ Similar problems occur when trying to translate "mir" into "peace." 12/ Since Russian utilizes no articles, attempts at measuring salience using translations of "the most important" versus "a most important" are also flawed.

A final area of controversy is the value of open-source data at all. All bureaucracies and governments need to communicate positions. Communication up the chain of command often serves to convince superiors, while communication down the chain may serve more to instruct subordinates. External communications may serve to warn. The author rejects the claim that all such open-source communications are propaganda and/or meaningless, since if 100% of all open-source data was a Potemkin village, it would imply that a total covert internal system exists which would be simultaneously performing the same function. The current "Aesopian means" of Russian communications in the open literature originated in Czarist times. 13/

Hypothesis Testing

The author experimented with 41 of Khrushchev's, Malinovsky's, and Gorshkov's writings from 1956 - 1964 in order to test his hypothesis that specific themes could be found, bureaucratic differences noted, and that a time series study was beneficial.

In creating themes, the author let the Soviet literature be his guide. He only brought into the research the limiting parameters of naval involvement and war (especially nuclear war). The author addressed the issue of war first, searching for statements regarding how victory in war is won. From these concepts of what it takes to win a war, he looked for the Soviet's specification of what types of missions and what types of forces were needed to perform those missions. The important distinction is the desire to uncover Soviet perceptions.

Since we cannot exactly think like a Russian without being one, tracing the logical presentation of arguments in their literature is probably the next best thing to actually getting inside their heads. If we are to avoid mirror-imaging concepts, we must use the Russian's concept, phrases, themes, and definitions.

From this initial hypothesis testing, the following lessons were learned and concepts identified: There appeared to be a slight difference in the perceived threat as articulated by the Soviet Navy C-in-C and by his seniors. Admiral Gorshkov appeared to utilize at least one theme (the use of Western navies to support the imperialists' foreign policy goals) that could be viewed as either describing the threat or as explaining how the Soviets could use an ocean-going navy for similar purposes. This theme is singled out since it might be of interest in a follow-on study using formal content analysis for naval diplomacy topics and is indictive of the "reading-in" into the literature that one can easily do.

Gorshkov appeared to follow the Ministry of Defense's lead in the 1956-1964 period on themes of military doctrine and strategy, making only tactful, modest, and subsequent comments. Despite the broad discussion of military doctrine and strategy in the other services during this period, Gorshkov generally remained outside the public debate. The navy primarily appeared to be responsible, however, for questions of naval art and tactics.

Gorshkov's declaratory major wartime roles for the Soviet Navy from 1956-1964 generally followed those previously announced by Khrushchev and Malinovskiy. Interestingly, Khrushchev and Malinovskiy were often very specific about targets for nuclear strikes, while Gorshkov was generally vague. There appeared to be disagreement over which types of forces were to destroy specific enemy naval targets.

The navy appeared to assign a higher status to naval surface and air forces than did the Defense Minister and Khrushchev from 1956-1964. Overall descriptions of the navy by Gorshkov during this period generally used the term "modern" with the capability to perform only "operational" tasks.

Gorshkov in this early period advanced the need for surface ships and aircraft for antisubmarine warfare and to support the striking force and naval forces in defended zones. One of his early articles had what appeared to be a "shopping list" for future weapons procurements. Interestingly, Malinovskiy and not the navy C-in-C first discussed the deployment of submarines under the ice and the need for other forces to provide mutual support for submarine operations.

Finally, regarding history, the author did not attempt to establish the correctness of Gorshkov's view of Russian/Soviet historical references. What was verified, however, was Gorshkov's use of history as a vehicle to make oblique complaints about policies and governmental behavior. A complete analysis of latent historical themes is presented in the chapter on Soviet military strategy since there has been so much made of this by other analysts.

Analysis Mechanics

Thematic reliability was verified by checking the presence of each major theme devised by the author against similar themes used in documents also coded by Ketron, or PASKEY. Additionally, a sample of 5% of documents was selected and subjected to an independent coder with a reliability of 86%. Documents were read sequentially regardless of author. This approach, rather than reading each author separately, aided comparison of the differences in positions and in theme initiation.

To describe the author's methodology, a sample set of manifest themes will be outlined in detail and the analysis explained.

> The USSR/Russia is a great naval/sea/maritime power
> vs.
> The USSR/Russia is a great land/continental power
> vs.
> The USSR/Russia is a great naval/sea/maritime
>   and land/continental power.

As can be quickly seen, the essential difference in these three related themes is whether or not the speaker stated that the USSR/Russia is a great sea, or land, or sea and land power. No latent or hidden meanings need be searched for.

Of the 275 documents used in this study, these three themes appeared 30 times, fairly consistently over the years. Table 2.1 shows the number of appearances for each theme in each indicated year. The total is greater than the sample size due to multiple themes within the same document.

Table 2.1

The USSR Is a Maritime Power

	Sea	Land	Sea and Land
1965	2		
66			
67	1		
68	2		
69	3		
1970	1		
71	3		
72			2
73		1	1
74	1		1
1975	1		4
76	1		
77			
78	1		2
79	1		1
1980			1
81	1		1
82			1
83	1	1	

Source: Author

Obviously, a shift occurred around 1971 to stress both the maritime and continental aspects of Soviet power. The next step in findings is to ascertain who is the author of each document. In the 30 documents that contained these themes, Gorshkov was the author in all but the following four cases:

In July 1971, Minister Marshal Grechko stated that the USSR was the largest continental state and at the same time an enormous maritime nation. He also said in the same article that recent exercises at sea demonstrated that the USSR was a world naval power. In a 1971 book, Grechko again claimed world naval power status for the USSR. The only other use by Gorshkov of any of these themes was Andropov in his 1983 Der Spiegel arms control interview when he said that the USSR was a land power.

Researchers must track both the presence and absence of themes in order to conduct proper analysis. The general absence from Defense Ministry and Politburo spokesman of the theme that the USSR is a sea power is significant. The Minister of Defense has the opportunity to use this theme in his annual Navy Day Order and his failure to do so must be deliberate. Party leaders also could have stated that the USSR is a maritime power during their many arms control policy announcements that deal with submarine launched ballistic missiles (SLBMs).

A pattern of advocacy of the maritime might of the Soviet state by Gorshkov appears rather steadily over time, with minor support by Minister of Defense Grechko and a general absence of support by the Politburo. Despite years of instruction by his navy C-in-C, Chairman Andropov in 1983 described the USSR as a land power.

Further analytic refinement takes place with identification of the object of the communication, or to whom the message was directed. Around half of these themes, were primarily aimed at internal general audiences and around half at an audience composed of primarily military recipients. Only a few were either to foreign locations or from foreign sources. It would thus appear that Gorshkov's message of Soviet sea power status is directed more at an internal audience. It may be concluded that Gorshkov is building a "unity of views" on the need for sea power.

Andropov's remark that the USSR is a land power appeared in a West German magazine, Der Spiegel, and does not appear to have been republished for domestic Soviet consumption. Gorshkov appears to have followed the Andropov remark with a subsequently published rebuttal that the Soviet Union was a sea power, but full investigation reveals that Gorshkov's statement was signed to press six days before the Andropov interview.

Gorshkov's claim of Soviet sea power greatness appears at least as early as July 1958. Khrushchev used the theme of the USSR as a continental power in his Central Committee Report of 1961. Rather than directly criticize Soviet spokesmen who argue that the Soviet Union is primarily a land power, Gorshkov states there are "those in the West" who incorrectly claim that the Soviet Union is a land power and does not need a navy.

Gorshkov refers to Western critics of Russia who falsify history by claiming that all Russia's military victories were on the land and not the sea. Such latent messages using surrogates allows the navy C-in-C to refute current critics of Soviet sea power and to align those critics with the forces of imperialism.

NOTES

1. Ole Holsti, "Content Analysis," Handbook of Social Psychology, 2nd Ed., Vol. II, Garner Lindzey and Elliot Aronson, Eds. (Reading: Addison-Wesley, 1968), p. 601; and Content Analysis for the Social Sciences and Humanities (Reading: Addison-Wesley, 1969), p. 14. The author also referred to: Bernard Berelson, "Content Analysis," Handbook of Social Psychology, Vol. I, Garner Lindzay, Ed. (Cambridge: Addison-Wesley, 1954), pp. 488-518; Fred Kerlinger, Foundations of Behavioral Research, 2nd Ed. (New York: Holt, Rinehard and Winston, 1973), pp. 525-535; and Klaus Krippendorff, Content Analysis: An Introduction to Its Methodology (Beverly Hills: SAGE, 1980).

2. Michael Cramer, "Admiral of the Fleet of the Soviet Union Sergei Gorshkov: An Operational Code and Thematic Analysis," unpublished M.A. thesis at the U.S. Naval Postgraduate School, 1975.

3. C.A.C.I., Inc., "The Application of New Methodologies to Analyze Soviet Perceptions of U.S. Policies," 2 Vols. (Arlington: October 1975); and "Further Methodological Development of Soviet Perceptions Content Analysis," (Arlington: November 1975; reports prepared for DARPA.

4. John McDonnell, "Content Analysis of Soviet Naval Writings" (Newport: Naval War College Center for Advanced Research, July 1977).

5. Ketron, Inc., "Soviet Perceptions of U.S. Antisubmarine Warfare Capabilities," 3 Vols. KFR 293-80, Report prepared for ACDA (Arlington: September 1980 & January 1981).

6. Frank Stech, "Estimates of Peacetime Soviet Naval Intentions: An Assessment of Methods," Technical Report by MATHECH prepared for the Office of Naval Research, March 1981; and Evaluating Intelligence Estimates of Soviet Naval Intentions (Boulder: Westview, 1985/86 forthcoming).

7. Stephen Walt, "Interpreting Soviet Military Statements: A Methodological Analysis," CNA 81-0260.10 (Alexandria: Center for Naval Analyses, Naval Studies Group, December 5, 1983).

8. COL P. A. Sidorov in The Officer's Handbook, MG S. N. Kozlov, Ed. (Moscow: 1971), English translation published under the auspices of the U.S. Air Force as Vol. 13 of the Soviet Military Thought Series, pp. 41-44. See also COL T. R. Kondratkov and MG N. D. Tabunov, "Historical Types of Wars - The Social Nature of Wars of the Modern

Era," <u>Marxist-Leninst Teaching on War and the Army</u>, LTG D. A. Volkogonov, Ed. (Moscow: Voyenizdat, 1984), pp. 36-44. There is no essential change in these views over the years.

9. MG S. A. Tyushkevich, <u>The Soviet Armed Forces: A History of Their Organizational Development</u> (Moscow: 1978), English translation authorized by the USSR and published by the U.S. Air Force as Vol. 19 of the Soviet Military Thought Series, p. 471.

10. John Erickson makes the point: "I fear that many of our 'Soviet experts' do not read Russian and must perforce wait on official translations, which may or may not materialize. They are not captives of 'Soviet disinformation' but rather of our information process and processing." See his "The Soviet View of Deterrence: A General Survey," <u>Survival</u>, November/December 1982, p. 250.

11. See on this point Peter Vigor, "The Semantics of Deterrence and Defense," <u>Soviet Naval Policy: Objectives and Constraints</u>, Michael MccGwire, Ken Booth, and John McDonnell, Eds. (New York: Praeger, 1975), pp. 471-478.

12. Paul Nitze, "The Word and the Woods," <u>Wall Street Journal</u>, March 23, 1984, p. 32; and "Living With the Soviets," <u>Foreign Affairs</u>, Winter 1985/85, pp. 360-374.

13. Robert Herrick private communication with author July 23, 1984.

3

Naval Influence on War

In order to analyze the declaratory role of the Navy in war and armed conflict, a number of methodological decisions were made. First, the literature itself provided the framework for the analysis. The author only enters his research with the desire to investigate a nuclear war involving superpower territory and how that war involved Soviet naval forces. What the Soviets themselves said is what drove the investigation.

Second, there was the question of "victory" in a nuclear war itself. This subject has been raised relative to the concept of a war-winning strategy or being able to fight and "win" a nuclear war. This book is only concerned with what the Soviets say about victory in warfare, not whether or not they could actually win, or, for that matter, whether anyone can win a nuclear war. In fact, the ability to attain victory in war is a frequent claim in the Soviet literature. From the concept of victory, we find the Soviets explaining what is needed to attain it.

The third decision was to let the Soviet literature identify the forces and types of actions that have the ability to influence the course and/or outcome of armed struggle and war. A parallel investigation dealt with the relative importance of the naval or oceanic theaters and served to cross check the evidence developed on the ability to influence war or armed struggle and thus achieve victory.

Another literature cross check had to do with the ability of the fleet to achieve "strategic goals" which by the Soviet own definition, can achieve the aims of war. Both the navy as a whole and specific combat branches of the fleet were analyzed to determine how they related to strategic goals. "Strategic missions" were also investigated to further cross check the ability of the fleet to influence wars or armed struggle.

It is appropriate to make the distinction between the Soviet use of the terms war and armed struggle. "War" includes diplomatic, economic, ideological, military, and other forms of struggle. "Armed struggle" involves the use of armed forces conducting combat activities to resolve strategic missions and attaining strategic goals. 1/ Armed conflict is thus only one part of the overall war effort.

By completing these specific avenues of investigation, it was possible to identify the types of forces and general means for the Soviet Union to attain victory and influence the course or outcome of armed conflict and war.

Victory in War

Victory in warfare is one of the easiest themes to trace in the Soviet literature consulted since it appears that a "canned" phrase is used to describe the concept. Over the past 25 years, the theme "victory can only be achieved by the participation of all armed forces" has consistently appeared in ten of Gorshkov's documents and ten from the Minister of Defense (MOD). The latter is probably only a modest sample, since only navy-related MOD documents were read, we can assume the subject is discussed in others. This phrase does not necessarily state that victory can be achieved, but rather that combined arms is the way to attempt to win a war.

It is interesting that Gorshkov follows the MOD line on military doctrine essentially to the letter. Gorshkov appears far too astute to challenge his superiors directly. His preferred technique is to use subtle shifts in emphasis or to have a more junior officer author an article if the navy differs with official doctrine.

For example, Gorshkov opens his "Navies in War and Peace" series and repeats in The Sea Power of the State that only ground forces can secure the results of victory. In The Sea Power of the State, he adds an additional phrase that victory in a present-day war is only attainable by action of the armed forces. Note, not all armed forces but the armed forces. Perhaps this is the beginning of a view that once a war is in progress, it is best left to the military to complete. According to the Soviet literature, however, the attainment of victory in either war or armed conflict is never associated with the navy alone.

Influence on Outcome of War

Since victory requires the participation of all services, we next need to analyze those services, theaters, or operations that are identified as having the ability to influence the outcome of war. To cross check, the author also investigated statements about which branch(es) of the Soviet armed forces are decisive or can resolutely defeat an enemy.

In 1965, Brezhnev implied in a discussion of types of ramps for rockets that subsurface forces were worthy of ranking with the Strategic Rocket Forces (SRF). In April 1966, Malinovskiy first used the theme that the "dyad" of the SRF and atomic rocket submarines can decisively route the aggressor in war. He used this theme three times in 1966 - 1967. In 1967 Grechko changed the concept by saying that the SRF (alone) was the decisive branch, although the reference to "in war" was dropped. Grechko refers to the SRF alone as the decisive branch at least three times until 1974, when he once again changed the concept by stating that all services had the capability for decisiveness in modern war.

Interestingly, the C-in-C of the navy used the theme of the decisiveness of the dyad (that included the navy) in war until February 1971, well after Grechko had shifted emphasis. Gorshkov directly differed with Grechko's view in a 1969 French naval journal article and in 1971 in a provincial Soviet newspaper. Perhaps this is an indication of the limits of tolerable debate. Apparently more can be said in Western journals or to provincial readers. Gorshkov called strategic missiles (in general), not the Soviet SRF itself, decisive in war in May 1975.

Grechko pairs the SRF and nuclear submarines in a general context in October 1967, soon after he had become MOD. By February 1968, he introduced the theme of a "triad" of Soviet "strategic nuclear forces": the SRF, atomic rocket submarines, and long-range aviation. He did not describe these forces as decisive but rather as warranting special attention.

Grechko is not the first military officer to have discussed the triad. The triad theme appeared at least as early as 1962 in Marshal V. D. Sokolovsky's <u>Military Strategy</u>. 2/ In February 1963 Malinovskiy discussed joint action by the navy, SRF, and air force against land and submarine rocket bases but did not specifically refer to these as "strategic nuclear forces." Reference to a triad of strategic nuclear forces continues today. 3/

Grechko departed from his use of the triad theme at least once. In July 1971, he made reference only to the dyad in the context that both were a reliable "shield" protecting the world socialist system. This anomaly appeared in Grechko's article in Morskoy Sbornik.

Admiral Gorshkov preferred to use the dyad theme (14 instances) to describe a (or the) main or primary Soviet military forces rather than the triad (3 instances) or the SRF alone (3 instances). Gorshkov makes a further claim, starting in February 1967, that the dyad is a (or the) most important weapon of the Supreme Command. In 1962 Sokolovsky stated it was the triad which would fulfill tasks of the Supreme High Command and attain victory. 4/ Gorshkov repeats through May 1970 the special role of dyad to the Supreme High Command. In February 1974 and November 1977, Gorshkov expanded the claim even further by stating that the Soviet Navy is a major strategic weapon of the Supreme High Command. Both statements, however, would have had a predominantly naval audience and the context was not the navy alone but rather the navy also.

Gorshkov stated in February 1974 that the Soviet Navy is able to substantially influence the outcome of an armed struggle. Note that the reference is to armed conflict and influence, not war and decisiveness. The claim is diluted by adding that it applies only to conflicts on great ocean and continental theaters of military operations. He did not state that the Soviet Navy can achieve victory in war.

In September 1977, Gorshkov states that the modern navy can influence the course and outcome of a war when operating against coastal objectives. It is not clear if his reference is to navies in general or the Soviet Navy. He also said the Soviet Navy and the SRF were capable of influencing the course of warfare (not the outcome), in vast theaters of military operations and referred to nuclear powered ballistic missile submarines (SSBNs) as strategic nuclear forces.

Gorshkov uses another technique to convey messages when he discusses the theoretical importance of navies and naval theaters in future wars. These passages cannot be directly tied to the Soviet Navy or the USSR. In seven documents, the C-in-C cites both the relative and absolute growth in importance of naval warfare in the future. Neither the MOD nor Politburo spokesman use this theme.

Gorshkov claimed in 9 distinct citations from 1974 - 1979 that naval forces/theaters in general will have an influence on the outcome of war. Gorshkov claimed influence in armed struggles three additional times. These claims on the ability to influence war appear in Gorshkov's books and Soviet Navy journal articles.

Generally, Gorshkov fails to identify the specific means by which armed struggles and wars will be influenced by naval forces/in naval theaters when discussed in theoretical terms. In three of these cases, however, Gorshkov states that operations involving fleets versus shore can influence the outcome of a war in continental theaters. In the other two cases, he identifies general strikes from the sea as being able to influence armed struggle. In all of these discussions of theoretical naval forces and theaters, the anticipated audience is military and primarily naval.

Sokolovskiy's <u>Military Strategy</u> contains an oft cited passage that military operations in naval theaters can hardly have a decisive effect on the outcome of a future world war. 5/ More complete analysis reveals that this passage is found as only one part (the general naval section) of a discussion of the four types of strategic operations. Rocket-carrying submarines were included earlier under the triad of strategic nuclear forces. Sokolovsky credits this triad with the capability of having decisive primary significance in the outcome of a modern war. 6/

We can thus conclude that according to Soviet military strategy, the ultimate means of defeating an aggressor will be the triad of strategic nuclear forces. All forces, however, will have a role in the attainment of victory and the ground forces will naturally have to actually occupy territory in order to consolidate the results of victory. The Navy C-in-C appears reluctant to articulate the role of the Soviet air forces have in contributing to the outcome of a war. He also inflates the role of the navy, often using theoretical discussions instead of direct claims.

The role of the Soviet Navy in the outcome of war is probably the best example of the differences in view depending upon the bureaucratic position of the speaker. The Politburo leaders analyzed do not appear to single out the navy as a whole but do accord the missile submarines special treatment. The MOD appears to have equated the SRF and sub force up until February 1968, at which time the reference shifts to the strategic nuclear triad. Gorshkov generally emcompases to the entire navy rather than specifically the submarine force when discussing significant roles and missions for the fleet.

Influence on Course of War

In August 1968, Gorshkov published an article in the German Democratic Republic which stated that after the strategic missile troops, the Soviet Navy was a (or the) most important instrument for exerting a decisive influence on armed conflict in theaters of war involving great distance. The theme does not claim equal status with the SRF nor the ability to decisively conclude a war, nor is the ability to influence universal. Influence on armed conflict is, by its nature, only influence on the course of a war.

Gorshkov states in February 1974 that the Soviet Navy can "substantially influence both the course and the outcome of armed conflict in oceanic and continental theaters." By April of the following year, Gorshkov waters down this claim to: Soviet naval strategic forces can have a decisive effect on the course of major operations occurring in theaters of war of great breadth and depth, including distant continents.

Gorshkov claims in July 1975 and November 1977, that the Soviet Navy can have a crucial effect on the course of armed conflict, mainly to military audiences. In his September 1977 booklet The Navy, Gorshkov says that the introduction of nuclear missiles and the impact it had on the fleet versus shore capability allows the modern navy to influence the course and even the outcome of a war. It is not clear from the context if the admiral was referring to the Soviet Navy or to navies in general.

Gorshkov also uses theoretical discussions of the influence of navies on the course of wars. In 17 different citations found in 7 documents, the navy C-in-C discusses the ability of fleets and naval theaters in general as being able to influence the course of war. Grechko even once refers to navies as being able to "have an enormous impact on the entire course of a future war."

Gorshkov is generally vague about which theaters of operation can be influenced. As in the theoretical discussion of navies influencing the outcome of a war, influence on the course of a war is generally used for navy audiences.

The last time Gorshkov directly stated that the Soviet Navy had the ability to influence the outcome of armed conflict (not war) was in 1974. The last time he discussed the theoretical possibility of navies being able to do this was in 1979. Since then, articles and books from other authors have stated that the Soviet Navy can influence the course (not the outcome) of a war. 7/

Means to Influence Outcome and Course of War

Although Gorshkov is distinctly vague about the specific theaters of operations in which naval warfare might be influential on a war or armed conflict, one can infer the theaters from his discussion of the means to attain influence. To influence the outcome of a future war, navies (in general) can: (1) crush an opponent's military-economic potential, (2) participate in fleet versus shore operations, or (3) destroy major groupings of the enemy. In the first and third, one can assume either oceanic or land targets. To influence the course of armed conflict or war, two additional means are identified: (1) fleet operations against the enemy's nuclear potential at sea and (2) atomic missile submarines versus shore.

Taking these themes and measuring salience by repetition, we find the following evidence. The major specific concept appears to be crushing military-economic potential, used six times evenly split between having an influence on the course and the outcome. Fleet versus shore (in general) was used eight times (three instances of influence on the outcome and three on influence on the course of warfare). Destruction of major enemy groupings is used three times, with only two citations that this can influence the outcome of war or armed conflict.

In addition to this quantitative assessment, it must be noted that Gorshkov claimed in July 1974 that the fleet versus shore role is a (or the) primary mission of navies in general and the Soviet fleet in particular. The controversy over whether or not Admiral Gorshkov was referring to navies in general or the Soviet Navy in this Pravda article was cleared up in his June 1975 Soviet Military Review interview in which the Soviet provided English translation includes that the "main task of the Navy today is to deliver attacks on ground objects." 8/

Gorshkov states in the introduction of The Sea Power of The State that direct action from the sea on vital centers of the shore can crush the military-economic potential of an enemy. In September 1977, Gorshkov specifically states that Soviet naval art clearly defines the two main missions of the Soviet Navy as fleet versus shore and fleet versus fleet. He says that the Soviet Navy's operations against the shore are dominant. Ballistic missile submarines, he adds, are a (or the) main component of the world's leading navies, including the Soviet Navy.

Strategic Missions and Goals

"Strategic missions" is a general phrase used by the Soviets to describe missions that can change the situations in vital sectors or theaters and thus attain strategic goals that impact upon the war as a whole or upon a theater of operations. 9/ The Soviet use is different than Western use, and mirror-imaging of the U.S. concept must be avoided.

Armed conflict is the means by which Soviet armed forces resolve strategic missions and attain strategic goals. Strategic goals, by definition, impact on the war as a whole. Gorshkov theoretically discusses the value of "strikes" and states that they can be used to achieve the strategic goals of crushing military-economic potential and shattering enemy nuclear sea power.

A number of Soviet documents specify the strategic missions necessary to attain strategic goals (and thus victory) in a future war. 10/ The list of strategic missions includes (1) strikes by strategic nuclear forces, (2) strategic operations on the continental theater, (3) strategic operations in naval theaters, and (4) operations to repulse or defend the nation from enemy strikes.

Admiral Gorshkov in 29 documents since 1959 that the Soviet Navy (as a whole) is capable of performing strategic missions. In 17 individual citations, the C-in-C associates strategic with general Soviet naval operations in oceanic theaters. In nine passages, strategic is associated with the delivery of blows on distant, primarily land targets. In seven cases, strategic is associated with countering aggression from the sea or protecting Soviet installations. In Gorshkov's booklet, The Navy, the fleet mission against enemy sea-based strategic weapons is described as "one of the main" missions and is designed to "weaken their attacks to the maximum extent possible."

In some of the passages, we find specific Soviet missions that contain phrases resembling those in Gorshkov's theoretical treatment of the ability to influence the outcome or course of armed struggles/wars or to attain strategic goals. For example, Gorshkov's specific Soviet Navy strategic missions are (number of times mentioned in parenthenses): delivery of blows against ground targets (8), preventing/countering aggression from the sea (4), actions against enemy ballistic missile submarines (4), protecting own installation (2), defense of the border (1), and unspecified operations at sea (12).

"Strategic" is also a descriptor associated with the capability of individual branches of the Soviet fleet. Marshal Malinovskiy associates in 1966 and 1967 rocket submarines with strategic tasks. In October 1967, the Soviet Navy Chief states that the subsurface, air, and surface branches were all capable of strategic missions.

It is only in 1971 that Gorshkov associates the Soviet submarine force (alone) with the term strategic. In eight subsequent citations, the Navy C-in-C credits Soviet submarines either with the capability of striking strategic targets or performing strategic missions. In three documents Gorshkov clearly states it was the equipping of submarines with nuclear warheaded submarine launched ballistic missiles (SLBMs) with ranges of thousands of kilometers that gave these ships a strategic capability. In two cases, the reference involves the strategic task of Soviet atomic submarines against an enemy fleet. In two cases, Soviet submarine ballistic missiles are associated with strategic targets ashore.

In seven additional citations, Gorshkov discusses the theoretical capability of submarines (in general) associated with the word strategic. In these cases, he is more specific than when discussing Soviet submarines. For example, in December 1974, he states that a single missile submarine can achieve strategic goals by making strikes against land targets. When this same sentence is recycled and used in The Sea Power of the State, the reference to the capability of a single combat unit is deleted.

In other passages concerning the theoretical capability of submarines (in general), strategic goals are associated with blows on targets ashore and nuclear submarines are called a "strategic resource" capable of blows against submarines and surface ships of the enemy and important targets ashore.

Gorshkov also associates strategic with other Navy combat branches. He associates strategic missions once even to surface ships in a passage that also mentions aviation and submarines. In four documents, Gorshkov pairs Soviet submarines and naval aviation and associates them with strategic missions.

In both editions of The Sea Power of the State, Gorshkov specifically credits Soviet submarines with ballistic and cruise missiles and missile-carrying and antisubmarine (ASW) aircraft with strategic missions in oceanic and continental theaters. These forces are then associated with a capability to strike and undermine the military-economic potential of an enemy and shatter his nuclear sea power. The specific targets of these strikes are given as military-industrial and administrative centers and the nuclear missile groupings of the enemy at sea.

These passages from The Sea Power of the State represent an excellent source letting us infer the use of Soviet naval forces in terms that were previously used to describe the ability to influence the course and outcome of wars. These passages bridge the gap between Gorshkov's theoretical discussions and his roles for Soviet forces. 11/

Strikes

The term strikes is frequently used by the Soviets to describe actions taken in combat. Gorshkov description of strikes in theoretical terms, includes their ability to achieve tactical, operational, and strategic goals Gorshkov relegates "battle" to the mere attainment of tactical goals. In eight passages that consider the theoretical role of strikes, Gorshkov directly associates such strikes with strategic goals in terms which were identified earlier as being the means of influencing the course and outcome of wars. Gorshkov stated that strikes can achieve strategic goals by devastating military-economic potential and shattering nuclear sea power. In addition, he specifically states that submarine missile strikes against land targets can achieve strategic goals.

Findings

By considering the Soviet literature treatment of types of targets, means of delivery associated with strikes and strategic missions, and by viewing these together with the ability to influence the course and outcome of wars, and attain strategic goals, it is possible to create an initial matrix of the declaratory policy for the strategic employment of the Soviet Navy in a major war. Table 3.1 presents this matrix. The means of delivery are in the left vehicle column; the horizontal column on top itemizes the means of influencing wars and attaining strategic goals. The center matrix lists specific targets and the number of times this theme is used. The means to influence wars and attain strategic goals do not always involve nuclear weapons.

Table 3.1

Strategic Missions/Targeting Associated with Influencing the Course and Outcome of War

Means of Delivery	Fleet vs. Shore (primary means)	Crush Military-economic Potential	Enemy Groupings (enemy nuclear sea power)
Soviet Fleet	8	1 military bases 1 acquiring capability to participate in such operations 4 prevent/counter aggression from sea	4 enemy rocket subs 1 enemy fleet
Soviet SSBNs/SSGNs/Missile and ASW Aircraft	2	2 strikes against military industrial, and administrative centers/undermine military economic potential	2 nuclear strikes against missile groupings/shatter nuclear sea power
Soviet Submarine			
-- Spokesman Gorshkov	2 strategic target	possibility implied	2 enemy fleet (by atomic submarines)
-- Spokesman MOD (submarines with rockets)	2 targets ashore	possibility implied	2 targets at sea
Submarines in General			
-- Submarines by missile strikes	3		
-- atomic submarines	2 important targets	possibility implied	2 enemy surface ships/submarines
Strikes in General	3 (by submarine with missiles)	4	2 shatter nuclear sea power 1 major groupings

Source: Compiled by author. Number indicates individual citations mentioning targets.

35

A sharp difference appears between the declaratory policy of the MOD and the C-in-C of the Soviet Navy. Gorshkov appears to give credit to the fleet as a whole, while the Defense Ministry appears to favor discussion of submarines with missiles. There is a correlation between this matrix and Gorshkov's often cited basic missions of great power navies in nuclear war. In February 1973, Gorshkov listed these primary missions as the participation in attacks by a nation's strategic nuclear forces, the blunting of nuclear attacks from the sea, and cooperation with ground forces in their operations on the continental theaters. In his booklet The Navy, Gorshkov lists the Soviet Navy's main missions as "operations against an enemy fleet and against a hostile shore."

To further investigate the question of role navies and naval theaters in a major war, further considerations must be given to types of targets and the means of destruction. It is to these questions that the next two chapters turn — consideration of the fleet versus shore mission and that of the fleet versus fleet. In doing so, themes that were identified in this chapter drove the investigation of new areas. For example, the military-economic potential of a nation needed to be investigated in terms that would make likely targets obvious. 12/

NOTES

1. Dictionary of Basic Military Terms, COL-GEN A. I. Radziyevskiy, Ed. (Moscow: Voyenizdat, typeset April 1965), English translation published under the auspices of the U.S. Air Force as Vol. 9 of the Soviet Military Thought Series, items 351 and 1428. See also LTG D. A. Volkogonov Marxist-Leninist Teaching on War and the Army (Moscow: Voyenizdat, signed to press September 30, 1983), pp. 26-27.

2. Marshal of the Soviet Union V. D. Sokolovskiy, Soviet Military Strategy, Ed. with analysis and commentary by Harriet Fast Scott (New York: Crane, Russak & Co., 1975), p. 282 used the "triad" concept in conjunction with decisive weapons.

3. Marshal of the Soviet Union N. V. Ogarkov, "Guarding Peaceful Labor," Kommunist, July 1981, pp. 80-91; Always Ready to Defend the Fatherland (Moscow: Voyenizdat, signed to press January 26, 1983), pp. 34 and 49; "Reliable Defense for Peace," Izvestiya, Morning Ed., September 23, 1983, pp. 4-5; and "The Defense of Socialist Experience of

History and the Present Day," *Krasnaya Zvezda*, 1st Ed., May 9, 1984, pp. 2-3. At the time, Ogarkov was the Chief of the General Staff and the ranking professional Soviet military officer. He did not claim decisiveness for the triad, but rather that strategic nuclear forces allow top-level military leadership to have a capability of significantly influencing the "achievement of strategic and political-military war aims and objectives." Michael Deane, Ilana Kass, and Andrew Porth have attempted to argue that Ogarkov was referring to a dyad and not a triad in his 1981-82 writing. See "The Soviet Command Structure in Transformation," *Strategic Review*, Spring 1984, pp. 63 and 69. There are a number of additional Soviet sources that support the view that the Soviets themselves think in terms of a triad. See for example: GEN V. F. Tolubko, C-in-C of the SRF, interview on Moscow Domestic Service at 1000 GMT on August 28, 1982; MG V. Samoylenko, "Ensuring Our Own and Our Allies Security," *Krasnaya Zvezda*, 2nd Ed., December 9, 1983, pp. 2-3; Marshal of the Soviet Union S. Sokolov, "Reliable Guarantee of Peace and Socialism" *Izvestiya*, Morning Ed., December 24, 1983, p. 3; Marshal of the Soviet Union S. Akhromeyev, Chief of the General Staff, "On Guard Over Peace and Socialism," *Krasnaya Zvezda*, 2nd Ed., February 22, 1985; and the charts used by Marshal Akhromeyev in the October 22, 1985 press conference reported by FBIS.

4. Sokolovskiy, *Soviet Military Strategy*, p. 282.
5. Sokolovskiy, *Soviet Military Strategy*, p. 299.
6. Sokolovskiy, *Soviet Military Strategy*, p. 282, 288-289. Although Sokolovskiy made the claim that nuclear weapons and the triad were decisive, Ogarkov today has rejected this claim (see above citations). There appears to have been a debate on this issue over the years. See MG S. A. Tyushkevich, *The Soviet Armed Forces: A History of Their Organizational Development* (Moscow: 1978), English translation authorized by the USSR and published by the U.S. Air Force as Vol. 19 of the Soviet Military Thought Series, pp. 460 and 473. Tyushkevich credits the SRF alone " . . . as the principal and decisive means of achieving the goals of a war . . . ".
7. Tyushkevich, *The Soviet Armed Forces*, p. 475, credits the navy. LTG M. M. Kir'yan, Ed., *Military-Technical Progress and the USSR Armed Forces* (Moscow: signed to press July 8, 1982), p. 289, credits nuclear powered missile carriers with the capability of influencing the course of a war. VADM K. Stalbo recently wrote that navies were only capable of exerting an often-times

decisive influence on the course of a war. See his "Some
Issues of the Theory of the Development and Employment of
the Navy, Morskoy Sbornik, April 1981, p. 25. James
McConnell's "Analyzing the Soviet Press - Spot Report
No. 1: The Irrelevance Today of Sokolovskiy's Book
Military Strategy, Research Memorandum 85-35 (Alexandria:
Center for Naval Analyses, May 1985) fails to account for
all the literature evidence yet reports that the Soviet
literature evidence includes that their SSBNs would
be decisive on the outcome of a war.

8. This point was raised by Michael MccGwire in
"Naval Power and Soviet Oceans Policy," Soviet Oceans
Development, a compendium of papers prepared by the
Congressional Research Service for the Committee on
Commerce and the National Ocean Policy Study, U.S. Senate,
94th Cong., 2nd Sess., Committee Print (Washington: U.S.
Government Printing Office, October 1976), p. 178. It is
always possible that the Soviet translators made an
error in their Soviet Military Review article, but the
sentence includes another reference to the role of navies
in general. It would appear that the capitalization was
deliberate and the reference is to the Soviet Navy.

9. Dictionary of Basic Military Terms, items 1465
and 1472. See also MG V. Kruchinin, "Contemporary Strategic
Theory on the Goals and Missions of Armed Conflict,"
Voyennaya Mysl', October 1963, pp. 13-14. An interesting
correlation is made by cross-checking goals that can be
achieved by the fleet as articulated by Gorshkov, and
those attainable by the SRF. According to Tyushkevich,
The Soviet Armed Forces, p. 460, the SRF can (1) undermine an enemy's military and economic potential, (2)
annihilate their strategic means of nuclear attack, and
(3) destroy main military groupings.

10. Sokolovskiy, Soviet Military Strategy, pp. 285
and 288-303; Kruchinin, "Contemporary Strategic Theory on
the Goals and Missions of Armed Conflict," pp. 19-20; MG
V. Zemskov, "Characteristic Features of Modern Wars and
Possible Methods of Conducting Them," Voyennaya Mysl',
July 1969, p. 20; Kir'yan, Military-Technical Progress
and the USSR Armed Forces, p. 315; and B. V. Panov et
al., The History of Military Arts, (Moscow: Voyenizdat,
signed to press October 28, 1984), p. 462. This latter
source clearly refers to the listing being valid during
the 1960s, hence this area will need additional research
in the future.

11. This bridging is necessary since in at least
one 1963 Voyennaya Mysl' article a General officer goes to

great lengths to explain that performing strategic missions by themselves might not have a decisive effect on the entire course of an armed conflict. See Kruchinin, "Contemporary Strategic Theory on the Goals and Missions of Armed Conflict," p. 14.

12. <u>Dictionary of Basic Military Terms</u>, item 312 defines the military-economic potential of a nation only in general terms. A more explicit definition can be found in MG S. A. Tyushkevich, "The Military Power of the State," <u>Marxist-Leninist Teaching on War and the Army</u>, pp. 211-212: that which can satisfy immediate needs of the armed forces and is concerned with the ability of the national economy to transition from peace to a war posture.

4

Fleet Versus Shore

The mission of fleet versus shore was identified by Admiral Gorshkov as the primary mission of fleets in general and the Soviet Navy in particular. Fleet versus shore has also been directly tied to the admiral's theoretical treatment of methods whereby navies in general can influence the outcome of wars. The fleet versus shore mission includes crushing the military-economic potential of an enemy which itself is a strategic goal and thus capable of impacting on a war as a whole.

The means, methods, and targets whereby the fleet versus shore (and crushing military-economic potential) mission can be carried out depended upon the speaker. Submarines with rockets against shore targets constitutes the one means accepted by <u>all</u> levels of the bureaucracy.

Admiral Gorshkov's descriptions of Soviet naval means to perform fleet versus shore missions include atomic submarines with ballistic (SSBN) and cruise missiles (SSGN) and missile and antisubmarine (ASW) aircraft, as well as the fleet as a whole. Gorshkov's generalities about means of undermining the military-economic potential of an enemy often include both operations against shore targets and also at sea targets.

This chapter will attempt to infer from the literature (1) what is specifically meant by fleet versus shore, (2) what means are to be utilized that are of sufficient magnitude to be able to influence the outcome of a war or attain a strategic goal and (3) what targets, if any, have been specified. The discussion of <u>when</u> fleet versus shore missions take place in a war are included in the chapter on Soviet military strategy.

Missions

The concept of fleet versus shore operations explained by Gorshkov in The Sea Power of the State includes a number of traditional general fleet missions that do not meet the test of being strategic nor are associated with strikes. These are amphibious landings, shore bombardment by guns from naval ships, and general assistance to the ground forces. These missions may be important but, do not appear in the Soviet literature associated with the ability to influence the outcome of a war. Hence, no analysis will be undertaken of Soviet Navy surface ships in a fleet versus shore role.

Since Gorshkov did refer to Soviet naval missile and ASW aviation as being able to perform strategic missions, a literature search was made to ascertain any declaratory policy for the use of Soviet naval aircraft in a direct fleet versus shore mission. The future combat utilization of Soviet Naval Aviation is discussed in some 41 primarily Gorshkov documents since 1961. One finds reference to an anti-shore mission in only a few.

There are two references by Gorshkov in July 1968 that Soviet Naval Aviation has a mission to strike land targets. In The Sea Power of the State, the C-in-C states in general, aviation attacks by fleets against fixed shore targets are now the exception. In September 1977, Gorshkov says that the appearance of SSBNs allowed naval aviation to redirect its efforts strictly to warfare at sea. In a widely distributed press release in Fall 1982, the admiral specifically stated that Soviet Naval Aviation was not intended for use against the American continent. 1/

Naval aviation strikes against ships in port or bases are considered by the Admiral to be a part of fleet versus fleet. Thus we can conclude Soviet Naval Aviation does not have a declaratory mission in direct strikes ashore, hence will not be considered herein.

According to the literature, the primary method of fleet versus shore strikes is the submarine missile. Gorshkov says they will be used to strike at strategic and economically important land targets. Ballistic and cruise missiles are both considered. Targeting objectives were analyzed to illuminate which may be considered part of military-economic potential.

Although one would not expect to find operations at sea in the general category of fleet versus shore, the disruption of the sea lines of communication (SLOC) will be considered in this chapter. Gorshkov states in

The Sea Power of the State that such operations are aimed at "undermining the military-economic potential of the enemy" and form "part of the general system of operations of a fleet against the shore."

Soviet Submarine Strikes

The wartime role of Soviet submarines to conduct strikes at land targets is a theme which appears in the statements of Alexey Kosygin and Marshals Malinovskiy and Grechko. In eleven documents from Politburo or Defense Ministry spokesman that discuss Soviet fleet versus shore, 100% specified submarines as the means, with all but one specifying in addition, submarine missiles. A check of similar citations from senior officials prior to 1965 reveals the same patterns, with four specific passages of submarines as the means for strikes ashore and only two vague references of unspecified Soviet naval forces.

When the spokesman is the Soviet Navy Chief, a much different pattern emerges. Gorshkov only singles out Soviet submarines (alone) as the means in 17 out of 44 citations. Submarine missiles are specified by him 11 additional times. Gorshkov describes the means for distant blows as the fleet (18 citations) or Soviet Navy missiles (3 citations) in general. There are two cases in which Gorshkov discusses strikes ashore by both the Strategic Rocket Forces (SRF) and navy missiles. To distinguish between the targets for each, it was necessary to search the literature for strikes by the SRF alone in order to compare what it is they will do.

Gorshkov also discusses fleet versus land targets in a theoretical sense without specific reference to the USSR. In 6 out of 15 such citations, submarines are given as the means of delivery. Since no other fleet branch has been given a declaratory role in strikes against distant shore targets, it does not appear that the use of general or vague means in nine cases is an attempt to describe other forces.

Targets of Soviet Submarine Strikes

In the citations that discuss the means of delivery of submarine and general fleet blows ashore, we find numerous references to types of targets. In 17 Politburo/ Minister of Defense (MOD) citations since 1958 referring to fleet strikes against the shore, we find the following targets: general (11), strategic or vital (3), and military (3). These latter (all earlier than 1965) include two cases of submarine missiles against naval and land bases and one of the joint action by the strategic nuclear triad against land and submarine rocket bases.

Admiral Gorshkov's statements contain more explicit targeting information. Gorshkov's targets are displayed in Table 4.1. Although most of the targets are general, like those given by the Politburo or MOD, we can learn a lot from the cases that are specific.

Table 4.1
Gorshkov's Specified Targets For
Soviet Fleet Versus Shore

Targets Means of Delivery	General	Strategic Vital Important	Administrative Political	Econimic	Military	Springboards Overseas Bases
Submarines	4	3				
Submarine Missiles (SLBMs)	9 4	4 3				
Navy Missiles	3				1	
Fleet in General	7	1		1	8	2
Aviation and Subs a/					2	
Aviation and Sub Missiles a/			2	2	2	
SRF and Navy Missiles	2					2

a/ Aviation portion of this assumed to be at sea.

Source: Author

Under the category of administrative-political targets, Gorshkov specified targets on the coast and deep in enemy territory. These passages are associated with Soviet atomic-powered submarines armed with ballistic (SLBM) and guided (SLCM) missiles as well as Soviet Naval Aviation, and included targets at sea as well. Since the aviation portion probably had to do with sea targets, hence, we can conclude the means of submarine missile strikes ashore is either is SLBMs or SLCMs.

Gorshkov declared in a July 1971 speech that "winged rockets" were primarily for use against sea targets, while submarines (no means specified) could hit enemy strategic targets at distances of 1,000 kilometers. In the first edition of The Sea Power of the State, Gorshkov states that SLCMs were initially developed by navies for use against surface ships and land targets, but he drops land targets in the second edition. 2/ From this discussion, we can conclude that the current means for targeting administrative-political centers and other land targets is the SLBM and not the SLCM.

Gorshkov twice makes reference to economic targets, the military-economic potential and military-industrial centers in coastal areas and deep inland. A third reference is that the Soviet Navy is in the process (February 1973) of acquiring the capability to crush the military-economic potential of an aggressor. Military-economic potential targets and military-industrial centers are sufficiently vague as to be taken as military, industrial, or military-related industrial.

Two direct military references come from Polish and Bulgarian articles where the passage specifies the targets ashore "that which comprises the nucleus of military might." From the context, it appears that Gorshkov is arguing for such a role, not announcing one. This seems illogical, since the intended audience would not include the Party or Soviet military, but it may have to do with the latitude given publications outside the USSR. Of the remaining nine instances of military targets, three specify bases, and the remainder are vague. The theme of fleet versus shore strikes against military targets received concentrated repetition between 1968-1972. During that time, it was directed to either general Soviet or foreign audiences and not the Soviet military.

The final category of targets is found in two 1967-1968 references to overseas enemy territory and two references in The Sea Power of the State to targeting springboards for attacks against the USSR. The means of attacking such bases are given as both SRF and navy missiles. Earlier Soviet Navy targeting identified by Gorshkov included one case (May 1963) where the intended targets were military bases including those in the North, Baltic, and Mediterranean Seas.

Thus Gorshkov's declaratory plan for the Soviet fleet to influence the outcome of war and attain strategic goals by SLBM strikes at shore targets appears to include at least: administrative-political centers, military targets, industrial centers associated with military potential, and bases that constitute a springboard for enemy attack.

As a cross check of this specific Soviet Navy targeting, reference to 15 discussions of the theoretical use of navies against shore installations reveals that important economic targets are twice associated with strikes by submarine missiles. There are also three vague references to the need to destroy weapons stores.

Marshal Grechko utilized the device of the theoretical strikes by navies in his July 1971 Morskoy Sbornik article. The Defense Minister stated that navies, in general, could deliver powerful strikes against military targets and troop dispositions. The specific means for such attacks were not given.

Targeting for the SRF was also investigated since the SRF was included in at least one passage in connection with navy missiles. Since the SRF was not the primary focus of this research effort, documents used probably represent only a modest portion of all that contain SRF targeting themes. The data is presented since it contrasts with Navy targeting in detail.

A January 1960 Khrushchev speech made general reference to the Soviet armed forces being able to deliver distant strikes on land targets. In an indirect passage from the same speech, Khushchev threatened destruction of capitals and administrative and industrial centers. On the very next day, the MOD repeated these themes and added enemy armed forces as a target. The MOD also illustrated the possible destruction of political, administrative, and industrial centers in a theoretical nation whose size equated to that of a larger European country.

By 1961, Malinovskiy expanded his discussion of targeting and tied it directly to Soviet ballistic missile systems. Communications centers, bases, and rocket sites in host nations close to the socialist community were added to the targeting list. The MOD also originated the targeting themes: "everything that feeds war" and "where the attack came from."

In February 1962, Gorshkov wrote that U.S. industrial, administrative, political centers, and U.S. bases overseas were targets, but did not specify the branch of the Soviet military that would deliver the attack. In February 1963 Malinovskiy associates the SRF with military and industrial targets. He made reference to general rocket strikes against the U.S. using the same target set that Gorshkov did in 1962.

Marshal Grechko stated in 1971 and 1972 that SRF targets including military administration, bases, means of nuclear attack, large concentrations of troops, industrial and transportation centers, rear services, and state administration and control. In his The Armed Forces of the Soviet State, the MOD associates general rocket strikes (not associated with the SRF directly) with rear area bases, lines of communications, communications and control centers. In May 1975, Gorshkov discussed the development of Soviet nuclear missile systems and stated that the primary object of military actions in a nuclear war including enemy armed forces, the economy, electrical power system, military industry, and administrative centers.

Soviet MOD's appear to have been very explicit about SRF targeting until about 1973 while during the same period, distinctly vague about SLBM targets. From this we can conclude that Gorshkov possibly may have had the authority to announce SLBM targeting. On the other hand, Gorshkov may have been arguing that SLBMs are capable of striking the same target set as the SRF by his specific references to the same quality of targets.

In Sokolovskiy's 1962 Military Strategy, the triad of strategic nuclear forces was associated with the destruction of: an enemy means of nuclear attack, military control centers, military-economic potential, enemy troop units, communications centers, bases, economy, and system of government. 3/

The SRF was described in 1978 as having the "principal and decisive means of achieving the goals of a war." They would be used to "undermine an aggressor's military and economic potential, annihilate his strategic means of nuclear attack, and destroy his main military groupage." 4/ In 1982 authors of a Soviet book state that their triad of strategic nuclear forces will destroy the aggressor's strategic nuclear forces, military-economic targets, troop units, and state and military control entities. 5/ Subsequent hardware analysis will have to consider what it is that SLBM strikes specifically can perform that the other portions if the triad cannot.

Sea Lines of Communication (SLOCs)

Gorshkov declared in The Sea Power of the State that actions to disrupt SLOCs now constitute a part of the general system of "fleet versus shore," a term used by him in that same book to describe missions capable of influencing the outcome of war. Gorshkov refers to the fleet versus shore anti-SLOC mission as "undermining the military-economic potential of an enemy," a term used in December 1974 and in The Sea Power of The State as also having the ability to influence the outcome of a war. In his booklet The Navy, the admiral mentions the ability of SLOC disruptions to undermine a nation's "economic potential," a term used by non-navy authors as having a decisive influence upon the course and outcome of a war. 6/

The subject of a Soviet SLOC mission, especially against North Atlantic reinforcement and re-supply shipments from North America to Europe, has been the subject of much heated and frequent debate in the West. Marshal Sokolovskiy is often cited for his description of the SLOC mission as being "among the main tasks" (which one might infer ranks it as not the most important) but in need of being developed in the very beginning of a war. 7/ In other places, he links the main tasks of SLOC disruption with defeat of an enemy fleet and as such constituting the type of operation which can be termed a strategic mission (although hardly decisive on the outcome). 8/ Sokolovskiy includes SLOC disruption in each of the three places where he describes strategic missions of the Soviet Navy. 9/

Gorshkov says in his booklet The Navy that SLOC disruption is "a part of a modern navy's main mission in a war." The SLOC mission also appears in the writings of other non-navy Soviet authors. 10/ The mission is still described as current in one of the latest pronouncements 11/ and naturally continues to attract the attention of Soviet naval authors. 12/

SLOC disruption receives nowhere near the same amount of attention as SLBM strikes at shore targets. Gorshkov only refers to it as a current Soviet Navy mission in 12 documents since 1961. Grecho referred to it twice in his book, and then only vaguely.

When Gorshkov specifically refers to SLOC disruption as a current Soviet Navy mission, he specifies the means as the fleet in general (4 times), submarines, naval aviation and surface ships (2 times), naval aviation (3 times), missile boats in closed and coastal seas (3 times), and by unspecified strikes across the seas (once).

Gorshkov's use of closed and coastal sea SLOC's is of special interest since not all references to SLOCs, convoys and transports as targets necessarily mean the North Atlantic or mid-Pacific. In fact, Gorshkov's references to the SLOCs might be those in the Baltic or the Sea of Japan whose disruption might be a strategic goal for that theater.

The one use of the theme: strikes across the sea as a means to sever SLOCs, could refer to missile strikes against SLOC terminals. The USSR might not want to make public a plan to target port terminals part of its declaratory policy, since ports are generally colocated with cities and therefore with non-combatant civilians.

In The Sea Power of the State the Navy Soviet C-in-C points out the vulnerability of Western economies to SLOC disruption and the military importance of convoys, especially in the North Atlantic. He also discusses the importance of ports in a unified transport system, although these passages might not be directly linked to military operations.

In one possibly historical passage in this book, Gorshkov states that once an aggressor is deprived of an opportunity to counterattack, the victor exploits his success by severing sea shipments of the enemy. In a more contemporary but again theoretical reference to SLOC disruption in The Sea Power of the State, Gorshkov states that submarines have been recognized by all fleets as the main threat to merchant vessels. In December 1982, Gorshkov once again points out the life-and-death value of uninterrupted communications to industrial developed coastal and island nations.

In a 1979 Morskoy Sbornik article, a Soviet Navy author discusses SLOC disruption in a modern war. 13/ The article cites the principal forces involved in the conflict as nuclear submarines, surface ships with aircraft, and shore-based aviation and missile forces. The article also points out the in ease in concentration objectives near terminals and states that SLOC combat operations include blockade and attacks. It further cites the potential of various types of armed forces participating in this mission and the advantage of nuclear weapons.

Findings

Fleet versus shore and strikes that undermine the military-economic potential of an aggressor are described by Gorshkov as influential upon the outcome of war. The primary means of fleet versus shore is strikes by SLBMs. The targets include political-administrative centers, military-industrial targets, military bases which constitute a springboard for attacks on the USSR, other military bases with a strong indication that SLOC terminals are also included.

NOTES

1. Interestingly, Gorshkov's claim <u>follows</u> the appearance of this theme in the first two <u>editions</u> of <u>Whence the Threat to Peace</u> (Moscow: Military Publishing House, 1982), 1st Ed. p. 70; 2nd Ed. p. 81. The theme is deleted in the 3rd Ed. (1984).
2. The 1979 Pergamon Ed. in English correctly translated a passage that is mis-translated elsewhere. See p. 205 in Pergamon where the passage states that guided missiles were given a role against ships and <u>land</u> objectives. A government translation incorrectly states that guided missiles have a role against ships and <u>large</u> objectives. Although the use of SLCMs against shore objectives is historically correct, and may be a future capability, both nations appear to have phased out this capability when they developed SLBMs. During the time frame of this study, it appears that SLBMs were primarily to be used for targets ashore and that SLCMs were to be used against targets at sea. This should finally end the debate over the meaning of Engineer Rear-Admiral N. V. Isachenkov's statement in "New Ship Weapons," <u>Krasnaya Zvezda</u>, November 18, 1961.
3. Marshal of the Soviet Union V. D. Sokolovskiy, <u>Soviet Military Strategy</u>, Ed. with analysis and commentary by Harriet Fast Scott (New York: Crane, Russak & Co., 1975), pp. 282, 284, 288-289.
4. MG S. A. Tyushkevich, <u>The Soviet Armed Forces: A History of Their Organizational Development</u> (Moscow: 1978), English translation authorized by the USSR and published by the U.S. Air Force as Vol. 19 of the Soviet Military Thought Series, p. 460.
5. LTG M. M. Kir'yan, Ed., <u>Military-Technical Progress and the USSR Armed Forces</u> (Moscow: signed to press July 8, 1982), p. 314.
6. MG S. A. Tyushkevich, "The Military Power of the State," <u>Marxist-Leninist Teaching on War and the Army</u>, LTG D. A. Volkogonov, Ed. (Moscow: Voyenizdat, signed to press September 30, 1983), p. 212.

7. Sokolovskiy, *Soviet Military Strategy*, p. 302.

8. Sokolovskiy, *Soviet Military Strategy*, pp. 299-300.

9. Sokolovskiy, *Soviet Military Strategy*, pp. 13, 285, 299-302

10. MG V. Kruchinin, "Contemporary Stratetic Strategy on the Goals and Missions of Armed Conflict," *Voyennaya Mysl'*, October 1963, pp. 19-20 (approx.), states that it was a strategic mission; COL I. S. Zheltikov, et al., "The Armed Forces of the USSR," *The Officer's Handbook*, MG S. N. Kozlov, Ed. (Moscow: 1971), English translation published under the auspices of the U.S. Air Force as Vol. 13 of the Soviet Military Thought Series, p. 117; MG M. I. Cherednichenko, "Conventional Weapons and the Prospects of Their Development," *Scientific Progress and the Revolution in Military Affairs*, COL-GEN N. A. Lomov, Ed. (Moscow: Military Publishing House, 1973) English translation published under the auspices of the U.S. Air Force as Vol. 3 of the Soviet Military Thought Series, p. 90.

11. Kir'yan, *Military-Techinical Progress and the USSR Armed Forces*, p. 321. Sovetskaya Voyennaya Entsiklopediya, Vol. 8, 1980, pp. 89-90 recognizes the value of SLOCs to NATO's abilities to continue military operations but only credits SLOC disruption with the capability to influence the course (not outcome) of a war.

12. CAPT 1st Rank B. Makeyev, "SLOC under Present-Day Conditions," *Morskoy Sbornik*, July 1979, pp. 19-22; and CAPT 1st Rank G. A. Ammon, et al., *The Soviet Navy in War and Peace* (Moscow: Progress Publishers, 1981), p. 99.

13. CAPT 1st Rank B. Makeyev, "SLOC Under Present-Day Conditions," pp. 21-22.

5

Fleet Versus Fleet

Fleet versus fleet is Admiral Gorshkov's term to describe the second of the two major roles of navies. Fleet versus fleet involves: the use of naval forces to combat an enemy's naval forces at sea and in his bases; and maintaining one's own sea lines of communication (SLOC). In past wars, it also involved disrupting an enemy's SLOC. Since the SLOC disruption mission is closely related to operations against naval forces at sea, and used to be a part of fleet versus fleet, it will once again be considered here. The mission of maintaining a Soviet SLOC will not be analyzed in this book since it is not associated with the term strategic nor has it been identified with any mission which has an influence upon the outcome of war. Obviously, SLOC maintenance may be crucial for the West, especially in Western eyes, but it is the Soviet strategic situation which is of interest to this study.

Two fleet versus fleet missions have been listed as strategic goals and thus are associated with the ability to influence the outcome of war. These are: crushing an enemy's military-economic potential (which was also a category for fleet versus shore), and destruction of major enemy groupings. Undermining the military-economic potential at sea probably involves operations against ships of the navy and on the SLOCs. Gorshkov included the shattering of an enemy's nuclear sea power as a specific strategic goal and the means to do so was given as the strike.

Gorshkov describes in The Sea Power of the State the two chief roles of fleets as: tasks associated with strikes against the shore (considered in the previous chapter) and protection of the homeland from strikes from an enemy fleet. Preventing and countering aggression from the sea, actions against enemy ballistic missile submarines, protecting own installations, and the defense of the sea borders have all been described by the Admiral as strategic missions.

Threats from the Sea

One of the most frequent sets of themes encountered in this research has to do with the threat from the sea. The threat is not always tied to a particular nation but most associated with the West or NATO. The U.S. is frequently singled out, as are West Germany, the United Kingdom, and France.

The threat from the sea is contained in 1/5 of all Politburo, 1/4 of all Minister of Defense (MOD), and 1/3 of Gorshkov's documents analyzed during the primary study period. The most often discussed threats are those posed by enemy nuclear-capable naval forces: submarines with missiles and attack aircraft carriers. Seventy-six percent of all documents that discuss the threat deal with these primary ones.

The stated threat from submarine launched ballistic missiles (SLBM) is the most often given threat and has changed over time; from Polaris to Poseidon and then to Trident. Since 1975, the submarine missile threat has expanded to include sea launched cruise missiles (SLCMs). The specific location of Western submarines is only rarely given. There are occasional references to the Mediterranean (first use July 1963) and the Atlantic and Pacific (first use February 1966) as the location of threat submarines. Marshal V. D. Sokolovskiy's Military Strategy, (first set in type March 1962), specified the western Pacific, Mediterranean, northeast Atlantic, northern seas, and Arctic Oceans 1/ as locations where Polaris submarines patrolled.

Generally there are no substantial differences between the subsurface threat as articulated by individual speakers from the different bureaucracies. One slight variation is that Gorshkov refers to enemy submarines as a threat other than in the context of strikes by them against Soviet territory.

The second most mentioned enemy naval threat is the attack aircraft carrier. We find it mentioned by Brezhnev, the MOD, and most frequently by the Soviet Navy Chief. Of interest is how this threat theme has changed over time.

Attack aircraft carriers were mentioned as a threat to the territory of the USSR in the 1960's with parallel mention of their vulnerability to Soviet weapons systems. The high costs and low combat potential of carriers were also cited. By 1970, Gorshkov wrote in the Great Soviet Encyclopedia that carriers were useful in local and limited wars and as a strategic nuclear reserve. In the event of a nuclear war, carrier-based attack aviation was described as primarily associated with combat actions at sea. No mention was made of major Western air strikes by carrier aviation against the territory of the USSR.

Gorshkov repeats in The Sea Power of the State and the Sovetskaya Voyennaya Entsiklopedia the theme that attack carriers form a strategic reserve. He did not repeat the theme in either of these two cases that attack aviation was associated with fleet versus fleet operations in a nuclear war.

Since 1981, the threat from aircraft carriers has most often appeared in the context of articles addressing the U.S.-Soviet naval balance and the need to account for "forward-based systems" in European theater nuclear arms control talks. Gorshkov published an October 1983 article in Krasnaya Zvezda that credited aircraft carriers (according to U.S. strategists) with a decisive role in a future confrontation between navies during a limited nuclear war.

The downgrading of the attack carrier threat to the Soviet homeland was one of the major pieces of evidence that James McConnell and Bradford Dismukes used to support their contention that Soviet fleet actions in the June War of 1967, the Jordanian crisis of 1970, and the October 1973 war, were primarily political in nature rather than necessitated by consideration of strategic defense of the USSR. Their logic is that had these events posed a threat to the Soviet Union, then the response was not sufficient to be characteristic of Soviet principles of war. 2/

Cruise missiles have been cited as a new threat since at least 1975. SLCMs are sometimes associated with the platform they would be launched from but more often appear in a general context. The cruise missiles threat has appeared in about one-third of all documents since 1982.

Periodically other themes of nuclear associated threats from the sea have appeared. In March 1972 Gorshkov cited Western plans for ocean floor bases for nuclear ballistic missile submarines (SSBNs). In the second edition of The Sea Power of the State, he claims that older U.S. Polaris submarines be placed into the reserves, 3/ which would imply that they could be reactivated. The Soviet Navy Chief made reference to U.S. neutron warheads from the sea in July 1977. Marshal Ustinov referred to the U.S. Trident missiles in July 1983 as a first-strike system.

The NATO multi-lateral force (MLF) was a favorite threat theme from 1963 - 1966. Other threat themes that appear include the opening of new ocean sectors to the enemy (since May 1975) and the ability of enemy navies to attack from varying directions (since November 1975).

The perceived threat posed by Western surface ships other than aircraft carriers, surface-launched SLCMs, and the MLF, has been generally minimal. Most passages credit Western surface ships with the role of protecting carriers, convoys, or amphibious units. One document in May 1975 specifically discussed light missile forces in NATO navies as a threat. There are occasional references to amphibious forces and the U.S. Marine Corps, but never in a context of being associated as a direct threat to the USSR. 4/

In the early 1960's, Gorshkov referred to the attack aircraft carrier and Polaris submarine as the main striking force of the U.S. Navy. Over time, the subsurface missile threat has clearly emerged as the predominant Western threat to Soviet territory, with aircraft carriers described as more of a threat to Soviet naval forces. Therefore we must conclude the protection of Soviet fleet assets is a separate category than protection of the homeland itself.

The major category of naval threats to the Soviet fleet is antisubmarine warfare (ASW). Grechko discusses the ASW threat twice and Gorshkov does so some 16 times. Since May 1963, ASW aircraft carriers and nuclear ASW submarines have been singled out. In his 1970 Great Soviet Encyclopedia article, Gorshkov identifies ASW forces as: ASW carriers, surface ships, diesel and attack nuclear submarines (SSNs). In fact, the only role given to the Western SSN in this article is ASW. The SSN as an ASW threat is repeated in the Sovetskaya Voyennaya Entsiklopedia and The Sea Power of the State.

Gorshkov uses the latter book to also introduce the theme that the U.S. fleet is tasked with conducting preemptive operations against enemy strategic forces before they can be used against the U.S. This is not necessarily against Soviet naval assets since the citation refers to counterforce against general strategic forces and Soviet "strategic" forces include more than what the U.S. terms "strategic." Missions to protect the USSR and its fleet assets will be consolidated into: (1) interactions designed to prevent nuclear attacks on the USSR, and (2) interactions designed to protect Soviet fleet assets, to ensure they carry out their fleet versus shore missions.

Prevention of Attacks on USSR

Destruction of the enemy missile carrier (the submarine) itself would qualify as the destruction of major enemy groupings and crushing military potential, both of which are included in Gorshkov's means to influence war and are strategic missions. Destruction of the enemy's nuclear sea power, according to the Admiral, is a strategic goal itself.

The destruction of enemy ships in their bases forms part of the fleet versus fleet mission. Land and rocket submarine bases have been on the declaratory list of targets since February 1963 for distant Soviet blows. Marshal Malinovskiy specified at that time the triad as the means of such blows. Gorshkov followed this declaration with one that the Soviet Navy would target Polaris bases in Europe and it would strike submarines at sea. Strikes are a method of performing strategic missions and attain strategic goals.

The mission to frustrate an enemy's attack does not necessarily have to be a total success in any one particular phase. Gorshkov says in The Navy that fleet operations against an enemy's sea-based strategic weapons will "weaken their attacks to the maximum extent possible."

Marshal Sokolovskiy discussed defense in depth in Military Strategy with the SRF and long-range aviation (LRA) striking the submarines in their bases, and LRA, ASW submarines, and other ASW forces being tasked with operations against submarines in transit and in patrol areas. He claimed that ASW submarines could use homing missiles and torpedoes against Polaris and LRA could use nuclear depth charges. 5/

Destruction of Western SSBNs is of the highest possible concern to both the West and the Soviet Union. Marshal Malinovskiy stated twice in 1962 and 1963 that Soviet submarine rockets would target Polaris submarines, but his reference could mean either while they were at sea or in their bases. Since that time, Gorshkov has specified Soviet submarines (not missiles) as the means to destroy Western SSBNs. In early 1965, Gorshkov stated Soviet Navy rockets were capable of dealing with a variety of naval targets including Polaris, but this is not necessarily a reference to at-sea targeting.

Marshal Grechko wrote in The Armed Forces of the Soviet State that naval operations include combat against enemy atomic missile submarines. In a December 1972 Krasnaya Zvezda article, Grechko stated the SRF would target naval forces in the theater, although not specifically SSBNs. This can be construed as the use of Soviet land-based ballistic missiles to target naval forces perhaps at sea, but possibly in theater anchorages or bases. Gorshkov discusses this issue once from a historical perspective.

Sokolovskiy included the Arctic Ocean as a Polaris patrol location. None of the Politburo spokesmen, MODs, nor Gorshkov ever refer to this area as a Western SSBN patrol area. Instead, they have stated since October 1961 that Soviet SSBNs deploy under the Arctic ice and that Soviet submarines in general have an under Arctic ice capability. There is no way in most passages to distinguish the Arctic as an area of deployment for Soviet SSBNs or an area for Soviet submarines to conduct a campaign against Western SSBNs (strategic ASW).

One unique passage appeared to discuss a different solution to the threat of Western nuclear missile strikes from SSBNs. In July 29, 1979, Gorshkov stated the Party and Government's . . . "way to neutralize that threat . . . consisted of creating qualitatively new strategic facilities in the shape of nuclear submarines carrying ballistic missiles." This appears to be a direct reference to the use of Soviet SSBNs to counter those of the West. But is it a reference to war-fighting damage limitation or a plan to deter use of Western SLBMs by a like Soviet threat implying withholding?

In general, the Soviet answer to Western SSBNs appears to be similar to the layered defense first outlined by Marshal Sokolovskiy. The SRF appears to have been tasked with destruction of SSBNs in bases. From the literature evidence of since 1965, it is possible to conclude that Soviet SLBMs might have either taken over this role or will participate in such strikes on bases.

Strategic aviation appears to have lost the role Sokolovskiy mentioned for LRA in countering SSBNs. There are still a few references to joint Soviet Navy-Air Force missions or air force missions in maritime theaters but not specifically tied to strategic ASW operations. In two cases where Gorshkov appeared to advocate a strategic ASW role for naval aviation, it appears more likely he was advocating this position not announcing it. The main weapon in combating enemy SSBNs at sea appears to be Soviet submarines.

Notably absent from any Soviet discussion of how to counter Western SSBNs are a number of other possible methods. There is, for example, no declaratory announcement that nuclear barrages by the SRF are considered against Western SSBN patrol areas nor as counter-battery fire once the first Western SLBM breaks the surface. Nor is there mention of anti-ballistic missile systems or other air defense forces and systems which could counter cruise or ballistic missiles launched from sea or transiting the ocean airspace.

Protection of the Soviet Fleet

The second most important mission in the Soviet Navy (but one that appears to be virtually equal in status) is prevention of strikes against the USSR including its fleet assets used in the primary missions of fleet versus shore. Soviet SSBNs as targets for Western ASW represents an opportunity to achieve a major military gain during the conventional or early nuclear phase of a war, at a potentially low cost. Despite the dearth of official statements in the past, 6/ that the West would mount a strategic ASW campaign, there is no question that the Soviets anticipate such actions.

Soviet spokesmen have specifically noted Western ASW forces as a threat, and Gorshkov has warned the U.S. fleet might pre-empt against Soviet strategic forces. There is evidence in the literature that implies that the Soviet plan to utilize all naval forces in a manner that the primary strike force (SSBN) will be allowed to carry out its mission in the face of a strategic ASW campaign by the West. Gorshkov even says in his booklet The Navy that the fleet versus shore mission created the fleet versus fleet problem.

The primary threat to Soviet SSBNs is from Western submarines. The U.S. has recently emphasized the need for a strategic ASW capability for its SSNs, and stated it will conduct an offensive in Arctic waters in the event of war. Land-based patrol aviation also constitutes an ASW threat especially to forward-deployed Soviet SSBNs. Western land-based air and carrier task groups could mount ASW campaigns in Arctic or other waters close to the USSR, but would then be subject to air strikes from Soviet air defense forces.

Naval Aviation

Soviet Naval Aviation has been discussed primarily with regard to fleet versus fleet. In some 35 documents which discuss Soviet naval air missions, there are 31 individual citations that mention ASW and 24 associations with an anti-surface ship role. In both editions of The Sea Power of the State, Gorshkov stated that naval aviation targets include the ASW forces of the enemy. As a general comment in this book, not tied specifically to the Soviet Navy, Gorshkov stated that the main task of naval aviation is ASW. Four additional references give convoys and transports as targets for Soviet naval air.

An interesting theme associated with Soviet Naval Aviation is that of cooperation with other naval forces. This theme originated at least as early as October 1961 but interestingly with Marshal Malinovskiy. Since then, Soviet Naval Aviation has been noted five more times as cooperating with submarines and four times with surface ships.

Soviet air forces also have a role in oceanic theaters against naval targets. This theme appears as early as February 1958, but is used only by the MOD. As we found Gorshkov reluctant to address the Soviet LRA and Strategic Aviation in discussion of the strategic triad, we also find him avoiding reference to air forces in the context of their mission to strike naval forces of the enemy. Gorshkov instead makes occasional references to "other forces" in oceanic theaters without specifying the name of the service.

Surface Ships

In a May 1965 Literaturnaya Gazeta article, Admiral Gorshkov stated that "war at sea still includes combat tasks which cannot be successfully resolved without surface ships." In July 1966, Gorshkov attempted to place surface ships on an equal status with submarines and aviation. In February 1968, surface rocket carriers were termed the "pride of the fleet." In July of that same year, he included ASW vessels in this special group. Five years later, he declared in a Pravda article that surface ships are technically equivalent to submarines.

In the first edition of The Sea Power of the State, we find the theme that Soviet surface ships are needed to solve a number of tasks facing the fleet. This specific theme is dropped in the second edition, although another reference is retained concerning the general need for surface ships to support submarines. In his 1977 booklet, The Navy and in the second edition of The Sea Power of the State, Gorshkov states that missile ships and small combatants are the pride of Soviet shipbuilding. In July 1980, he repeats the claim that surface ships are still important.

In the 42 documents that contain references to Soviet surface ship missions, the most often mentioned ones are ASW: (41 citations) and anti-surface (14 citations). Notably absent in the literature is the use of surface ships to fire cruise missiles against land targets or to specifically engage missiles enroute to targets ashore in the USSR. In general, Politburo spokesmen or the MOD only associate Soviet surface ships with ASW.

Gorshkov specifies additional targets for Soviet surface forces such as enemy strike forces and transports. In The Sea Power of the State, missile boats in coastal waters and closed seas are credited with a capability against enemy surface ships and transports. Convoys are repeated as targets in the Sovetskaya Voyennaya Entsiklopedia. Transports and enemy ASW forces appear as targets in September 1977.

Gorshkov stresses the multi-purpose nature of Soviet surface ships or their capability for a wide variety of tasks 17 times since 1965. In theoretical discussions of both surface ships in general and specifically Soviet surface ships, Gorshkov states in The Sea Power of The State that they are capable of strikes, missions against the SLOCs, and "often the sole combat means of ensuring deployment of the main strike forces of the fleet - submarines."

This latter capability is tied directly to the Soviet Navy in the Sovetskaya Voyennaya Entsiklopedia and Gorshkov's booklet The Navy, which state that Soviet surface ships will "assure the combat stability of submarines." Soviet surface ships cooperating with submarines and aviation also appears in The Sea Power of the State. Gorshkov has made it clear that Soviet carriers and air-capable cruisers are primarily for ASW purposes.

Submarines

Soviet submarines also have a role in fleet versus fleet. Submarines are capable of laying mines, firing torpedoes, or using missiles. Despite a long involvement in mine warfare and much concern about this threat by the West, the Soviet authors whose writings were consulted in this study were generally silent about any future Soviet use of mines. Mine warfare is not openly associated with the term strategic. The use of torpedoes is a frequent theme. The Soviet Navy Chief and MOD have stated on ten occasions since 1962 that Soviet torpedoes have nuclear warheads.

As was noted in the fleet versus shore chapter, passages referring to the object of attack by submarine missiles have often included both land and sea targets. Over the years, there has been lively debate in the West over the possibility that ballistic missles might be used against targets in the oceanic theater. 7/

In October 1961, Chairman Khrushchev made a specific reference to submarines' target-seeking rockets being used against ships. Following this report, Engineer-Rear Admiral N. V. Isachenkov stated in a Krasnaya Zvezda interview what appears to be the plan to use SLCMs against ships and SLBMs against the shore. 8/ This article was re-analyzed to conclude that he could have meant SLBMs against ships. 9/

Marshal Sokolovskiy stated in the 1962 and 1963 editions of Military Strategy that submarines guided missiles launched from under the surface were a threat to surface vesssels and that such methods of operation replaced the standard method of torpedo attack. 10/ Subsurface-launched cruise missiles had not yet appeared in 1962, and the only subsurface-launched missiles at that time were ballistic. As late as April 1965, cruise missiles were listed in the Dictionary of Basic Military Terms as being only fired from submarines on the surface. 11/

In a February 1966 Malinovskiy article appearing in Bulgaria, a passage discussing the use of submarines in fleet engagements included submarine missiles striking "targets" from a submerged position. The type of missile is not specified, but only operational subsurface launched missiles at the time were ballistic. Malinovskiy could have meant SLBMs against ships in port or anchorages rather than on the high seas.

Marshal Grechko's October 1967 Supreme Soviet speech contains the passage:

> Submarines armed with ballistic rockets
> are capable of destroying ships from a
> distance of hundreds of kilometers and

delivering blows from underwater on
strategic enemy targets thousands of
kilometers away.

This is a direct citation threatening the use of SLBMs against ships at a distance that might imply on the high seas. Additional Soviet articles by other authors have appeared that might imply that SLBMs were intended for targets at sea including ships in formation. 12/ One must certainly question the possibility of such a major conceptual breakthrough in strategy/military art being hidden in light of other public pronouncements of military and naval capability.

It is possible, naturally, that the Soviet military does not want to emphasize the possibility of using SLBMs against surface ships or submarines. This may be for internal domestic needs rather than to ensure surprise. Maintaining support for naval programs might be undermined if the Party continually had naval vulnerability discussed in such terms that the survivability of Soviet ships was also in question.

There are references to Soviet submarines against transports and amphibious forces only in two of Gorshkov's encyclopedia articles. In The Sea Power of the State, and the Sovetskaya Voyennaya Entsiklopediya, the Admiral includes enemy merchant ships as the target for submarines (not specifically Soviet) on three additional occasions. This book also contains reference to the use of Soviet submarines to engage the enemy fleet in areas of the ocean chosen by the USSR and criticism of the centuries-old practice of the Russian fleet being tied to coastal areas and closed theaters.

A widely cited passage from a 1975 Morskoy Sbornik article contains reference to the use of "operational-tactical submarines . . . to support the combat patrolling of strategic submarines." 13/ Unfortunately, this entire article is a discussion of Western practices and is not a direct reference to Soviet submarine patrolling with and protecting their SSBNs. Similarly, Gorshkov's Sovetskaya Voyennaya Entsiklopediya article on "Naval Tactics," in 1979 discusses submarine tactics (in general) as now including their use in screens around other screens.

Soviet submarine cooperation with other submarines in war is a historical fact. 14/ In the naval campaign against German SLOCs in WW II, Soviet submarines were deployed in groups including groups of 2-3 when engaging convoys. A 1979 Sovetskaya Voyennaya Entsiklopediya article on "Tactical Groups" describes groups of 2-3 submarines in present terms. 15/ Gorshkov makes no <u>direct</u> mention of <u>Soviet</u> submarines protecting SSBNs nor does he mention submarine missiles against aircraft.

The "Blue Belt of Defense"

There are problems associated with the translation of the Russian words "zashchita" and "oborona" into English as "defense." The former generally is used as a protective shield between enemy and victim, while the latter is more of an active insertion of the shield between oneself and the enemy. "Defense" of Soviet borders is one of the most frequent themes appearing in all documents, appearing some 87 times since 1965.

According to the literature evidence, defense of the <u>sea</u> borders appears to be primarily a Soviet Navy task. The participation of other services appears from time to time but not on a regular basis. The mission of homeland defense appears to be definitely an active one using terms such as "repel" or "repulse" attacks from the sea.

Gorshkov uses the phrase of protecting own targets, objectives, and installations, four times from October 1967 - October 1969. It is not clear whether the targets to be protected are ashore or at sea. In July 1963, Gorshkov used the term "defended zone of a naval theater" when discussing forces needed to combat the enemy and to support to the Soviet Navy's main assault forces.

Marshal Malinovskiy's April 1966 speech to the 23rd Congress of the Communist Party of the Soviet Union included a unique passage that "the construction of our <u>blue belt defense</u> has been completed." The closest parallel to this theme was Gorshkov's July 27, 1968 radio address statement that the Soviet Navy was "capable of taking its defense line out into the ocean."

Exactly what the MOD meant by this "blue belt defense" has been the subject of much speculation in the West. 16/ The German Democratic Republic Defense Minister, General Heinz Hoffman stated in 1966 that Soviet atomic submarines operating in every sea in the world were part of the "blue defense belt." 17/ A Hungarian officer wrote the next year in an army publication in Budapest that the Soviet Union now had a nuclear sword and also a shield referring to the "blue belt." The article, however deals, mostly with anti-ballistic missile defense. 18/

An East German radio broadcast from Moscow in 1970 on the Soviet Navy Okean maneuvers used the "blue belt defense" term with reference to maritime defense. It listed only <u>naval</u> forces as being assigned to the "blue belt defense," and associated those units with strategic tasks. The report also stated that the Okean maneuvers tested the "blue belt defense" and the operability of the fleet "as well as all branches of service in such exercises." 19/

In <u>The Sea Power of the State</u>, Gorshko states that under conditions of modern war, where submarines are the main branch, and the main strategic orientation is fleet versus shore, there is a need for "all-round backing of the actions of the forces solving strategic tasks."

> Therefore, the struggle to create, in a particular time, favorable conditions for successfully solving by a large grouping of forces of the fleet, the main tasks facing it, and at the same time creating conditions such as would make it more difficult for the enemy to fulfill his tasks and prevent him from frustrating the actions of the opposing side, will apparently be widely adopted. . . . Among these measures are the creation and preparation of the necessary forces and resources for keeping them in readiness to solve combat tasks, form groupings of forces and such deployment of them in a theater as to ensure positional superiority over the enemy . . .

Gorshkov is saying that in order to accomplish strategic tasks, sea control is only required over particular ocean areas and only during particular times.

Findings

Soviet declaratory policy does <u>not</u> include fleet versus fleet engagements as interactions such as decisive battles for their own sake. All major naval engagements have been tailored to contribute in a formalized system of strategic goals and missions capable of influencing the outcome of a war.

The long-range naval threat to the USSR, according to the literature, is from Western naval forces still in their home bases and waters and by Western SSBNs deployed at sea. The long-range threat can be countered by ballistic missiles from the SRF and possibly also from Soviet Navy submarines. Strikes will be conducted against enemy fleet units in ports and at bases. Ships in their bases (especially SSBNs and carriers) are magnets for Soviet strikes, since major benefits would result from the expenditure of only a few missiles. U.S. SSBNs on distant patrol are targets of Soviet submarine ASW action.

A closer-in threat is posed by shorter range SLBMs, carriers of SLCMs, and surface carrier task forces, especially their ASW assets including submarines. These Western units pose a direct threat against the Soviet homeland itself or against the Soviet fleet.

This author concludes that open Soviet literature evidence includes a declaratory policy for the active defense of Soviet SSBNs. Such a defense would bait Western navies to combat in areas chosen by the USSR. It would allow protection of Soviet fleet assets and the homeland while simultaneously providing the opportunity for destruction of major enemy groupings. Calling this area of active defense a "bastion," appears proper.

There is only modest evidence of a declaratory Soviet open-ocean anti-SLOC mission. The anti-SLOC means, rather, appears to be the missile strikes described previously as fleet versus shore. Finally, the use of ballistic rockets against surface ships appears to be historical declaratory policy.

NOTES

1. Marshal of the Soviet Union V. D. Sokolovskiy, Soviet Military Strategy, Ed. with analysis and commentary by Harriet Fast Scott (New York: Crane, Russak & Co., 1975), p. 301.
2. Soviet Naval Diplomacy, Bradford Dismukes and James McConnell, Eds. (New York: Pergamon, 1979) p. 292.
3. Gorshkov should have known that this was not possible under the provisions of the SALT I Interim Agreement. Consequently, we can surmise either poor research by the staff tasked with updating the book, or deliberate falsification of data.
4. An interesting exception is found in MG M. Yasyukov, "CPSU Military Policy: Essence, Content," Kommunist Vooruzhennykh Sil, October 1985, pp. 14-21 which cites U.S. amphibious forces and aircraft carriers as direct threats to the Soviet homeland.

5. Sokolovskiy, <u>Soviet Military Strategy</u>, pp. 290, 302.

6. The plan to have U.S. naval forces conduct strategic ASW against the USSR in the event of a war was openly resurfaced by Chief of Naval Operations James Watkins. See May 19, 1983 articles based upon an interview with the CNO in the <u>Wall Street Journal</u>, p. 1; New York Times, p. 17; <u>Washington Post</u>, p. 5; and the August 1983 <u>Air Force Magazine</u>, pp. 88-94. More recently, the CNO published these views in a special January 1986 <u>Maritime Strategy</u> supplement to the <u>U.S. Naval Institute Proceedings</u>, pp. 11 & 14.

7. See for example, K. J. Moore, et al., "Development in Submarine Systems, 1956-76," in <u>Soviet Naval Influence: Domestic and Foreign Dimensions</u>, Michael MccGwire and John McDonnell, Eds., (New York: Praeger, 1977), pp. 151-184.

8. Engineer Rear-Admiral N. V. Isachenkov "New Ship Weapons," <u>Krasnaya Zvezda</u>, November 18, 1961 stated: "Ballistic rockets are basically assigned to the destruction of coastal targets. The Soviet Navy is faced with the task of destroying on the sea the ships and vessels of the enemy. The most efficient means of combat on the oceans and seas are self-homing rockets."

9. K. J. Moore, et al., "Development in Submarine Systems, 1956-76," pp. 171-172. One critical sentence was left out of their reprint of the Isachenkov's November 18, 1961 statement. This sentence is the second sentence included above in footnote 8.

10. Sokolovskiy, <u>Soviet Military Strategy</u>, p. 301.

11. <u>Dictionary of Basic Military Terms</u>, COL-GEN A. I. Radziyevskiy, Ed. (Moscow: Voyenizdat, typeset April 1965), English translation published under the auspices of the U.S. Air Force as Vol. 9 of the Soviet Military Thought Series, item 797.

12. Carl Clawson, "The Wartime Role of Soviet SSBNs-Round Two," <u>U.S. Naval Institute Proceedings</u>, March 1980, p. 66, cites three references to Soviet SLBMs perhaps being used against surface ships. Two of the original sources were checked and the appropriate passages do not necessarily support such a conclusion.

13. CAPT 1st Rank N. V'yunenko, "Some Trends in the Development of Naval Tactics," <u>Morskoy Sbornik</u>, October 1975, p. 22.

14. V. I. Achkasov and N. B. Pavlovich, <u>Soviet Naval Operations in the Great Patriotic War 1941-1945</u> (Annapolis: Naval Institute, 1981) translation of the 1973 Russian edition, p. 205; and CAPT 1st Rank G. Karmenok, "Control

of Navy Submarines in Operations on Enemy Sea Lanes," *Morskoy Sbornik*, May 1983, p. 24.

15. "Tactical Group," *Sovetskaya Voyennaya Entsiklopedia*, Vol. 7, 1979, p. 638.

16. Robert Herrick, "The USSR's 'Blue Belt of Defense' Concept: A Unified Military Plan for Defense Against Seaborne Nuclear Attack by Strike Carriers and Polaris/Poseidon SSBNs," *Naval Power in Soviet Policy*, Paul Murphy, Ed., published under the auspices of the U.S. Air Force as Vol. 2 in the Studies in Communist Affairs (Washington: U.S. Government Printing Office, 1978), pp. 169-178.

17. East Berlin ADN Domestic Service in German at 1421 GMT on May 25, 1966.

18. LTC Jozef Bojcsuk, "The Antimissile—A Contribution by Our Military Expert," *Nepszabadsag* (Budapest), April 30, 1967.

19. Jonny Marhold Moscow dispatch carried on East Berlin Domestic Service in German at 0756 GMT on May 7, 1970.

6

Soviet Military Strategy

The theory by official Washington of the strategic employment of the Soviet Navy ballistic misiles in the event of war is generally that forward-deployed nuclear ballistic missile submarines (SSBNs) would be employed against soft military targets in the U.S. and Europe, i.e., bomber bases, command and control centers, and industrial facilities. 1/ Certain older submarines in European and Asian waters are assigned theater strike missions. Newer submarines would be deployed in Arctic-defended bastions where they constitute a strategic reserve 2/ that could be withheld from an initial Soviet strike in order to be used for inter- or post-war negotiations and a peace settlement.

It is to this general conception of an employment plan that the content analysis will now turn. Some of the more recent criticisms of existing analyses is that the evidence in the Soviet literature does not necessarily support these Western conclusions. 3/ The ability of the Soviet fleet to carry out its wartime missions cannot be harshly criticized in internal Soviet publications or speeches for fear of undermining deterrence credibility. This chapter will review the literature for both manifest and latent evidence.

General, Limited Nuclear and Conventional War

The literature during the Khruschev era clearly presented a declaratory policy to strike the West with massive nuclear attacks in "response" to an attack on the USSR and that the USSR rejected the concept of limited nuclear war. Since that time, Soviet military authors and leaders have stressed the importance of conventional warfare and the ability to "respond" with other than a spasm nuclear attack.

Minister of Defense (MOD) Grechko stated in February 1968 that a future war can be waged either with or without nuclear weapons. He also said in February 1969 that a future war could commence with nuclear or conventional weapons. In February 1970 he added that it might be a conventional war only. Grechko stated in <u>The Armed Forces of the Soviet State</u> that conventional weapons might be <u>decisive</u> and that nuclear weapons cannot solve all the problems of war.

The MOD's emphasis on conventional warfare does not necessarily mean that a future Soviet war with the West will take the form of a conventional-only attack on NATO Europe. His statement may have referred to the need for conventional capabilities to complement nuclear warfare or exploit the use of nuclear weapons. Alternatively, the context might have been for a capability to fight limited wars (such as in Afghanistan) or to provide similar international military "assistance."

Admiral Gorshkov has generally remained outside the debate over the character of a future war, making only infrequent statements that directly support the MOD. Apparently, the question of the character of future war is beyond the domain of the Soviet Navy Chief. The Soviet Navy position parallels that of the MOD: a future war might be conventional or nuclear. Although it is the latter that this book is focused on, we cannot dismiss complementary conventional naval operations, such as strategic antisubmarine warfare (ASW), that might be conducted prior to the nuclear phase of a future war and that could impact on successful strategic nuclear forces mission completion.

In the West, many have the view that there is conventional war, and there is nuclear war, with some accepting that limited nuclear war is possible. Many Western observers of war consider the type of weapon as the major determinant of the type of war being fought. From certain aspects of the Soviet literature, their view of the firebreaks in escalation and the characteristics of war might be the political goals and not the weapons used. 4/

Even if this political distinction is the essential question in escalation, we must also conclude that a primarily nuclear offensive is one possible option for the means, that a conventional armed struggle is another, and that a mix of combined nuclear and conventional a third. From the author's reading of the available literature concerning land warfare, recent Soviet emphasis has been decidedly conventional with nuclear as a complementary alternative. 5/

A frequent question in analysis of Soviet military thought has been whether or not the USSR would engage in a limited or tactical nuclear war. A few years ago, one could read into the literature or note from land exercise behavior that limited nuclear war ashore was contemplated.

In recent years, Chairman Brezhnev and Marshal Ustinov specifically rejected the notion of a limited nuclear war (November 1981 and February 1982). Other senior officers have supported this view more recently. 6/ Marshal Nikolay Ogarkov, former Chief of the General Staff, has also consistently spoken against any Western notion of limited nuclear war and emphasized the decisive nature of the initial period of a future war. 7/

Admiral Gorshkov describes general war in October 1967 in terms that include the need to suppress aggression at its inception. Gorshkov repeats this theme at least seven times through 1979. Gorshkov made one reference to limited nuclear wars (October 1983) but attributed the plan to U.S. strategists (U.S. plans to use aircraft carriers in a decisive role during a limited nuclear war between navies).

Ustinov also mentions the need to prevent military conflicts from growing into nuclear ones (July 1982) implying a recognition of a nuclear firebreak. He implies a need to deter nuclear attack in the event of a conventional-only war.

Deterrence

The Soviet means of deterrence has been often described in the West as "war-fighting." In other words, the Soviet method of deterrence is not just to threaten a retaliatory blow but to prevent successful attacks in addition to threatening retaliation. Marshal Ogarkov supported this view when he discussed Soviet military doctrine in 1982 and stated:

> The point is to be able not simply
> to defend oneself, to oppose the
> aggressor with appropriate passive
> means and methods of defense but
> also to deliver devastating
> response strikes on the aggressor

and to defeat the enemy in any
situation conditions. 8/

There are two main literature themes relating to
naval forces and deterrence. The first is that the
Soviet Navy is restraining aggression and adventurism
by the imperialists on the high seas. This theme appears
as early as June 1969 and appears 30 times only in statements by the Soviet Navy Chief. Gorshkov credits fleets
(in general) in his "Navies in War and Peace" series with
the capability of achieving political objectives in war.
He adds to this claim, when it is revised in The Sea Power
of the State, that navies can achieve political goals by
threatening military action without actual armed struggle.
The context of the latter passage is clearly peacetime
naval diplomacy. The restraint on imperialism theme cannot
be tied directly to either nuclear forces as the means of
restraint nor to deterrence of nuclear war.

In some additional 22 passages, however, the means to
restrain, or the behavior restrained, is more closely
associated with nuclear/general war. This is the second
main literature theme dealing with deterrence and naval
forces.

In three citations (1966-1967), Marshal Malinovskiy
initiates that the dyad of the Strategic Rocket Forces
(SRF) and Navy atomic rocket submarines are the chief means
of restraining/resisting/containing aggression. Marshal
Grechko, on the other hand, in five passages from 1968-
1972, cites the SRF alone as the chief means of deterring/
restraining/curbing aggression. Only in his July 1971
Morskoy Sbornik article, does Grechko credit the dyad with
deterrence, stating that both constitute a shield.

In February 1968, the Soviet Navy Chief asserted that
the SRF (alone) was a powerful means of containing imperialism (in a clearly nuclear context). At the time that this
article appeared, Grechko had already published his
view that the SRF alone was the chief means of deterring
aggression and was the decisive service.

In July 1969, Gorshkov advances the idea that submarine launched ballistic missiles (SLBMs) were a barrier
to aggression. The context was that naval forces also, not
alone, contributed to deterrence. By October 1969, Gorshkov
stated that the dyad was a fundamental means of deterring
aggression. Gorshkov repeats this theme twice in February
1971 adding that the dyad was a shield over the socialist
system. He ignores numerous Grechko statements that the SRF
was the main service and alone was the chief means of restraint

The Soviet Navy Chief continued using this dyad deterrence theme (including the shield concept) in five additional cases through July 1973.

In July 1979, Gorshkov made a cryptic statement that Soviet SSBNs could neutralize (in the sense of off-setting) the threat of enemy SSBNs. In February 1980, he referred to strategic missile forces as a nuclear shield. In July 1983, Gorshkov stated that Soviet Navy strategic arms deterred aggression. The deterrence of nuclear war is accomplished by all strategic nuclear forces, according to Marshal N. V. Ogarkov and other senior military officers.

Withholding

Since 1973, a frequent theme has been that the Soviet Navy restrains ocean-originated threats to the USSR. This theme was first introduced in Gorshkov's February 1973, "Navies in War and Peace" article where the Admiral described the Soviet Navy as a "shield from enemy attacks from the sea and a real warning of the inevitability of retaliation for aggression." In his February 1980 Kommunist article, the Soviet Navy Commander-in-Chief (C-in-C), again states that the navy will contain aggression coming from the ocean and if necessary, retaliate.

The question of the inevitability of retaliation is tied to the scope and length of a future nuclear war. Under Khrushchev, declaratory policy was that Soviet nuclear use would be swift, total, and widespread. With the conventional-only campaigns as a new option, the Soviet Navy still has strategic missions to prevent Western naval operations against the Soviet SSBN fleet and homeland, and to be prepared to initiate or retaliate with its nuclear capability if called upon. Strategic missions do not go away in a conventional phase of a war.

Soviet global nuclear war is obviously not the automatic response to any or all types of aggression. The question remains, however, how much of the Soviet nuclear forces will be fired once the political decision is made to go nuclear? Here, the evidence begins to get extremely thin and is inconclusive.

On the one hand, we have Gorshkov's statement in July 1979 that Soviet SSBNs are a counter to Western SSBNs. One can read into this a threat to withhold these as long as the West does; in other words nuclear forces deter opposing nuclear forces. We also have Gorshkov's October 1983 mention of limited nuclear war involving naval forces. On the other hand, most of the commentary from MOD and Politburo spokesman about the inevitable retaliation include the statement that it will be "crushing" and not limited or withheld.

From the content analysis alone, it is impossible to measure exactly what the Soviets mean by a "crushing" blow or response. They appear to emphasize that the response will be a large one, but Soviet comments since January 1981 have discussed both the danger of unlimited nuclear war (implying that global escalation is not automatic) and that nuclear war cannot be conducted by prearranged rules.

In January 1960, Chairman Khrushchev discussed Soviet hidden reserves of rockets. In February 1968, Gorshkov stated that an attack on the USSR would be followed by Soviet SLBM retribution from the sea but the retaliation was not described as immediate or swift. In July 1982, the Navy C-in-C again stated that Soviet SSBNs would provide inevitable retribution to Western strategic submarine missile systems.

The manifest evidence on withholding is simply inconclusive. There is no direct evidence in the literature alone to support a declaratory policy of withholding SSBNs from the initial nuclear strike for inter- or post-war bargaining and negotiations. Therefore, the author expanded his research into related but more indirect themes of naval art.

Advantages of Naval Forces

One of the more common themes from all naval leaders is the uniqueness of naval warfare and the advantages of fleets in peacetime or in war. Gorshkov is no exception. His writings on the use of navies to support foreign policies of states demonstrating that a nation's military might beyond its borders, supporting friends, and operating in a no-man's land are well known in the West and have been analyzed by others.

Gorshkov's related comments in December 1972 and The Sea Power of the State that naval forces can demoralize an enemy, intimidate him, and achieve political goals by the mere threat of military action, can be viewed in a number of ways. One can read into them nuclear deterrence, but this author thinks that naval diplomacy is the more correct context. Naval diplomacy could be a surrogate for other contexts, however.

The Soviet Navy Chief does make frequent reference, starting in 1973, to the concealment of atomic submarines in

general and of SSBNs in particular. He also cites their
stability from nuclear weapons and great survivability.
Grechko adds a discussion of the survivability of missile
submarines to the 2nd Edition of The Armed Forces of the
Soviet State. One cannot infer from these passages, withholding of weapons.

Those of us in the West generally assume that the
West will not conduct a first strike on the USSR, although
defense of NATO may require the first use of tactical
nuclear weapons even if the Soviets remain conventional.
Therefore, the Soviets must assume the potential for a
Western first nuclear strike in their war plans. Thus
submarine' survivability may be explained as an attribute
allowing an inevitable and a crushing counter-blow even if
the West eliminated all Soviet land systems. Grechko in
The Armed Forces of the Soviet State, refers to nuclear missiles (land systems) as being only relatively invulnerable.

Naval forces also have some advantage in a more
offensive military context. Gorshkov frequently cites
their ability to form into powerful groupings and their
great maneuverability (including that of SSBNs). He also
discusses the ability of fleets to strike from different
directions. One such comment is directly associated with
SLBMs (July 1973) and two with a Western capability (in The
Sea Power of the State). Striking from different directions
can be viewed as a potential threat to the USSR since it
would complicate Soviet anti-ballistic missile systems.
It can also be viewed as a Soviet advantage since it
might frustrate U.S. warning systems. The ability of
fleets to deploy rapidly is also a Gorshkov theme tied
to SSBNs twice in The Sea Power of the State.

Command and Control

Another frequently analyzed area of commentary in
the Soviet literature deals with the needs of naval
command and control. Gorshkov has gone on record as
pointing out the problems posed by independent and distant
deployments creating problems for command and control.
Most of his passages discussing the need for flexibility
are probably of a more tactical nature, since independent
military initiative involving the initiating nuclear war
would appear to be an anathema to any political group
running any country. On the other hand, nuclear war at sea
might be viewed as necessary, controllable, and not necessarily escalatory. If the war ashore is nuclear, the war
at sea will probably also be.

In viewing statements involving command and control, one notices that an often-overlooked aspect is that comments are in the context of ensuring control. Malinovskiy referred at least as early as February 1958 to the need to control the new means of warfare. In July 1982, Ustinov openly discussed the need to ensure tight control to prevent the non-sanctioned launch of nuclear weapons.

Gorshkov, Marshal Orgarkov, and the new Chief of the General Staff, Marshal Akhromeyev have endorsed Soviet centralized control on the same basis as it was in the Great Patriotic War. Gorshkov also points out in The Sea Power of the State that fleet versus fleet operations are more independent than fleet versus shore. In May 1980, he states that centralized control is necessary for guided missile weapons and other situations in which there can be no delay. Marshal Grechko does acknowledge in The Armed Forces of the Soviet State that naval operational art is somewhat different. This author feels that the context of the literature emphasizes that initiation of any nuclear operation would be a political decision and not military.

Naval Art Versus Military Strategy

Rather than discussions of specific problems of command and control in the open literature, we more often encounter more detailed but open debate over the concepts of military strategy and naval art. Debate is permissible under the category of military science. The most interesting subject of debate involves the degree of independence of naval operations and what theoretical framework should govern operations by forces other than naval forces in oceanic theaters. In other words, the debate is deliberately vague but can be directly related to service roles.

Military strategy decides the employment of all Soviet military forces. There is no independent naval strategy. Military art generally determines how land and air forces will carry out the strategy, as naval art determine the role for naval forces. The running debate is that since naval forces must be subordinated to military art when operating in or in support of a military theater, then should not naval art determine the employment of other forces when they operate in oceanic theaters?

We know from the review of fleet versus fleet that the air force has a role in oceanic theaters. We also know that the SRF has a declaratory role in fleet versus fleet actions against ships in port and achorages and possibly also at sea. It has been Gorshkov's view since February 1965 that the Soviet Navy, as the determinant of naval art, should manage the employment of other services in oceanic operations.

With the 2nd Edition of The Sea Power of the State, Gorshkov revises his position slightly by discussing a unified strategy but with options for the strategic employment of individual forces. Furthermore, he states that there cannot be one sphere where one branch of the military is sovereign.

Following this revision to his book, a series of nine articles appeared in Morskoy Sbornik from April 1981 through April 1983, in which the subject of the "Theory of the Navy" was debated openly. 9/ Vice Admiral K. Stalbo, a leading navy theoretician, opened up the series with his views that: there cannot be an independent naval science, a future war would likely be protracted and global in nature, and that the Soviet Navy could influence the course of such a war. He was also critical of those who underestimated the strategic employment of SSBNs, and appeared to argue that naval operations must include actions against the enemies' main and most heavily defended forces. Stalbo stated that the primary strategic effort of the fleet involved strategic nuclear missile submarines.

In July 1983, Gorshkov ended the debate with a restatement of the theme that there cannot be a separate naval science. There can only be a separate theory, which is allowable for each service. He emphasizes that the procurement of new weapons is limited by Soviet Navy roles, missions, and economic realities. The strategic employment of the navy is determined by a unified military strategy. Naval operational art is considerably more independent. Naval art is primarily determined by the Soviet Navy, although it is linked to and based upon military art. It appears from Gorshkov's article that operations by other forces in remote oceanic regions will be governed by naval operational art.

Stalbo described the strategic employment of the navy as being concerned with the objectives of armed conflict at sea and in coastal sectors of continental theaters where strategic missions are accomplished with the navy's participation. This ties navy missions previously described as strategic to the overall unified military strategy. Independent navy strategy does not exist.

Stalbo described naval operational art as governing both independent and joint service actions in oceanic theaters. Naval operational art as a concept falls between the theory of the strategic employment of the navy and naval tactics. Operational art is essentially the standardization of naval operations.

The point is that the Soviet Navy does not determine the major questions of how to fight or deter wars but rather is primarily concerned with maximizing the implementation of strategy. The Soviet Navy appears to be interested in gaining command and control over other forces assigned to oceanic theaters for operational-tactical purposes. The Soviet Navy does not and cannot have an independent view of how wars will be fought.

Hence statements by Admiral Gorshkov that are at odds with his seniors must be viewed extremely carefully. Unfortunately, this does not answer questions raised earlier about whether or not Gorshkov is empowered to articulate SLBM targeting, since his statements do differ from those of the MOD. It is not clear whether or not those passages are part of a debate or are announcements of strategy. Thus, we need to analyze the hardware and deployment patterns to decide this question.

Naval Operational Art and Tactics

Discussions of naval operational art and tactics are generally found only in writings of Soviet Navy authors. Marshal Grechko did enter the field on a few occasions. For example, he mentions in The Armed Forces of the Soviet State that sudden attack is a navy tactic. Since tactics are structurally subordinate to doctrine or strategy, one cannot infer a Soviet nuclear first-strike from such statements. Gorshkov makes similar comments about suprise blows by Soviet naval forces, including a comment in April 1966 involving submarines against land and sea targets. The advantages of surprise in conjunction with nuclear weapons is cited in December 1974 by the Soviet Navy C-in-C as a general comment not tied to the USSR.

Grechko also introduces the theme in February 1971 that the Soviet Navy has the means for simultaneous and prolonged combat. This is repeated in The Armed Forces of the Soviet State and then picked up by Gorshkov in July 1975 and in The Sea Power of the State.

Gorshkov uses this book to make specific reference to problems of the Soviet fleet in carrying out strategy. The Soviet Navy Chief cites the lack of overseas bases, choke points, and bad weather in home bases. As a general comment, he states that battle forces may have to pre-deploy.

Gorshkov repeats in April 1983 mention of choke points and that Western fleets are able to inhibit Soviet fleet actions. In September 1977 and July 1983, he implies that the proper method of establishing a fleet's balance is to do so in each individual theater.

Boldness and initiative are also frequent Gorshkov tactical themes, usually tied to discussions of increased tempo of operations at a tactical level. Battle will probably be determined in short order, and success may hinge on seconds. Battle is associated with tactical, not strategic, objectives.

In discussions of the tactical use of nuclear weapons at sea, Gorshkov has become more vague over the years. In May 1965, he pointed out the advantages of nuclear weapons in rapidly and with certainty, destroying objectives. In July of that year, he boasted to a foreign audience that massive Soviet nuclear use would be employed on short notice against a variety of land, air, surface, and sub-surface targets.

In May 1966, Gorshkov stated that the fleet must be prepared to use nuclear weapons in response to enemy first use. The advantage of destroying targets with one missile that has a powerful warhead, appears in Gorshkov's statements in July 1972 and March 1973. Since then, the Navy C-in-C has made three general comments about tactical nuclear weapons as a powerful means of battle and one that air-launched nuclear missile strikes are especially effective. In his booklet, The Navy, he claims that nuclear missiles are the main weapons.

From the literature evidence alone, it is impossible to make conclusions about the Soviet view of a limited tactical nuclear war at sea. The literature evidence supports the view that if the Soviets go nuclear, all forces will go nuclear. If the land campaign would be better served by a nuclear offensive, according to their literature, one must conclude that nuclear use would also occur at sea. On the other hand, use at sea alone, or first use in maritime sectors, appears to be governed by a Soviet declaratory policy rejecting limited nuclear war.

Latent Lessons of History

Over the years, Gorshkov has changed his emphasis on the value of the lessons of history relative to current military strategy and naval art. In July 1963, he first stated that the role of the Soviet Navy today was greater than its role in the Great Patriotic War. In May 1965

Gorshkov said that military art had changed significantly since the war and that many obsolete theories had been abolished.

In May 1975 the Soviet Navy Chief changed his emphasis and stated that current questions must include investigation of the experiences of the Great Patrotic War. Gorshkov stated in September 1977 that the gap between capability and tactics had been eliminated. In October 1977 he added the need to study Leninist principles and in July 1983 the need to study the experiences of imperialist local wars.

The experiences of the military in a historical context is one of the most frequent methods of articulating concepts in the Soviet literature. It is necessary to analyze this material both due to its volume and to the fact that both Gorshkov and Grechko state that historical military experiences (especially the Great Patriotic War) still have value today. This section will analyze latent military strategy themes and historical surrogates to see if they parallel and supplement current ideas.

Czarist History

James McConnell has done outstanding pioneering analysis of latent themes using historical surrogates. McConnell's summation of hidden messages in historical lessons 10/ was substantiated by this author's review of the literature.

Specifically, analysis of history prior to the Russian revolution does validate emphasis on navy political roles and their influence on the outcome of wars and on peace talks. McConnell does not stress a concurrent Gorshkov theme that land forces have are extremely important and are needed to consolidate victory. McConnell uses various examples from Czarist history to argue that Gorshkov is sending a message that the Soviet Navy will win the peace in a future nuclear war.

Of interest is the place of publication of these references to historical experiences prior to the revolution. All but one occur in "The Navies in War and Peace" series or in the revision and reprint of these passages found in The Sea Power of the State. The one additional place of publication is a March 1972 article in Voyennaya Mysl'. Thus the intended audience is primarily military, not general audiences or foreigners. One can assume, however, that the Soviets know the U.S. does read internal documents and that therefore that the internal audience includes foreigners.

Some other themes of interest not previously emphasized by Western analysts include: enemy sea lines of communication (SLOCs) should be cut if the enemy depends upon them, the value of bases for inter-theater maneuver, and the ability of navies to geographically escalate. One interesting passage in the 1972 Voyennaya Mysl' article is the appearance of a passage that is never used elsewhere.

> The Russian Navy was always confidently guided by the dictate of the first naval regulations: 'Do not adhere to regulations as to a blind wall, for in it orders are written, but not times and instances'.

Historical references to the Czarist days contain explicit criticisms of short-sighted leaders who failed to understand the value of navies, or misused them, and failed to provide the Russian fleet with the materials necessary in future wars. The value in constantly building and of technological superiority is pointed out. These passages appear only in Soviet Navy publications.

World War I

Gorshkov states that in certain areas navies had a profound influence on the course and outcome of World War I. These areas include: the German submarine blockade of Britain, convoying reinforcements to Europe from North America, the allied blockade of Germany, and the influence of Allied navies on neutrals' decisions to eventually declare war on Germany.

The lack of influence on the Battle of Jutland was indeed rejected by Gorshkov in May 1972 and in The Sea Power of the State. Yet in a subsequent discussion of this battle in that same book, Gorshkov said Jutland did not have "any strategic or operational link with the combat actions on the land." Furthermore, in the Sovetskaya Voyennaya Entsiklopedia, Gorshkov wrote "that not one of the sides achieved its objectives." McConnell argues that Gorshkov's treatment of the Jutland Battle is a message that less than decisive battles (and mere fleets-in-being) can have a major influence on the course of the armed struggle.

On a tactical plane, Gorshkov points to German failure to coordinate other forces with their submarine campaign against the SLOC. He also mentions the high cost of the ASW forces mounted against German submarines. All World War I commentary appears in publications designed for military and primarily navy audiences.

Inter-War Years

Admiral Gorshkov includes the Leninist principles governing military operations in his discussion of the Soviet Navy in the revolution. Naval analyst commentary in the West 11/ noted the presence of these passages in "The Navies in War and Peace" series but failed to uncover their prior publication. In 1970, the centennial year of V. I. Lenin's birth and the 25th anniversary of the victory over fascist Germany, Marshal Grechko published an article in Kommunist that discussed these Leninist principles. Grechko again discusses these principles in Kommunist in 1974 as well as both editions of The Armed Forces of the Soviet State. Gorshkov refers to the Leninist principles in The Sea Power of the State and in October 1977 says that they are still important today.

Leninist principles governing military operations are summarized as follows:

(1) Determine the primary threat and study all possible means of military employment by the enemy.
(2) Concentrate the means and forces at the decisive place and time.
(3) Be flexible in the use of forces.
(4) Seize the initiative and strike sudden blows.
(5) Make blows decisive.

A sixth principle is used by Grechko but not by Gorshkov. In his 1970 article, the MOD discusses the Great Patriotic War and states "Lenin's concept to the effect that war in our days is a people's war and that 'he who has greater reserves, greater sources of strength and greater endurance within the thick (mass) of the people' emerges as the winner." In that Kommunist article, Grechko pointed out how Lenin built up strategic reserves and the Party provided for industrial base reserves prior to World War II. In his book, Grechko adds the need to create reserves in war.

The subject of reserves is intimately tied to roles and missions for Soviet Navy SSBNs. There has been an excellent attempt to trace the role of reserves in the Soviet literature and tie the submarine force to these roles. 12/ Perhaps the best direct evidence for an SSBN reserve from the open literature is from a discussion of strategic reserve mission is a 1964 Voyennaya Mysl' article, that states strategic reserves include "reserves of nuclear weapons and rockets," 13/ The value of reserves is tied to Lenin's dictum that "victory in war goes to the side who people has greater reserves, greater sources of strength, and greater endurance." 14/

The literature evidence, using the sources herein, that submarines are part of a strategic nuclear reserve simply does not exist in either direct manifest or latent passages. Reaching this conclusion on the basis of the open literature alone is speculative and is based upon the interpretation reading certain passages that have multiple possible meanings.

Should, as McConnel suggests, we accept these latent themes as evidence that the Soviet Navy has the major role in the creation of the peace? If it does, then why is this message directed primarily at navy audiences? Is it to explain approved strategy, or does Gorshkov utilize his own service journals and military journals to advocate? If he is advocating, why not target an audience that could do him the more good (the party).

Gorshkov is not reluctant to criticize Soviet policies during the inter-war years. In July 1963, the Soviet Navy Chief quotes Army General M. V. Frunze (People's Commissioner for Military Affairs in 1925) at a 1924 conference:

> Some comrades, as a result of our in-
> adequate means, have the idea that it
> would be better to concentrate our entire
> attention on the land army. This point
> of view is extremely erroneous. . . The
> Revolutionary Military Council takes the
> firm and unshakeable point of view that
> the navy is extremely necessary to us . . .

The quotation reappears in both editions of The Sea Power of the State. The Frunze name is associated with a prestigious military academy and an annual award by the Council of Ministers for excellent military or military historical writing. There can be no doubt that Gorshkov is using a historical surrogate to get across a message to today's audience. Non-naval authors place Frunze's message in a context of coastal defense. 15/.

In discussing the Soviet Navy of the 1920's, Gorshkov both points out that the "small war" or "mosquito fleet" was defensive in nature" and also that it corresponded to the economic realities of the time. The association of any military form with the defensive is to associate it with the disgraced Trotsky rather than with Lenin and the offensive. 16/ All discussions which include criticism of the 1920's era appear in Soviet Navy publications.

In addition to using history to criticize, Gorshkov uses it also to reinforce positive actions. In discussing the economy of the 1930's and the possibilities for building a large navy, Gorshkov makes repeated reference to the party decision made before World War II to build such an oceangoing fleet. This theme appears 20 times in a wide variety of domestic publications.

The decision cited generally is associated with the end of the 1930's implying a recognition that the threat was perceived and that the correct solution was reached well before the start of hostilities in the Great Patriotic War. A related theme is that this war interrupted the planned ship buildings which Gorshkov obviously thinks were wise.

Related to the planned pre-war buildup is commentary on military thought. MODs generally refer to pre-war military thought as essentially correct, although Grechko made reference to faulty concepts based upon the limited experiences of the Spanish Civil War. Gorshkov frequently points out that a defensive mind-set for the employment of the Soviet Navy was created because of earlier "small war" theories that impacted on support for naval building.

Gorshkov specifically criticizes the pre-war fleet since it was capable of only local defensive operations. He also faults pre-war military doctrine and strategy because they only considered the Soviet Navy capable of local defense operations. Gorshkov rebukes the armed forces leadership for underestimating and having disdain for the fleet. Gorshkov stresses the pre-war lack of appreciation for the potential of attack naval aviation. It appears certain that Gorshkov's use of these concepts constitute examples of historical surrogates. In all cases, the intended audience is military and not necessarily only navy.

The Soviet Navy C-in-C also cites the prewar maldeployment of submarines and problems associated with joint combat operations. The fleet itself is described as deficient in anti-air protection, ASW equipment and forces, minesweepers, and auxiliaries. Naval aviation deficiencies included the lack of aircraft designed specifically for sea warfare. Gorshkov implies in The Sea Power of the State that an aircraft carrier would have been useful. Amphibious hardware problems receive the most frequent commentary and are virtually the only criticisms that are published outside military circles.

In an attempt to ascertain the importance of these latent comments to current needs, a cross check was run to those statements that discuss needs of the current Soviet fleet. Today's surface ships have also been described once as needing anti-air defenses in a passage tied to the lessons of the past war. ASW ships were cited as being required in 1963. Auxiliary vessels are also needed to balance today's fleet. Gorshkov makes it clear that the pre-war fleet was not balanced. The current need for aviation being able to overcome anti-air defenses is associated with the lessons of the war. Current ASW aircraft problems parallel similar pre-war criticism.

Subsurface needs are both quite explicit and most interesting. A paragraph was added by Grechko to the 2nd Edition of the Armed Forces of the Soviet State which discusses the need for Soviet SSBN quietness, greater depth and endurance. This passage does not appear in the U.S. translation authorized by the Soviet All-Union Copyright Agency.

Gorshkov discusses in July 1983 the need for greater submarine depth, a new powerplant, the necessity for concealment, and sensors to ensure the submarine gathers necessary intelligence. The Soviet Navy C-in-C makes reference to the possibility of close coordination between subsurface, surface, and air platforms in three passages tied to the lessons of the past war. Thus there appears to be some but not total correlation between manifest current fleet needs and that of the fleet in 1938.

World War II

Both Grechko and Gorshkov have specifically stated that the past war holds lessons of value today. The MOD uses the war as a warning to the West that an attack will result in defeat.

Gorshkov repeatedly implies that the current Soviet Navy has roles of greater importance than those in the past war due to the composition of the modern fleet, advances in technology, and the improved economic opportunity. Soviet Navy wartime roles of interest to this study which Gorshkov refers to are as follows (number of documents containing theme):

Support to the army in general	53
Amphibious operations	46
Attacking surface ships including disrupting SLOCs	43
Maintaining Soviet SLOCs	41

It has been widely reported that the primary Soviet fleet mission was to support the army. Gorshkov's discussions of amphibious operations and maintaining supply lines at sea are generally all tied to the support they provided the army. Other tactical fleet support operations include gunfire (23) and aviation (16).

Of interest is Gorshkov's treatment of the Soviet campaign against enemy SLOCs. He often goes to great lengths to explain how the interruption of supplies to the Germans was felt on the land fronts. In July 1982, he states that "all this attests to the great strategic importance of the naval actions on the naval communications lines for victory over the enemy."

Gorshkov cites a number of positive achievements and lessons from the Great Patriotic War: Northern fleet operations that kept open supply lines to allies were described as strategic; the diversion of significant numbers of German Navy units to the flanks contributed to the allies victory in the battle of the Atlantic; the value and correctness of Stalin's centralized command and control. This latter theme of Grechko's is modified by Gorshkov in July 1982 when he cites the successes of navy-controlled SLOC disruptions.

Gorshkov acknowledges that the war was won on land. Grechko associates victory with strategic reserves in 1970 but says in The Armed Forces of the Soviet State they were decisive only on the course of the war. Three times Grechko cites the importance of the buildup of strategic reserves in the pre-war period.

One of McConnell's main points is that Gorshkov states that navies rarely have an impact on the outset of a war but exercise more influence as it progresses. One can certainly infer this from earlier historical discussions. From discussions involving the Great Patriotic War, the war that Grechko and Gorshkov say is most important, a different pattern emerges.

We find 29 distinct citations by Gorshkov and one by Grechko that refer directly to the Soviet Navy's contribution to the armed struggle in its <u>initial</u> period. In passages that specifically discuss the Soviet Navy doing its duty "right to the end," we find only 14 citations. The initial value of the Soviet Navy is cited regularly over the years whereas the "duty to the end" appears less regularly, from 1963-1967 and then since 1975.

Not all experiences from the Great Patriotic War were positive, however. Gorshkov admits that during the war the employment of the navy was primarily local and merely defensive, and that some commanders had disdain for the fleet and did not understand its potential. He cites examples of poorly coordinated joint amphibious landings and naval base defense. The Admiral specifically cites the lack of surface and air units for support of Baltic fleet submarines because these surface and air forces were diverted to support the army.

The lack of shipbuilding production is a negative factor blamed on the loss of shipyards to the enemy, the assignment of the remaining to produce items for the army, and actual wartime naval losses exceeding all forecasts. In Gorshkov's September 1977 book and his 1980 <u>Kommunist</u> article, he says the rear supplied the navy everything it needed. It was <u>not</u> the job of the Rear Services to provide <u>new</u> ships.

Other less frequent lessons include: that the Soviet Union was hampered in inter-theater maneuver between fleets (meaning that each fleet essentially remained unsupported); and that ships had to perform missions for which they were never designed. Gorshkov acknowledges the contribution of 1,600 ships mobilized by the Peoples Commissariat of Internal Affairs, the merchant and river fleets, new construction, and allied aid but states that these were of low quality, secondary importance, and did not solve the lack of balance in the fleet. All negative comments are found in publications primarily aimed at military audiences.

Gorshkov draws on the experiences of the USSR's former allies. He points out the massive amounts of support for allied amphibious operations, the tremendous ASW assets tied up but their limited results (which he says, in November 1972, is of interest today), and the value of the SLOCs, both economically and for the military. In his booklet <u>The Navy</u>, the Admiral emphasizes the role of submarines in the World War II SLOC campaign but not in the historical section. Instead, it appears in the post-war review.

World War II SLOC campaigns are associated in <u>The Sea Power of the State</u> with undermining military-economic potential. In that book, Gorshkov also points out the Pacific war as being instructive for wars between nations separated by oceans. He also points out that Pearl Harbor had no unified commander responsible for defense.

Gorshkov emphasizes the need for air supremacy/capability for distant-water operations and amphibious landings. He points out in <u>The Sea Power of the State</u> that the British attitude that carriers were mere auxiliaries was faulty. Most comments on allied experiences are destined for military readers.

In both editions of <u>The Armed Forces of the Soviet State</u>, Grecko states that atomic bombs are only decisive if used on a massive scale and that the "American command used the new weapon not on enemy forces, but on cities having little strategic or economic importance." 17/

In assessing the experiences of her former enemies in World War II, Gorshkov points out the value of Norway to Germany, the loan of non-naval aircraft to the German Navy as a proven bad idea, and the ability of the German command to maneuver fleet units against the USSR and use geography to their advantage.

Gorshkov's most frequently cited criticism of the German Navy is its failure to allocate air and surface units to support submarines in the battle of the Atlantic and its failure to attack ASW forces. In discussing Japan, Gorshkov cites her wartime navy as being unbalanced and that Japan grossly underestimated her dependency upon SLOCs. The comment is about Japan, but the message applies currently to the U.S. and Europe. All commentary about axis war experiences appear in Soviet military publications.

Post-War Era

Gorshkov criticizes the postwar Stalin era for its mistaken views that the fleet should revolve around a defensive strategy and assisting the army. He faults relying on large gun ships that lacked air and submarine defenses. Building gun ships so dominated the shipyards that it precluded building amphibious ships and craft. Gorshkov complains that naval aviation was too defensive in orientation and specifically lacked ASW capability. In February 1967, he said that military theory in this era was deficient. All criticisms generally appear in Soviet military publications.

Criticism of the Khrushchev era begins in February 1967 with commentary about the mid-1950's decision to expand the fleet. Gorshkov criticizes "authorities" who thought that nuclear weapons had made the fleet obsolete and those who dismissed amphibious operations. He claimed that "defensive tendencies held up forward movement of our theoretical military thought."

Gorshkov mentions in February 1967 that a "frequent assertion of the time was that single missiles, placed on land launchers would be sufficient for destroying . . . surface warships, and even submarines." Yet in December 1972 Grechko made specific reference to the SRF targeting naval forces in the theater.

The Navy Chief repeats in The Sea Power of the State his criticism of those who thought fleets were obsolete, attributing such views to no one in particular, or to imperialist circles who genuflected to the "omnipotence" of nuclear weapons.

In one extremely convoluted passage from an article in Voprosy Filosofii, (May 1975), Gorshkov points out that initially Soviet Navy plans for the use of nuclear weapons and missiles were "within the framework of already existing principles and views." Nuclear weapons were simply viewed as intensifications of weapons of the Great Patriotic War.

He says that when Soviet Navy missiles with nuclear warheads were actually built, the theoretical employment of these weapons was then based upon the U.S. experience of nuclear weapons in Japan and the experience of other powerful means of armed combat. Following further investigation and testing, Gorshkov states that later the proper role and targeting objectives of strategic missiles was determined.

Of interest here is Gorshkov's historical reference to the early consideration of nuclear weapons for routine tactical use and an apparent disdain for the targeting of cities. This parallels Grechko's comments. Targeting objectives might be in cities, which was perhaps unfortunate or irrelevant, but it was specific strategic, military, and economic objectives that were settled upon as the objects of attack.

This Voprosy Filosofii article is simply too vague to allow the analyst to definitely conclude that the Soviets are telling us they will use nuclear weapons in a limited nuclear war, but it does reinforce military targeting in order to achieve distinct war aims. If the political decision were made to use nuclear weapons in warfare, the declaratory policy for their use does not appear to include deliberate use against civilians or cities.

Value of Historical Analysis

In order to illuminate more fully Soviet declaratory policy involving a future nuclear war, it has been argued in the West that one must include the use of historical latent themes. Such themes are supposed to show that the Soviets intend to withhold a part of their submarine missile fleet to be employed for escalation control, deterrence (or its restoration), and inter- or post-war negotiations conducted from a position of strength.

If this view is accepted as declaratory policy, historical surrogates must first be accepted as real. From reviewing the literature, there appears to be no question that historical surrogates are used by Soviet writers to impact hidden messages. There is no doubt that Gorshkov has used latent themes to demonstrate the value of navies and the wisdom of previous party decisions to support the navy. Similarly, he uses history to illustrate problems in peace and war when a nation, including the USSR, had an unbalanced navy or when a navy was inadequate for national needs.

If the most significant latent themes of Czarist era history are those involving navies winning the peace, then the intended audience being primarily navy is a problem. We simply do not know whether this is a case of publishing ideas in navy journals, since censorship controls are perhaps looser, or, if it is an attempt to explain policies internally to the navy. There is always the possibility that the use of Czarist era history might simply be to illuminate the general worth of navies and not to convey a special message for nuclear war.

Discussions of Leninist principles governing military operations are associated with today's political-military situation. The emphasis on reserves is most often cast in terms of land forces and economic stockpiles. Inferring that a message regarding reserves of all forces is logical, 18/ even so, withholding as a strategy involving only submarines is not an automatic next step.

Criticism of the defensive tendency of the Soviet Navy in the 1920's, pre-war period, Great Patriotic War, and postwar eras is constant. Yet the bastions theory would involve a defensive strategy with offensive (active defense) tactics. The weight of the evidence due to both the quantitative amount and the repeated emphasis to study the Great Patriotic War would suggest that a defensive-only strategy in a future war is not declaratory policy, rather that active defense against western SSBNs and attack carriers should be expected.

Latent historical themes and manifest themes regarding specific fleet building deficiencies were correlated. There was some degree of similarity but no general analogy, hence criticisms of the fleet in 1938-1941 may simply have been used to demonstrate that previous decisions can be erroneous, not to infer specific needs today.

A similar lack of correlation is evidenced by Gorshkov's constant discussions of the need for balanced navies. He frequently points out historical instances of lack of balance and associates this lack with failures. We might, therefore, expect to find him mentioning the need to balance the Soviet Navy today, or, at least no mention of the subject. Gorshkov has stated nine times (from May 1965 to July 1982) to a variety of military, general, and foreign audiences that his fleet is balanced. One does not find a separate external message that the Soviet fleet is balanced and a different internal message that the navy needs balance. Both editions of The Sea Power of the State only refer to having the foundation of a balanced fleet.

If we take Gorshkov's advice and focus on the last war, the latent message is that Soviet naval operations in war will not be purposeless fleet versus fleet operations. Rather the operations would be expected to support the land campaign. Cutting the SLOCs is an important method that undermines the military-economic potential of the enemy and influences the war ashore.

One can attempt to show history demonstrating navies as valuable in longer wars or after the armed struggle is well underway. Yet the worth of the Soviet Navy in the initial period of the Great Patriotic War is consistently stressed.

It appears, therefore, that there is value in the investigation of historical surrogates but that their validity can be diminished by selective extraction and lack of cross check with manifest themes. Marshal Ogarkov has said that the current international situation reminds him of the years preceding World War II. 19/ By taking the extra effort and analyzing a wider data set, analysis of declaratory policy is possible.

Arms Control Impact

In June 1971, Chairman Brezhnev gave an election speech in Moscow where he proposed solving the situation of the navies of great powers cruising for long periods far from their shores. In a February 1982 letter to an Australian disarmament group, the Party Chairman repeated this position. Since 1982 restrictions on Western SSBNs, SLBMs, and sea-launched cruise missiles have been a recurring theme in the context of on-going bilateral arms control negotiations. The Soviets have proposed extensive and various naval arms control regulations. 20/ Proposals call for limitations on ASW forces and aircraft carriers. 21/

In general, it would appear that naval arms control is a matter for Politburo spokesman to initiate and the MOD and Soviet Navy C-in-C to simply endorse and more fully explain. Soviet proposals would directly hamper Western deployments and the ability of Western navies to strike the USSR. Few proposals would appear to be related to Soviet home waters. 22/

There appears to be a direct correlation with perceived threats from the sea and willingness to regulate such threats by arms control. As threats are identified, they appear to be met, in the literature, by a combinations of Soviet military programs and arms control. Arms control as a solution appears to be most frequent in areas where the literature indicates the Soviets are weakest militarily.

NOTES

1. Office of the Chief of Naval Operations, Understanding Soviet Naval Developments, 5th Ed. (Washington: U.S. Government Printing Office, April 1985), p. 28. The previous edition listed "pin-down" of U.S. intercontinental ballistic missiles as a mission (on p. 15) instead of industrial targets found in this version.

2. Statement on February 28, 1984 of RADM John Butts, Director of Naval Intelligence, contained in Fiscal Year 1985 Department Authorization and Oversight Hearings, Part 3, Seapower and Strategic and Critical Materials Subcommittee, Armed Services Committee, House of Representatives, 98th Cong., 2nd Sess. (HASC No. 98-34) (Washington: U.S. Government Printing Office, 1984), p. 5.

3. The Soviets own view of the mission-completion capability of their own SSBNs in defended bastions appears to be less that assured. See Ketron, Inc., "Soviet Perceptions of U.S. Antisubmarine Warfare Capabilities," KFR 293-80, Vol. I pp. S 27-S 28 and Vol. II pp. III 298-III 299, III 333, and IV 10-IV 12, Report prepared for ACDA (Arlington: September 1980). More recently, Jan Breemer has raised the issue of the wartime missions of

the Soviet Navy in "The Soviet Navy's SSBN Bastions: Evidence, Inference, and Alternative Scenarios," RUSI Journal, March 1985, pp. 18-26. See my follow-on letter in the September 1985 issue, pp. 77-78.

4. RADM V. Shelyag, "Two World Outlooks—Two Views on War," Krasnaya Zvezda, February 7, 1974, pp. 2-3; and a condensed version in English "Two Ideologies—Two Views on War," Soviet Military Review, November 1974, p. 9.

5. John Hines and Philip Peterson have written extensively on this subject. See for example their concise "Strategies of Soviet Warfare," Wall Street Journal, January 7, 1983, p. 16. See also COL-GEN M. A. Gareyev, M.V. Frunze-Military Theoretician (Moscow: Voyenizdat, 1985), p. 240.

6. Interview with Marshal V. Tolubko, Commander-in-Chief of the Strategic Rocket Forces, "Constantly on the Alert," Moscow News in English, July 8, 1984, p. 5; and Marshal S. Akhromeyev, Chief of the General Staff, "The Great Victory and its Lessons," Izvestiya, Morning Ed., May 7, 1985, p. 2.

7. Marshal of the Soviet Union N. V. Ogarkov, "Guarding Peaceful Labor," Kommunist, July 1981, pp. 80-91; Always Ready to Defend the Fatherland (Moscow: Voyenizdat, signed to press January 26, 1982), pp. 16 and 47; "The Victory and the Present Day," Izvestiya, Morning Ed., May 9, 1983, pp. 1-2; "Reliable Defense for Peace," Izvestiya, Morning Ed., September 23, 1983, pp. 4-5; "The Defense of Socialism: Experience of History and the Present Day," Krasnaya Zvezda, 1st Ed., May 9, 1984, pp. 2-3; "On the 40th Anniversary of the Great Victory," Kommunist Vooruzhennykh Sil, November 1984, p. 26; and History Teaches Vigilance (Moscow: Military Publishers, 1985), p. 89.

8. Ogarkov, Always Prepared to Defend the Fatherland, p. 58; reiterated in History Teaches Vigilance, p. 77: ". . . Soviet military doctrine demands not only to defend the country, using massive defense means but also to be able to strike the enemy and crush him in any possible situations."

9. Moroskoy Sbornik: April, May, and November 1981; January, March, April, July 1982; and March and April 1983.

10. James McConnell, "The Gorshkov Articles, the New Gorshkov Book, and their Relation to Policy," Soviet Naval Influence: Domestic and Foreign Dimensions, Michael MccGwire and John McDonnell, Eds., (New York: Praeger, 1977), pp. 586-592.

11. Michael MccGwire, "Advocacy of Seapower in an Internal Debate," <u>Admiral Gorshkov on "Navies in War and Peace</u>," CRC-257 (Alexandria: Center for Naval Analyses, September 1974), pp. 29-30.

12. Roger Barnett, "Soviet Strategic Reserves and the Soviet Navy," <u>The Soviet Union: What Lies Ahead?</u>, K. M. Currie and G. Varhall Eds., published under the auspices of the U.S. Air Force as Vol. 6 in the Studies in Communist Affairs (Washington: U.S. Government Printing Office, 1985), pp. 581-605. The strategic reserve role for Soviet SSBNs has been given official sanction in the statement of RADM Butts, <u>Fiscal Year 1985 Defense Department Authorization and Oversight Hearings</u>, p. 5.

13. MG Kh. Dzhelaukhov, "Combatting Strategic Reserves in a Theater of Military Operations," <u>Voyennaya Mysl'</u>, November 1964, p. 2.

14. V. Ryabov, <u>The Soviet Armed Forces Yesterday and Today</u> (Moscow: Progress Publishers, English translation 1976), p. 73.

15. MG S. A. Tyushkevich, <u>The Soviet Armed Forces: A History of Their Organizational Development</u> (Moscow: 1978), English translation authorized by the USSR and published by the U.S. Air Force as Vol. 19 of the Soviet Military Thought Series, p. 163.

16. Y. Korablev, <u>Lenin-The Founder of the Soviet Armed Forces</u> (Moscow: Progress Publishers, English translation, 1977), p. 147. The Russian fascination with the "offensive" has been rediscovered of late in the West. For an excellent precursor see D. Fedotoff White, "Soviet Philosophy of War," <u>Political Science Quarterly</u>, September 1936, pp. 321-353.

17. Similar criticism of allied targeting of cities are found in COL M. Shirokov, "The Question of Influences on the Military and Economic Potential of Warring States," <u>Voyennaya Mysl'</u>, April 1968, p. 38.

18. See Samuel Cohen and Joseph Douglass, "Selected Targeting and Soviet Deception," <u>Armed Forces Journal International</u>, September 1983, pp. 95-101, for an excellent discussion of the possibility of land-based reserves.

19. Ogarkov, <u>History Teaches Vigliance</u>, p. 93.

20. "Averting the Growing Nuclear Threat and Curbing the Arms Race," a memorandum submitted to the United Nations, distributed by TASS (in English) and contained in a Soviet Embassy press release of June 17, 1982.

21. Andrei Gromyko letter to U.N. Secretary General Javier de Cuellar, distributed by TASS (in English) on

April 14, 1984 and contained in a Soviet Embassy press release of April 16, 1984.

22. A noteable exception invovles Yuri Andropov's speech of June 7, 1983, which raises the issue of a nuclear-free Baltic. See <u>Kraznaya Zvezda</u>, 2nd Ed., pp. 1 and 3; and a Soviet Embassy press release of that same day. According to a <u>New York Times</u> report on that same date, COL-GEN V. Chervov stated some time before the speech that if the Baltic were indeed made a nuclear-free zone, then the Soviet Navy would withdraw its six missile-carrying submarines based there.

7

Findings of Declaratory Policy

This chapter contains the author's findings of declaratory policy for the strategic employment of the Soviet Navy in a future major nuclear war. These findings represent a synthesis of the manifest and latent themes as discussed in detail previously. Alone they do not represent predictions for Soviet behavior. Such predictions must include consideration of hardware, deployments, and exercises.

Bastions

The theory that the Soviets will deploy their fleet in home waters in defended bastions designed to protect their nuclear powered ballistic missile submarines (SSBNs) appears to be well substantiated by manifest evidence. Falling into the category of fleet versus fleet, concepts have been openly described that likely would apply to any such bastions, including the presence of defended zones, cooperation between branches, and the need to support the main striking arm — their SSBNs. The threat to Soviet SSBNs is described as Western antisubmarine warfare (ASW) forces, including submarines and aircraft carriers.

Bastion defense also appears to be associated with the need to protect Soviet territory itself. The defense perimeter that protects the SSBN also protects the homeland against shorter-range threats from the sea, such as cruise missiles and older ballistic missiles and carrier aviation.

Latent evidence for bastions appears to be plentiful. The need to provide combat stability to submarines, which are the main striking arm, is a message in discussions of World Wars I, II, and Soviet Baltic Fleet operations in the Great Patriotic War. The failure of Germany to attack allied ASW forces is also mentioned. There is additional latent evidence in the claim that Western submarines will support their SSBNs, a concept that is not found in the Western literature.

Bastion defense may be defensive strategy, but involves aggressive tactics and offensive operations. Bastions will not be passively defended. Defense of bastions may take place in the conventional phase of the armed struggle even though the primary object of attack by the West and subject of defense by the Soviet Union are nuclear forces.

Withholding SSBNs

The theory that the Soviets will withhold some of their SSBNs for escalation control, deterrence, or to aid inter- or post-war negotiating positions is not well substantiated by the manifest evidence. Rather, the latent evidence for withholding, is for withholding <u>all</u> types of nuclear forces and not specifically those in the navy.

According to literature evidence, Soviet declaratory policy now includes the potential for an initial conventional phase or a total conventional war. These may not necessarily have anything to do with a possible war with the U.S. The fleet has also been described as having the capability for prolonged combat operations.

Nuclear retaliation from the sea and elsewhere is "inevitable," not only automatic. Chairman Brezhnev and Marshal Ustinov stressed that limited nuclear war is impossible and a future war could not be fought assuming prearranged rules. The context appears to be that if Soviet territory is hit by Western theater systems, U.S. soil will also suffer.

If war is to come about, Soviet declaratory policy is to end it quickly and on terms favorable to the USSR. A case can be made from the literature that long-range nuclear weapons will be withheld initially from attacks on the soil of each superpower and would serve as a deterrent to the conduct of such operations. Thus Soviet long-range strategic nuclear forces, including SSBNs, must be able to survive Western strike during any phase of the war.

Land-based systems are not necessarily considered invulnerable. The emphasis on sea-based systems survivability, therefore, may have nothing to do with withholding, since it could equally be a part of a general strategy to delay nuclear attacks on superpower territory and fear of a

Western first strike or strategic ASW campaign against Soviet SSBNs.

There is no manifest evidence that if the nuclear tripwire is crossed in Europe, that the use of nuclear weapons by the Soviet Navy will be delayed; rather the fleet's ability to immediately participate is stressed. One can infer that withholding Soviet SSBN strikes from attacks on the U.S. itself could deter similar strikes by American SSBNs. Withholding might be a strategy to deny advantage to the U.S., which has openly discussed maintaining a secure force capable of assured destruction of the USSR. The U.S. might be deterred from using its final military capability due to withheld Soviet reserves.

The withholding of submarines as part of a reserve appears likely but not unique. It would appear illogical, based on the literature, that the nuclear reserves would be allocated to only one service. Soviet victory in war is always described as requiring the participation of all services. Naval forces and theaters are described only by navy sources as being capable of influencing the outcome of war. In non-navy documents, the claim is diluted to influence in armed struggles.

The evidence from latent themes does support the use of navies to win the peace, but so do similar historical passages written by Western authors. Rather than conclude that Admiral Gorshkov has made a unique contribution in stressing naval forces in winning wars, one need only re-read Admiral Mahan on how the American Revolution was really won and how Napoleon was really defeated.

Despite many historical examples of the value of navies over the long run in a war, Admiral Gorshkov stresses the lessons of the Great Patriotic War, which emphasize the value of the Soviet Navy in the initial phase. If anything can be gained from these latent messages, it is that there is a role for navies both in the beginning and at the end of a future war.

Targeting

Soviet ballistic missile declaratory targeting includes major Western naval combatants (SSBNs, ASW forces including carriers and submarines) in ports and at bases. The Strategic Rocket Forces (SRF) and the navy appear to be assigned this mission. All operations would be nuclear.

Open ocean fleet versus fleet operations receive little mention. Modern U.S. SSBNs probably do not have to enter the local defended bastions in order to fire their missiles, and therefore they must be the target of Soviet ASW submarines conducting distant operations. Such operations could be entirely conventional. There is also a possible declaratory policy (not reinforced of late) that SRF and navy nuclear ballistic missiles will be used against enemy ships in the theater (which may mean at sea). Admiral Gorshkov criticized such views in 1967, but Marshal Grechko did make direct reference to SRF targeting naval forces in the theater in 1972. Gorshkov himself discussed the use of Soviet SSBNs to counter similar Western systems in 1979.

Targeting for fleet versus shore operations appears to involve ballistic missile strikes against political-administrative centers, military-industrial targets, terminals for the sea lines of communication (SLOCs), and military bases. As such, all operations would be nuclear. Gorshkov is much more specific in his targeting objectives than are his seniors. This needs to be further analyzed by consideration of deployment patterns and hardware capability.

Of interest is the targeting of military bases that constitute springboards for attack against the USSR. This can certainly be taken as air bases and would thus confirm official Washington's version of Soviet SLBM targeting.

Latent evidence supports the contention that the USSR does not plan to target cities per se, but it does not answer the question if they view civilian casualties as something to avoid, unavoidable and unfortunate, or a bonus. Unless they planned to occupy the U.S., Soviet collateral damage avoidance may not be the same as in Europe.

Sea Lines of Communication (SLOC)

The manifest evidence for a SLOC mission involves nuclear war and strikes against terminals. The importance of SLOCs in history is cited as being both strategic and capable of undermining an enemy's military-economic potential (a current strategic goal). The difficulty in defending against a submarine campaign in historical passages as well as the diversion of assets it causes is pointed out.

A SLOC campaign at sea is not important in a short nuclear war involving the U.S. or Europe. If Soviet doctrine in fact now recognizes a conventional phase or even a lengthy conventional war (declaratory policy according to the literature), then the disruption of SLOCs without nuclear strikes on the terminal ends would still be a strategic mission that the Soviet military would have to perform. An at-sea SLOC campaign could involve conventional or tactical nuclear weapons.

This could explain Gorshkov's continual criticisms, using historical surrogates, of defensive-only navies. A conventional SLOC capability would involve an offensive strategy that could influence the outcome of a war. The evidence of capability in hardware should provide insight into Gorshkov either arguing for this role or announcing it as approved strategy.

Tactical Nuclear War at Sea

Based upon the literature, the possibility for tactical nuclear warfare initiated at sea and limited to that theater cannot be supported or dismissed. It is clear that the Soviets do not want a nuclear world war, but there may be advantages for the Soviets in threatening to go nuclear immediately in Europe. The Soviets have also been emphasizing conventional capabilities.

Gorshkov has pointed out what all naval officers intuitively understand—that nuclear weapons can guarantee tactical success in battle (one weapon = one surface ship). Whether or not operations could be confined to the sea is another question. On the other hand, if the Soviets go nuclear ashore, there is no reason to doubt they will go nuclear at sea.

Ustinov made direct reference to the non-sanctioned use of nuclear weapons, and Gorshkov is obviously concerned with getting release authority to his deployed forces. Based upon the general tone of the literature, the seriousness with which nuclear war is addressed, and the absence of statements to the contrary, this author finds no literature evidence to support the view that release authority for tactical nuclear weapons is a navy matter nor that a nuclear war at sea (alone) would be initiated by the Soviets.

Based upon the author's understanding of the literature concerning the nature of a future land war against NATO Europe, the author must conclude that once nuclear weapons are used ashore, they will be used at sea as well. The decision to initiate tactical nuclear war at sea appears to be neither a Soviet Navy decision nor one that will hinge upon naval matters. Rather, it will depend upon the political context, such as participants in and desired length of the war.

PART TWO

Hardware Analysis

8

Methodology

The ability of a nation actually to use its military or to threaten to use force is a function of the capability of those forces and of the opposing forces, and the credibility that they can and will be used as planned. Capability of military hardware is a measurement of what a military force can actually do. Capability is generally thought to be easier to measure, the result of intelligence gathering and expert analysis of the threat.

As opposed to what a military force can do, intent involves what the enemy will do with its force. Intent can be partially determined by analysis of declaratory policy, which was done in the content analysis section of this book. Intent can also be ascertained by analysis of capability, exercise behavior, and deployment patterns. This section will analyze those concepts.

Credibility is more difficult to measure than capability, since it is not easily quantified. Credibility can be inferred from open source literature information by measuring the repetition of themes and the emphasis they are given. This, too, was done in the previous content analysis section.

Capability can also be a measurement of credibility, since it also represents a measurement of determination or will. The final capability of forces is the end result of inter-service debates over roles and missions, debates over percentages of budgets to go to each service or the military versus non-military sectors and occurs after the actual technical abilities of the economy, scientific community, and military are factored in. Hence, capability is more than just a measurement of what weapons systems can do.

This section will deal primarily with measurements of capability. Since measurements of capability may be dependent upon one's perception of intent, intent can and will be manipulated or tested against all reasonable possible uses for a weapon system.

One of the first problems in assessing capability is whether the analyst should adopt a "worst-case," "worst-plausable-case," "most-likely-case," or "best-case" view of the perceived threat. In other words, should he view what is the worst that the opponent can do if everything works in his favor, or vice versa, or should analysis be based upon conditions somewhere in between.

Adopting a worst-case or worst-plausable-case threat to strategic nuclear forces has always been doctrine in the U.S. In looking at the statements of former and the successive Secretaries of Defense, one finds remarkable consistency over the years. In discussing the need for sufficient U.S. capability to threaten the USSR, the following statements reflect the worst-case assumption made:

1962	McNamara	. . . . even in the face of a massive surprise attack. . . . 1/
1965	McNamara	. . . . even were the attacker to strike first 2/
1967	McNamara	. . . . even after our absorbing a surprise first strike 3/
1974	Schlesinger	. . . . even in the aftermath of a well-executed surprise attack 4/
1977	Rumsfeld	. . . even after a highly effective first strike . . . 5/
1980	Brown	. . . . even if the Soviets were to attack first, without warning 6/
1983	Weinberger	. . . . survive a first strike 7/
1986	Weinberger	. . . our forces must be able to survive a pre-emptive attack. 8/

In matters of a possible nuclear war, taking the worst-case threat to the U.S. has been the rule and not the exception. That worst-case is the well executed surprise attack on an unalerted U.S., i.e., the bolt from the blue.

Since this study involves the threat posed by Soviet Navy strategic nuclear forces to U.S. strategic nuclear forces, the reader can be justified in preferring to view the threat in its worst-case form. The author will present the range of evidence for the extremes of a worst and best case and one case in between.

Worst-cases have been criticized as being extremely unlikely, although, in theory, if one develops his own forces based upon the worst-case threat, it is likely that he will have sufficient capability to meet any actual threat. The worst-case is usually not acceptable politically in the U.S. for other than strategic nuclear forces since it can result in a never-ending commitment of resources. The best example of this is NATO where the worst-case surprise attack is never used as a programs planning assumption.

It is the job of the analyst to calulate the extremes of both the worst and best-case. This will set the parameters of the problem and will provide the decision-maker with sufficiently accurate assessments that he can make an intelligent choice of the most-likely-case.

Taking into account the purposeful high levels of uncertainty regarding military force capability and the scenario dependency of various aspects of hardware analysis, this section will proceed as follows. First, a common data base of facts will be established based upon items that most or all major sources agreed upon. This will include fleet disposition and forward deployments. Second, a set of scenario aggregated fleet task groups will be based upon the author's assessment of the logical employment of forces considering declaratory policy, peacetime force deployment, and design characteristics.

The author will then attempt to ascertain whether or not the capabilities of the forces permit accomplishment of missions articulated as declaratory policy. Essentially these are nuclear strikes from ballistic missile submarines on shore targets of varying types and protection of a portion of the ballistic missile submarine fleet in bastions.

A full assessment of Soviet capability would have to include dynamic interactions with opposing Western defenses and forces. That is well beyond the scope of this research effort, since it would involve, among other things, a major gaming effort that would need to be classified. This research effort will instead, examine only half of the equation. It is the author's opinion that since the U.S. is virtually defenseless against ballistic missiles, sufficient information can be gained from this one-sided presentation for the nuclear strike mission. The data base generated herein can be used by others interested in gaming to model the dynamic interactions.

Following completion of this basic analysis, the researcher will subject those findings to sensitivity analysis. 9/ Sensitivity analysis is an attempt to determine how sensitive results are by deliberately varying the quantitative assumptions. Contingency analysis is similar but involves the manipulation of context or environment rather than numbers alone. In other words, intent can be manipulated in order to see the impact upon capability.

Sensitivity analysis has been noteably absent from most of the hardware studies in the past. Although certain sophisticated methods exist with which to vary a large number of variables simultaneously, the author feels that a major contribution can be made simply by varying one or two key assumptions once those driving factors become obvious.

A number of other points will be considered in the analysis. Prominent will be whether or not a surplus in capability exists beyond what is minimally necessary for the accomplishment of the primary mission of nuclear strikes and bastion defense. The most logical mission for surplus general-purpose forces involves interdiction of the sea lines of communication.

Another flag will be whether or not offensive forces are more likely to be used in counterforce (including active defense by damage limitation) or countervalue (the threat of punishment). Types of targets for Soviet Navy strategic weapons may be ascertainable from certain key design features.

There is the question of time frame: 1985 will be the year for a snapshot analysis of hardware. The intent is to provide a guide on how to do one year so as to aid subsequent researchers attempting to create such a model.

A number of factors must be included in this type of hardware analysis. These include the types and numbers of ships in the Soviet Navy, their location, their mobilization potential, and the capability of certain individual weapons systems. Many of these factors can be identified and quantified with relative certainty. Other factors, however, such as fleet logistics capability for sustained operations, qualitative factors of individual units, and personnel are beyond the methodology used.

For example, in May 1984 the press reported a major explosion in the Soviet Northern Fleet ammunition depots. There is no way to account for the impact of the loss of weapons. At one extreme, it might prevent the Northern Fleet from carrying out vital wartime missions. On the other hand, it may have involved obsolete weapons or perhaps a few nuclear devices. We have no way of knowing.

Hardware analysis will consist of two parts. The first will deal with the strategic offensive nuclear forces assigned to the Soviet Navy. The second will deal with general-purpose forces. In general, this parallels the content analysis of fleet versus shore (strategic nuclear forces) and fleet versus fleet (general purpose forces). For both parts, the author has selected three major sources from which to draw the raw numbers necessary to create data bases. These sources are as follows:

1. Captain John Moore, RN (Ret.), Ed., Jane's Fighting Ships 1985-86. London: Jane's Publishing Co., Ltd., 1985 (currency varies).

2. International Institute for Strategic Studies, The Military Balance 1985-86, Autumn 1985 (current through July 1, 1985).

3. U.S. Defense Intelligence Agency, Unclassified Communist Naval Orders of Battle, DDB-1200-124-85, (current through October 1, 1985).

Other sources used to establish the data base or expand the hardware analysis (especially nuclear warhead characteristics) will be individually cited. The methodology utilized herein was developed by the author and was used in part by the Rand Corporation and published by them as "Soviet Navy Data Base: 1982-83," P-6859, April 1983. The data base in this book will not replicate the detail given to general-purpose forces published in the Rand version but will significantly expand in the areas of nuclear weaponry.

In Part Three of this book, a full comparison of declaratory policy and hardware capability together will be undertaken. One of the key goals will be to search for a match or mismatch between declaratory policy and capability. It is the author's opinion that if mismatches are found, available unclassified data is insufficient to explain them fully.

Mismatches as perceived by the Western analyst may not be obvious to the Soviet decision-maker. Furthermore, in the real world, people do not always complete what they have set out to do. Hence, a mismatch may be due to bureaucratic inefficiency, structural failures, human blindness, etc. Hence mismatches, as perceived by the author, will be identified, but no effort will be made to explain why they exist. Part Three will include the author's assessment of capability and the credibility of intended missions as gleaned from the declaratory policy.

NOTES

1. Robert McNamara, address given at Ann Arbor, Michigan, June 16, 1962; contained in American Defense Policy, 4th Ed., John Endicott and Roy Stafford, Eds. (Baltimore: John Hopkins University Press, 1977) p. 74.
2. Robert McNamara, statement of February 24, 1965 before the Committee on Armed Services and the Subcommittee on Department of Defense of the Committee on Appropriations, U.S. Senate, 89th Cong., 1st Sess.; contained in American Defense Policy, p. 75.
3. Robert McNamara, statement of September 18, 1967 before the Annual Convention of United Press International Editors and Publishers at San Francisco, California; contained in Department of State Bulletin, October 9, 1967, p. 443.
4. James Schlesinger, Annual Defense Department Report, FY 1975, March 4, 1974; contained in Nuclear Strategy and National Security: Points of View, Robert Pranger and Roger Labrie, Eds. (Washington: American Enterprise Institute for Public Policy Research, 1977), p. 92.
5. Donald Rumsfeld, Annual Defense Department Report, FY 1978, January 17, 1977; contained in Nuclear Strategy and National Security: Points of View, p. 190.
6. Harold Brown, Annual Defense Department Report, FY 1981 January 29, 1980 (Washington: U.S. Government Printing Office, 1980), p. 65.
7. Caspar Weinberger, Annual Defense Department Report, FY 1984, February 1, 1983 (Washington: U.S. Government Printing Office, 1983), p. 34.

8. Casper Weinberger, *Annual Defense Department Report, FY 1987*, February 5, 1986 (Washington: U.S. Government Printing Office, 1986), p. 33.

9. E. S. Quade, *Analysis for Public Decisions* (New York: Elsevier 1975), p. 220.

9

Strategic Nuclear Forces

Static Measurements

From the content analysis section, it was determined that the Soviets consider ballistic missile submarines as part of their strategic nuclear forces. Those that are nuclear powered are termed SSBNs in the West while those with diesel propulsion are SSBs. For purposes of this research, Western hardware terms will be used.

The Soviets had some twelve classes of ballistic missile submarines in service during 1985. Seven classes of ballistic missile submarines are accountable under the bilateral U.S.-Soviet SALT I Interim Agreement and are generally termed "strategic" in the West.

The total number of SALT accountable or "strategic" missile submarines, however, does not equal the total number of ballistic missile submarines available to the USSR. Additional units are not accounted for under SALT since they have shorter range theater weapons or may not have undergone official sea trials. Many are thought to be exempt since they are relatively unique prototype or research and development subsmarines. This analysis will include all militarily useful weapons and will not be artificially limited to consideration of the lesser numbers of SALT accountable systems. SALT numbers will be tabulated to demonstrate the contrast.

The first need in assessing the Soviet Navy's strategic nuclear forces is to decide how many of what class submarines actually exist. In order to do this, each of the primary sources was consulted, the total numbers per class were averaged (rounded), unless otherwise noted and an agreed upon figure was derived. Table 9.1 contains the findings of this data.

Table 9.1

Soviet Navy Ballistic Missile Submarines (1985)

Class	Jane's	IISS	DIA	Assumed
*Typhoon SSBN	3	3	3	3
*Delta IV SSBN	1	1	1	1
*Delta III SSBN	14	14	14	14
*Delta II SSBN	4	4	4	4
*Delta I SSBN	18	18	18	18
*Yankee II SSBN	1	1	1	1
*Yankee I SSBN	20	21	21	21
Hotel III SSBN	1	1	1	1
Hotel II SSBN	1	0	0	0
Golf V SSB	1	1a/	1	1
Golf III SSB	1	1	1	1
Golf II SSB	13	13	13	13
All SSBN/SSB	(78)	(78)	(78)	78
All SSBN	63	(63)	(63)	63
All SSB	15	(15)	(15)	15
*SALT I Accountable Hulls (limit 62)	(61)	62	(62)	62

Source: Final assumed number by author.

Notes:

a. Golf V is not tabulated by IISS or in Soviet Military Power under operational forces but rather under research.

From an agreed-upon number of submarine hulls, we can now proceed to the number of missile tubes per hull and therefore the number of missiles able to be carried. The possibility of reloading missiles into submarines has not yet been considered. Since the DIA did not give the number of missile tubes per submarine, an alternate official U.S. government document was used, the Department of Defense (DOD) Soviet Military Power, 4th Ed., published in April 1985. Table 98.2 presents the data for submarine launched ballistic missile (SLBM) launchers.

Table 9.2

Strategic Soviet SLBM Launchers (1985)

Class	Missile Type a/	No. Subs b/	Jane's	IISS	DOD	Assumed No. of c/ Launchers
*Typhoon	SS-N-20	3	20	20	20	60
*Delta IV	SS-N-23	1	16	16	16	16
*Delta III	SS-N-18	14	16	16	16	224
*Delta II	SS-N-8	4	16	16	16	64
*Delta I	SS-N-8	18	12	12	12	216
*Yankee II	SS-N-17	1	12	12	12	12
*Yankee I	SS-N-6	21	16	16	16	336
*Hotel III	SS-N-8	1	6	6	6	6
*Golf V	SS-N-20	1	1			1
*Golf III	SS-N-8	1	6	6		6
Golf II	SS-N-5	13	3	3	3	39
						980

Totals: *SS-N-23   16
         *SS-N-20   61
         *SS-N-18 224
         *SS-N-17   12
         *SS-N-8   292
         *SS-N-6   336
          SS-N-5   39

* SALT I accountable launchers (Limit 950)   941

Source: Final assumed number by author.

Notes:

a. All sources agree upon type missile carried.
b. Taken from assumed number in Table 9.1.
c. Number of submarines x number of launchers.

Each missile contains a certain number of warheads. These warheads are either single (one warhead per missile) or multiple. Of the latter, some are independently targetable (MIRVs) while others (MRVs) are multiple but not independently targetable and will fall on the same target.

In general, both strategists and arms controllers consider MRVs as one warhead since they will fall essentially in the same place. A multiple-warheaded MRV missile could only be used against one target area while MIRVed missiles can target more than one. For the purposes of this research, MRV capability will be noted but will be counted as one nuclear warhead.

Table 9.3 presents the best information available in the major sources for the number of warheads carried by each type SLBM. Again, <u>Soviet Military Power</u>, 4th Ed. was used as the official U.S. government source. Where SS-N/1 or 2, etc. appears, this indicates the modification or model number of that missile. For example, SS-N-18/3 means SS-N-18 Mod 3.

Table 9.3

Possible Static Soviet SLBM Warheads (1985)

Missile Type	No. of Launchers [a]	Jane's	IISS	DOD	Possible No. of Warheads [b]
SS-N-23	16	7[c]		7	112
SS-N-20	61	6-9	9	6-9	366 - 549
SS-N-18/3	224	7	7	7	1568
SS-N-18/2[d]		1	1	1	0
SS-N-18/1[d]		3	3	3	0
SS-N-17	12	1[c]	1	1	12
SS-N-8/2	292	1	1	1	292
SS-N-8/1[d]		1	1	1	0
SS-N-6/3[e]	336	1	1	1	336
SS-N-6/2[d]		1	1	1	0
SS-N-6/1[d]		1	1	1	0
SS-N-5	39	1	1		39
					2725 - 2908

Source: Final assumed numbers by author.

Notes:

a. Taken from assumed numbers in Table 9.2.
b. Number of launchers x minimum number, and, number of launchers x maximum number.
c. Jane's data inconsistent. Section on missiles says SS-N-23 has 10-12 warheads and SS-N-17 has MIRV; section on submarines says SS-N-23 has 7 warheads and SS-N-17 has 1 warhead.
d. IISS states none are operational.
e. SS-N-6/3 MRV capable. 2 RV according to Jane's, IISS, DOD.

Table 9.4 reflects the same data but expressed in terms of types of misiles and warheads for each submarine class. The number of RVs carried aboard each SS-N-20 is assumed to be 9.

Table 9.4

Assumed Static Soviet SLBM Warheads (1985)

Missile Type	Sub Type	No. of Launchers	Total No. of Warheads
SS-N-23	Delta IV	16	112
SS-N-20	Typhoon	60	540
	Golf V	1	9
SS-N-18/3	Delta III	224	1568
SS-N-17	Yankee II	12	12
SS-N-8/2	Delta II	64	64
	Delta I	216	216
	Hotel III	6	6
	Golf III	6	6
SS-N-6/3	Yankee I	336	336
SS-N-5	Golf II	39	39
			2908

Source: Author.

The static number of warheads on missiles as a measure of military capability is a poor indicator, despite its frequent use by the press. It does not account for missiles actually deliverable due to range limitations, a submarine going through overhaul etc. At best, it is a rough measure of the number of targets capable of being hit (discounting colocated targets). As such, it will be utilized later in the dynamic assessment section.

Since not all warheads are equal in size, the next step is to determine the estimated yield for each type warehead. Table 9.5 presents the findings in raw megatons. Raw megatonnage itself is of value in the construction of other units of measurement. It may also serve as an input assisting in computing lethal fallout areas and measurements of damage that will be considered later.

Table 9.5

Static Soviet SLBM Warhead Raw Megatonnage (1985)

Missile	Jane's	IISS	Assumed Raw Yield	Total Force a/ Raw Yield
SS-N-23			.1b/	11.2
SS-N-20		.2c/	.2b/	109.8
SS-N-18/3	.2	.2	.2	313.6
SS-N-17		1.0	1.0	12
SS-N-8/2	.8	.8	.8	233.6
SS-N-6/3	1.0	2x.5	2x.5	336
SS-N-5	.8	1.0	.8	31.2
				1047.4 Megatons (MT)

Source: Final totals by author.

Notes:

a. Assumed Raw Yield x number of warheads from Tables 9.3 and 9.4 except that the SS-N-20 will be assumed to have 9 warheads.
b. No sources estimated the yield for the SS-N-23. Rather than <u>not</u> account for this weapon, the author assumed the minimal yield that any ICBM or SLBM is credited with by IISS or in John M. Collins <u>U.S. - Soviet Military Balance 1980 - 1985.</u>
c. IISS data inconsistent. Reports 100KT in one section and 200KT in another. Assumed 200KT.

In an effort to make each of the effects of various types of warheads relatively standardized for analytic purposes, equivalent megatonnage (EMT) can be calculated from raw megatonnage. One needs to do this is because it takes roughly an increase in yield of 8 times in order to double blast damage. In other words, an 8 MT nuclear blast is not 8 times as powerful as 1 MT blast, but rather twice as powerful.

The formulas used to construct EMT reflect the lethal radius of a weapon is proportional to its yield to the 1/3 power and its lethal area is proportional to the square of the lethal radius. For individual warheads below 1 MT, EMT = yield 2/3. Above 1 MT, EMT = yield 1/2. Obviously, EMT is biased to increase warheads yield below 1 MT and reduce it above 1 MT. Aggregate EMT is computed by totalling the figures from individual warheads calculations, not by computing the total yield and then applying the correction factor.

There has been specific criticism of the present method of computing EMT. 1/ Nevertheless, the standard formula represents an analytic measure recognizable in much of the defense community. Despite its flaws, EMT continues to be utilized in analysis since it can be found associated with charts giving urban-industrial damage and is used to compute counter-military potential. It also is a standard unit of measurement used to describe the level of deliverable force often described as needed to assure the destruction of the USSR (400 EMT).

Table 9.6 presents individual, missile, and total force EMT based upon raw megatonnage and the warheads assumed.

Table 9.6

Static Soviet SLBM Warhead EMT (1985)

Missile	EMT/Warhead	EMT/Missile	Total Force EMT
SS-N-23	.22a/	1.54	24.6
SS-N-20	.34	3.06b/	186.7
SS-N-18/3	.34	2.38	533.1
SS-N-17	1.0	1.0	12
SS-N-8/2	.86	.86	251.1
SS-N-6/3	1.0	1.0	336
SS-N-5	.86	.86	33.5
			1377.0 EMT

Source: Author.

Notes:

a. Assumes .1 MT per warhead.
b. Assumes 9 RV per missile.

Thus far, the units of measurement have not been specifically associated with any particular target set. Warheads and yields assist an analyst in determining the countervalue potential of nuclear forces against relatively unprotected cities, harbors, airfields, etc. To assess potential against protected targets, such as missile silos, an assessment must be made of the accuracy of the warheads.

CEP is the radius of a circle around a target into which there is a 50% chance that the warhead will fall. CEP varies with range, but the given figures will be assumed valid at nominal useable range. Data concerning warhead accuracy are difficult to find in authoritative unclassified government documents. Table 9.7 represents the best assessment of accuracy available expressed in circular error of probability (CEP) in meters. No DOD sources were available, hence a Congressional Research Service (CRS) source was used: John Collins U.S. - Soviet Military Balance 1980-1985, Report No. 85-895 (Washington, D.C.: Congressional Research Service, Spring 1985).

Table 9.7

Soviet SLBM Warhead CEP (Meters) (1985)

Missile	Jane's	IISS	CRS	Assumed CEP
SS-N-23				unknown
SS-N-20			556	500 - 640
SS-N-18/3	1,280	900	926	900 - 1,280
SS-N-17		1,400	1,389	1,389 - 1,400
SS-N-8/2		900	1,482	900 - 1,482
SS-N-6/3		1,300	1,296	1,296 - 1,300
SS-N-5		2,800	2,778	2,778 - 2,800

Source: Final figures and conversion to meters by author.

There is obviously a great deal of uncertainty over the accuracy of certain of these missile warheads. To make matters worse, slight variations of CEP in formulas which assess counterforce potential (against hardened targets) can result in major fluctuations in assessment. Rather than average CEP, a worst and best-case must be presented.

Prior to delving into formulas, it is possible to infer the hard target kill potential of Soviet SLBMs. Admittedly hard target kill is a poor unit of measurement but in this case we have an opportunity to assess capability by comparison to U.S. systems.

Hard target kill potential assumes that one warhead will be delivered against one target of approximately 2000 - 2500 psi hardness. Obviously not all silos are of this hardness, nor would one warhead be targeted against one silo. However, like EMT, hard target kill represents a standard measure recognized by analysts as an acceptable basis for comparison.

For example, the Reagan administration has been attempting to develop a new Trident II missile which is described as being capable of counterforce silo targeting. The single-shot hard target kill potential for Trident II is supposed to be just over 82%. 2/ The current Minuteman III with a MK-12A warhead has about a 56% probability of hard target kill. This relatively unsatisfactory rating is cited as the need for upgrading the U.S. intercontinental ballistic missile (ICBM) force.

The U.S. Trident I missile had about a 18% hard target kill rating and was described as a weapon incapable of serious counterforce targeting. By referring to the IISS data on these U.S. missile CEP, we see that the Minuteman III/MK-12A is rated at 220 meters and the Trident I at 450 meters. The best Soviet SLBM warhead (the SS-N-20) is rated at 500 meters CEP.

Since hard target kill is dependent on both yield and accuracy, we must attempt to compare Soviet systems in both areas. The closest Soviet SLBM warhead yield comparable to the Minuteman III/MK-12A (335 KT) is the SS-N-20 (200 KT). The accuracies of these two systems are not even close. The best estimate of the SS-N-20 (500 m) is 2-1/4 times the radius of the Minuteman III/MK-12A. The Soviet warhead is 135 KT less than the U.S. system.

Comparison of the SS-N-20 (200 KT) to the Trident I (100 KT) shows nearly the same accuracy. The U.S. system is 50 meters better than the SS-N-20. The Trident I was described as having an unnsatisfactory (18%) hard target kill potential. To significantly increase its potential, the accuracy (not yield) would have to be substantially better. By inference, we can see that at best, the SS-N-20 is not much more capable than the Trident I which is _not_ considered a counterforce weapon. Similarly Soviet SLBMs accuracies are well outside the 250 meter CEP of Soviet ICBMs (SS-18) that have been described as being counterforce capable.

To cross check this conclusion that Soviet SLBM warheads have little utility in counterforce destruction of silos, another unit of measurement, counter military potential (CMP) will be used. Again, this measure by itself is unsatisfactory since it is extremely biased toward accuracy and does not account for the reliability of warheads nor the effects of electromagnetic pulse (EMP). However, it is a tool used and recognized by analysts.

CMP = the EMT of a warhead divided by the square of the CEP. CEP = Y 2/3 / CEP2. This formula shows that a fourfold increase in CMP occurs if accuracy is halved. To match a fourfold increase using yield only, if above 1 MT, a 16 times increase is needed. If below 1 MT, a 8 times increase is required.

Table 9.8 presents the CMP value computed for each missile warhead. Variations are due to the use of all combinations of possible CEP. CEPs have been converted to nautical miles (nm). Hard target kill probability is then given. The CMP necessary to destroy a U.S. ICBM silo hardened to 2000 psi with 95% certainty has been given as 150. 3/

Table 9.8

Soviet SLBM Warhead CMP (1985)

Missile	Y 2/3	CEP(nm)	CMP	Kill Probability Against 2000psi Target a/
SS-N-23	.22	unknown	unknown	unknown
SS-N-20	.22	.26995- .34554	2.8-4.7	8 - 10%
SS-N-18/3	.34	.48591- .69107	.7-1.4	nil - 2%
SS-N-17	1.0	.74992- .75586	1.8	3%
SS-N-8/2	.86	.48591- .80013	1.3-3.6	2 - 9%
SS-N-6/3	1.0	.69971- .70187	2.0	7%
SS-N-5	.86	1.49984-1.51172	.4	nil

Source: Author.

Notes:

a. Derived using Bruce Bennett Assessing The Capabilities of Strategic Nuclear Forces: The Limits of Current Methods, N-1441-NA (Santa Monica, CA: The Rand Corporation, June 1980) p. 58.

As a comparison to the CMP for other warheads, using IISS data, the Trident I (non-counterforce) has a CMP of 3.6, the Minuteman III/MK-12A (insufficient counterforce) has 34 and the Soviet SS-18/3 (counterforce) is 125.

Thus, by a different route we can see that existing Soviet SLBM warheads are not significantly usable against hardened silos (not greater than 10%). Even if we assume the worst-case (for us), most accurate estimates, the largest warhead estimated yield contained in Table 8 (1.0 MT for the SS-N-17) and combine it with the greatest accuracy for any Soviet SLBM (500 meters), the result is a CMP of 13.7 which still does not approach that of a nominal counterforce weapon. A CMP of 13.7 equates to a kill probability of around 32%.

The most important finding of this section is that current Soviet SLBMs cannot be used with any degree of success against hardened silos. Soviet weapons of this caliber do exist, but they are a part of the land-based forces, not the navy. 4/ There are also alternative measures that would accomplish the same results that navy SLBMs can perform. These will be analyzed later.

Dynamic Measurements

To a large degree, static measurements must be supplemented with additional considerations in order to assess military capability. It is not enough to know that Soviet Navy warheads are only capable against softer targets, we must know what is the deliverable amount of that force.

The most effective illustration of the importance of dynamic measures is number of warheads. We know that the Soviets have around 2900 SLBM warheads in deployed submarine launchers. Yet by accounting for the number of submarines on routine patrol, a significantly lower number is the actual day to day threat. For example, if 5 Yankees and 5 Delta I with SS-N-8 missiles were routinely at sea on patrol, the maximum number of warheads posed by the close in Yankee threat is 80 and the nominal number of Delta warheads posing a long range threat would be 60 (assuming other Deltas will not fire from their berths). This section will estimate the routine threat of deliverable warheads, megatonnage, etc.

To further develop dynamic measurements, we must account for Soviet fleet deployment of submarine hulls, various missile ranges, the potential for surge, mobilization in addition to normal patrols, and make some assumption as to how many weapons will work. From these measures, we can then assess the threat to the U.S. The first breakdown must be the allocation of submarine hulls to each of the four Soviet fleets (Northern, Pacific, Baltic, and Black Sea).

The DIA Unclassified Communist Naval Orders of Battle, however, has broken out the specific fleet location for each class of SSBN/SSB. Since the DIA hull data base and the one used in this study are identical, it is possible to utilize DIA as the authority for fleet location. Table 9.9 presents this data.

Table 9.9

Soviet SSBN/SSB Fleet Assignments (1985)

Class	Northern	Pacific	Baltic	Black
Typhoon	3			
Delta IV	1			
Delta III	7	7		
Delta II	4			
Delta I	9	9		
Yankee II	1			
Yankee I	12	9		
Hotel III	1			
Golf V				1
Golf III	1			
Golf II		7	6	

Source: DIA.

The single tube research and development Golf V was reported by IISS and in Soviet Military Power as being in a research and development status. Therefore, it will be discounted from further considerations of routinely available forces.

The next step for analysis will be to account for the number of submarines on normal routine patrol in peacetime. Naturally, this number is a closely guarded secret and will fluctuate over time. There have been sufficient "leaks" to the open press to give us a reasonable assumption of the numbers of submarines on station. 5/

In early 1984, the Soviets increased the numbers of SSBNs by sending out additional Delta SSBNs to mid-Atlantic patrol stations and upsetting the normal pattern of deployed units. 6/ For the purposes of this research, we will assume tht a maximum of 5 Yankees will be on patrol off both U.S. coastlines and an additional 5 Deltas/Typhoons maximum are patrolling in all Soviet home waters.

The patrol areas for Soviet SSBNs are identified in Soviet Military Power. They include the Atlantic and Pacific near North America, the Norwegian and Baltic Seas, and the Bering, and Seas of Japan and Okhotsk. 7/

The reason why Soviet SLBMs can target the U.S. while close to their own waters is a function of missile range. The SS-N-6 systems aboard Yankee I need to be relatively close to their targets while newer missiles aboard Delta and Typhoon classes can reach the U.S. from Arctic waters. SS-N-5 equipped submarines and Yankees found in Soviet home waters will be considered theater systems.

The next stage in the dynamic measurement is to account for the ability of the fleet to unexpectedly surge additional units or to mobilize for war or exercise. No navy can put 100% of its fleet to sea at any given time, nor can we expect any military force to be able to count on total participation from its forces. There will always be units undergoing overhaul, outfitting, scheduled and unscheduled maintenance, conversions, etc.

For purposes of this study, a low threat and high threat will be presented using the same procedures developed by the author in his earlier "Soviet Navy Data Base: 1982-83." 8/ Two conditions will be analyzed. The first will present the fleet's capability to rapidly surge forces (implying a lack of planning/warning). The second will be the mobilization threat based on a planned deployment for a show of force or war. Naturally, the second case assumes strategic warning or Soviet intentional use of the fleet.

The low threat scenario will assume that at least one-third of the fleet can get underway under normal peacetime conditions and two-thirds if the Soviets planned in advance or mobilized. No specific timetable of days is specified for a surge, but within a few days is assumed as reasonable. The high threat will assume one-half of the fleet can surge deploy rapidly and that three-fourths could mobilize.

Obviously all of these assumptions are just that — assumptions. They are based upon familiarity with U.S. force capabilities and discussions over the past years with numerous analysts who obviously would prefer to remain uncited. 9/

It is important to realize that the part of the fleet that is deployable under each condition includes those ships assumed to be already at sea. Although the number of Yankees and Deltas at sea has already been assumed as five each, an accounting needs to be made of other forces normally on patrol. The 10-15% figure appearing in the unclassified literature as a rule of thumb will be utilized for all other classes.

Table 9.10 indicates the SSBN/SSB threat assessment using assumed deployments, surge, and mobilization potential. Rounding has been used to account for whole submarines. For Yankees, additional units must be accounted for due to transit distances involved. Transit calculations will not be presented here but are found in the author's earlier published data. 10/

Table 9.10

Soviet SSBN/SSB Threat Tabulation (1985)

Fleet	Submarine	On Patrol/ Transit	Home Waters Total If Surge	Home Waters Total If Mobilize
Northern	Typhoon	0	1-2	2
	Delta	3	7-10	14-16
	Yankee	3/2	0-2a/	3-5a/
	Hotel III	0	0	1
	Golf III	0	0	1
Pacific	Delta	2	5-8	11-12
	Yankee I	2/1	0-2a/	3-4a/
	Golf II	1	2-4	5
Baltic	Golf II	1	2-3	4-5

Source: Author.

Note:

a. Locally available Yankees in addition to units on forward deployment or in transit to those locations.

The point of Table 9.10 is to use it as the key to calculate deliverable nuclear warheads or megatonnage. In addition to the 10 Yankees and Deltas routinely on patrol within missile range of the U.S., the additional 3 Yankees in transit might be quickly deployable against North America. As such, the likely case involving a rapid increase in Yankees is not additional surged units but rather the extension of the off-going submarine patrol date.

In the Soviet home waters, the situation is different, since, in theory, Delta or Typhoon could strike the U.S. from its home base. If we assume 5 already on local patrol, this number could be at least increased by 8 and perhaps by as many as 16. The mobilization threat is naturally much higher. 11/

Theater threats are highly variable. Obviously, Golf and Hotel submarines that are surged or mobilized are theater systems, but what about the additional Yankees? Should these be considered as a theater threat, or will they go into the deep Atlantic and Pacific and attempt to reach the U.S. coastlines? In order to answer these questions, all likely cases will be analyzed as alternative scenarios.

NOTES

1. Bruce Bennett, *Assessing the Capabilities of Strategic Nuclear Forces: The Limits of Current Methods*, N-1441-NA (Santa Monica: Rand, June 1980), pp. 67-73.

2. Information on U.S. hard target kill potential for missiles taken from February 23, 1982 statement of Richard Perle, Assistant Secretary of Defense for International Security Policy; contained in *Military Posture (Strategic Programs), and Fiscal Year 1983 Defense Department Authorization*, Hearings, Part 2, Armed Services Committee, House of Representatives, 97th Cong., 2nd Sess. (HASC No. 97-33) (Washington: U.S. Government Printing Office, 1982), p. 75.

3. Steve Smith, "MX and the Vulnerability of American Missiles," *ADIU Report*, May/June 1982, p. 2. Hardness of Minuteman silos confirmed by Secretary of Defense Caspar Weinberger written statement of October 6, 1981; contained in HASC 97-33, p. 12.

4. James McConnell, "Possible Counterforce Role for the Typhoon" PP-345 (Alexandria: Center for Naval Analyses, March 1982), is an argument for a counterforce role for the SS-N-20. No calculations are presented to substantiate hard target kill potential. Apparently McConnell is really presenting a case for soft target counterforce. Similar arguments also lacking supporting calculations can be found in Harold Feiveson and John Duffield, "Stopping the Sea-Based Counterforce Threat," *International Security*, Summer 1984, pp. 187-202.

5. *Los Angeles Times*, November 28, 1982, Part IV, p. 7 (8-10 subs); *Aviation Week and Space Technology*,

November 28, 1983, p. 17 (8-10 SSBN/SSBs); and Bryan Ranft and Geoffrey Till, The Sea in Soviet Strategy (Annapolis: Naval Institute, 1983), p. 169 (9-10 Delta/Yankees). John Collins, U.S.-Soviet Military Balance 1980-1985, Congressional Research Service Report No. 85-89S, p. CRS-100, states that about 25% of Soviet SSBNs are at sea on any given day and another 25% are probably on alert in port.

6. Washington Post, January 27, 1984, p. 23 reported 2-3 Deltas in the Atlantic.

7. Department of Defense, Soviet Military Power, 4th Ed. (Washington: U.S. Government Printing Office, April, 1985), pp. 116-117. The Baltic is not depicted on the map as an "SSB/SSBN Operating Area," although the text (p. 37) states that Golf II submarines are stationed there. Tracing the differences in this particular map over time reveals that until the 3rd. Ed., the Seas of Okhotsk, Japan, and the Norwegian Sea were omitted and it was not until the 2nd Ed. that the Bering Sea was depicted as a patrol area for Soviet submarines.

8. "Soviet Navy Data Base: 1982-83," P-6859 (Santa Monica: Rand, April 1983).

9. Michael MccGwire attempted similar calculations in "Maritime Strategy and the Superpowers," Adelphi Paper 123, papers presented at the 1975 Conference of the International Institute for Strategic Studies. MccGwire used the term "ready" to describe a force on patrol or able to deploy within 4 hours. He described forces on "standby" as those able to deploy within 1 day. MccGwire's "surge" force was those aditional forces able to deploy after 1 week. He calculated that the total force that could be deployed in a surge case was 45% of the total. Similarly, he calculated a "mobilized" force as being 65% of the total and requiring 1 month to deploy the additional assets.

10. The exceptions are that for my previous data base, two unlocated Yankees were assumed for gaming purposes (1 in the Atlantic and 1 in the Pacific) and in this book, two Yankees are assumed to be off the U.S. Pacific coast.

11. A similar accounting was presented by John Moore in Jane's Fighting Ships 1980-81 (p. 127). Moore concluded that a maximum of 16 SSBNs with long-range missiles could be mobilized by the Northern Fleet in home waters with another 15 carrying shorter-range missiles available for deep-water Atlantic operations. In the Pacific, Moore calculated that 8 submarines with long-range missiles could be mobilized in home waters and

another 10 SSBNs could forward deploy. Moore also assumed
that Soviet SSBNs would deploy to the Indian Ocean and the
Mediterranean (5 units).

10

Nuclear Threat Assessment

For the purposes of analysis, some probability needs to be assigned to the likelihood of what type of Yankee or Delta or if it will be a Typhoon that is found on patrol. The single Delta IV is not assumed to be performing operational patrols in 1985. Table 10.1 presents the probabilities assumed and are based upon percentages found in that fleet.

Table 10.1

Analytic Probabilities Assumed

Likelihood Northern Fleet Yankee is a	Yankee II	8%	(limit 1 sub)
	Yankee I	92%	
Likelihood Northern Fleet long range SLBM submarine is a	Delta I	40%	
	Delta II	17%	(limit 4 subs)
	Delta III	30%	
	Typhoon	13%	
Likelihood Pacific Fleet Delta is a	Delta I	56%	
	Delta III	44%	

Source: Author.

Bolt from the Blue

For the purposes of analysis, the bolt from the blue threat must be calculated since it represents one end of the spectrum. It assumes a calculated war initiated by the Soviets with no strategic and essentially no tactical warning. In other words, it means they will fire forces already in place without any overt sign of preparation. Based upon the data constructed thus far, with no manipulation of forces, this threat can be assessed. One *can* view the bolt from the blue as the worst case, since this is the one in which they can strike without doing anything new.

Since the number of submarines on patrol is more of less known, we can assign probabilities to assume their type and missiles carried. Numbers of warheads and equivalent megatons (EMT) on patrol will be calculated and serve as the primary two units of measurement since it has already been shown that hardened silos are not a credible target for submarine launched ballistic missiles (SLBMs).

Not all missiles can be expected to work or be serviceable on the date of need. The serviceability and reliability of Soviet missiles is probably not even known with certainty to the Soviets themselves. The author has based his estimates upon a composite of varying U.S. government, the International Institute for Strategic Studies (IISS), and other sources.

In general, IISS gives a maximum reliability rating of 80% to any weapons system. The Congressional Budget Office (CBO) has assessed a reliability of 70% in their assessment of Soviet SLBMs. For comparision, U.S. SLBM reliability is assessed by the CBO to be 80%. 1/ Table 10.2 presents an assessment of the bolt from the blue threat from Soviet SLBMs. In the subsequent sensitivity analysis, reliability ratings will be manipulated.

Damage to the U.S. possible from a bolt from the blue strike as well as the other scenarios to be quantified will be presented later. At this point, only the number of deliverable warheads and EMT is calculated.

Table 10.2
Bolt from the Blue (1985)

Fleet	No. Subs on Patrol	Assumed Class	Assumed No. and Missile	No. Warheads on Patrol	EMT on Patrol	Reliability	Deliverable warheads	Deliverable EMT
Northern (forward)	3 Y	3 Y-I	48 SS-N-6/3	48	48	70%	34	34
(local)	3 D	1 D-I	12 SS-N-8/2	12	10.3	70%	8	6.9
		1 D-II	16 SS-N-8/2	16	13.8	70%	11	9.5
		1 D-III	16 SS-N-18/3	112	38.1	75%	84	28.6
Pacific (forward)	2 Y	2 Y-I	32 SS-N-6/3	32	32	70%	22	22
(local)	2 D	1 D-I	12 SS-N-8/2	12	10.3	70%	8	6.9
		1 D-III	16 SS-N-18/3	112	38.1	75%	84	28.6
	1 G-II	1 G-II	3 SS-N-5	3	2.6	60%	2	1.7
Baltic	1 G-II	1 G-II	3 SS-N-5	3	2.6	60%	2	1.7

Source: Author

From the data in Table 10.2, we can conclude that the likely bolt from the blue attack on the U.S. might involve 56 deliverable SLBM warheads from close-in Yankees capable of 56 EMT. An additional 195 deliverable warheads and 80.5 EMT is carried aboard submarines on patrol in Soviet home waters. The theater threat is 2 deliverable warheads on Europe, or 2 on Asia, Alaska, or Pacific islands.

Mobilization

At the other end of the spectrum, a greater number of weapons could target the U.S. if the Soviets fully mobilized. A mobilization could take place under conditions of escalation in which both sides were aware of the mobilization or else under the guise of an exercise.

For example, in the Spring of 1984, the Soviet Navy conducted a major Northern and Baltic Fleet exercise in which hundreds of ships got underway. If this "exercise" were to suddenly take the form of a real war, mobilization could have been achieved without the West taking appropriate countermeasures. Thus one can consider a mobilized USSR and an unmobilized West as another possible worst-case. The method by which mobilization would occur (under the guise of exercise or not) is not the issue—only the numbers of units that constitute the resultant threat.

For the mobilization scenario to be considered, an assumption needs to be made about the location of submarines once at sea. Two situations will be presented. In the first case, all Yankees will deploy to forward positions. This clearly would be the worst-case for the U.S. since Yankees off the North American coastline represent a unique threat due to the shorter range of their missiles hence shorter warning time.

In the second, no increase in forward-deployed Yankees will be assumed other than a delay in off-going subs. In other words, only those in transit will supplement those off the U.S. coastline. Additional Yankees will be deployed in Soviet home waters. Tables 10.3 and 10.4 present the data for both cases assuming high-risk threat percentages (75% of the fleet can deploy), rounded as necessary.

Table 10.3
Mobilization - Yankees Forward Deploy (1985)

Fleet	No. Subs on Patrol	Assumed Class	Assumed No. and Missile	No. Warheads on Patrol	EMT on Patrol	Reli-ability	Deliverable Warheads	Deliverable EMT
Northern								
(forward)	10 Y	9 Y-I	144 SS-N-6/3	144	144	70%	101	101
		1 Y-II	12 SS-N-17	12	12	70%	8	8
(local)	2 Typ.	2 Typ.	40 SS-N-20	360	122.4	70%	252	85.7
	15 D	7 D-I	84 SS-N-8/2	84	72.2	70%	59	50.7
		3 D-II	48 SS-N-8/2	48	41.3	70%	34	29.2
		5 D-III	80 SS-N-18/3	560	190.4	75%	420	142.8
	1 H-III	1 H-III	6 SS-N-8/2	6	5.2	70%	4	3.4
	1 G-III	1 G-III	6 SS-N-8/2	6	5.2	70%	4	3.4
Pacific								
(forward)	7 Y	7 Y-I	112 SS-N-6/3	112	112	70%	78	78
(local)	12 D	7 D-I	84 SS-N-8/2	84	72.2	70%	59	50.7
		5 D-III	80 SS-N-18/3	560	190.4	75%	420	142.8
	5 G-II	5 G-II	15 SS-N-5	15	12.9	60%	9	7.7
Baltic	5 G-II	5 G-II	15 SS-N-5	15	12.9	60%	9	7.7

Source: Author

Table 10.4
Mobilization - Yankees Withheld (1985)

Fleet	No. Subs On Patrol	Assumed Class	Assumed No. and Missile	No. Warheads on Patrol	EMT on Patrol	Reli- ability	Deliverable Warheads	Deliverable EMT
Northern								
(forward)	5 Y	5 Y-I	80 SS-N-6/3	80	80	70%	56	56
(local)	5 Y	4 Y-I	64 SS-N-6/3	64	64	70%	45	45
		1 Y-II	12 SS-N-17	12	12	70%	8	8
	2 Typ.	2 Typ.	40 SS-N-20	360	122.4	70%	252	85.7
	15 D	7 D-I	84 SS-N-8/2	84	72.2	70%	59	50.7
		3 D-II	48 SS-N-8/2	48	41.3	70%	34	29.2
		5 D-III	80 SS-N-18/3	560	190.4	75%	420	142.8
	1 H-III	1 H-III	6 SS-N-8/2	6	5.2	70%	4	3.4
	1 G-III	1 G-III	6 SS-N-8/2	6	5.2	70%	4	3.4
Pacific								
(forward)	3 Y	3 Y-I	48 SS-N-6/3	48	48	70%	34	34
(local)	4 Y	4 Y-I	64 SS-N-6/1	64	64	70%	45	45
	12 D	7 D-I	84 SS-N-8/2	84	72.2	70%	59	50.7
		5 D-III	80 SS-N-18/3	560	190.4	75%	420	142.8
	5 G-II	5 G-II	15 SS-N-5	15	12.9	60%	9	7.7
Baltic	5 G-II	5 G-II	15 SS-N-5	15	12.9	60%	9	7.7

Source: Author

From the worst mobilization case (for the U.S.) in Table 10.3, we find that if the Soviets mobilized and sent all available Yankees off the North American coastline, they might threaten the U.S. with 187 medium-range deliverable warheads/EMT that provide little warning time. Since it might be argued that this scenario is unrealistic, the alternate mobilization scenario in Table 10.4 presents a more likely threat where only the in-transit and off-going Yankees supplement those already on station. In this case, 90 deliverable warheads/EMT would threaten the U.S.

The force that could be mobilized in Soviet home waters capable of hitting North America is identical in either case. The Soviets can probably deliver 1252 long-range warheads totaling 508.7 EMT on the U.S.

As for the theater threat, one must decide whether or not Yankees in home waters would be used or withheld. If these forces are to supplement SS-N-5 equipped submarines in theater strikes, the threat is 62 deliverable warheads and 60.7 EMT on Europe and 54 deliverable warheads and 52.7 EMT in Asia, Alaska, or against Pacific islands. On the other hand, if Yankees in local waters are not used, the theater threat is again only modest.

Surge

A third case will be that of an unplanned, immediate surge. The scenario will be that the fleet has been instructed to respond rapidly to a crisis and thereby put on a show of force. The data used will be based upon the high-threat surge in Table 9.10 that assumes 50% of the fleet can deploy giving the Soviets the benefit of the doubt as to capability to get their forces underway.

As was done with the mobilization scenario, the surge will present the dual deployment Yankee alternatives. Tables 10.5 and 10.6 present the findings. The surge case represents a mid-range threat between the bolt from the blue and the mobilization case. It should not be looked upon as a most likely case since it is only reflective of the assumptions upon which it is based. If anything, it can be considered another worst-case (for the U.S.) since the environment likely to be unplanned and highly unstable.

Table 10.5
Surge - Yankees Withheld (1985)

Fleet	No. Subs on Patrol	Assumed Class	Assumed No. and Missile	No. Warheads on Patrol	EMT on Patrol	Reli- ability	Deliverable Warheads	Deliverable EMT
Northern								
(forward)	5 Y	5 Y-I	80 SS-N-6/3	80	80	70%	56	56
(local)	2 Y	1 Y-I	16 SS-N-6/3	16	16	70%	11	11
		1 Y-II	12 SS-N-17	12	12	70%	8	8
	1 Typ.	1 Typ.	20 SS-N-20	180	61.2	70%	126	42.8
	9 D	4 D-I	48 SS-N-8/2	48	41.3	70%	34	29.2
		2 D-II	32 SS-N-8/2	32	27.5	70%	22	18.9
		3 D-III	48 SS-N-18/3	336	114.2	75%	252	85.7
Pacific								
(forward)	3 Y	3 Y-I	48 SS-N-6/3	48	48	70%	34	34
(local)	2 Y	2 Y-I	32 SS-N-6/3	32	32	70%	22	22
	8 D	4 D-I	48 SS-N-8/2	48	41.3	70%	34	29.2
		4 D-III	64 SS-N-18/3	448	152.3	75%	336	114.2
	4 G-II	4 G-II	12 SS-N-5	12	10.3	60%	7	6
Baltic	3 G-II	3 G-II	9 SS-N-5	9	7.7	60%	5	4.3

Source: Author

Table 10.6
Surge - Yankees Forward Deploy (1985)

Fleet	No. Subs on Patrol	Assumed Class	Assumed No. and Missile	No. Warheads on Patrol	EMT on Patrol	Reli-ability	Deliverable Warheads	Deliverable EMT
Northern								
(forward)	7 Y	6 Y-I 1 Y-II	96 SS-N-6/3 12 SS-N-17	96 12	96 12	70% 70%	67 8	67 8
(local)	1 Typ. 9 D	1 Typ. 4 D-I 2 D-II 3 D-III	20 SS-N-20 48 SS-N-8/2 32 SS-N-8/2 48 SS-N-18/3	180 48 32 326	61.2 41.3 27.5 114.2	70% 70% 70% 75%	126 34 22 252	42.8 29.2 18.9 85.7
Pacific								
(forward)	5 Y 8 D 4 G-II	5 Y-I 4 D-I 4 D-III 4 G-II	80 SS-N-6/3 48 SS-N-8/2 64 SS-N-18/3 12 SS-N-5	80 48 448 12	80 41.3 152.3 10.3	70% 70% 75% 60%	56 34 336 7	56 29.2 114.2 6
Baltic	3 G-II	3 G-II	9 SS-N-5	9	7.7	60%	5	4.3

Source: Author

In this surge case, the most likely scenario would involve keeping off-going Yankees on station off North America and surging the extra Yankees into home waters. In this case, depicted by Table 10.5, the threat to the U.S. is identical as in the mobilization case (90 deliverable warheads/EMT from Yankees).

The surge scenario results in a long-range missile threat to the U.S. from Soviet home waters, totalling 804 deliverable warheads and 320 EMT. The theater threat would be 24 deliverable warheads and 23.3 EMT on Europe and 27 deliverable warheads and 26.3 EMT on Asia, Alaska, and Pacific islands if Yankees are withheld.

Assessment of Counterforce Damage to U.S.

Although counterforce is often associated with the destruction of land-based intercontinental ballistic missiles (ICBMs) silos, this study will assess the impact of Soviet Navy SLBMs in each of the three cases outlined above against other strategic offensive systems based in the continental U.S. Three distinct classes of counterforce attack will be analyzed: disruption of command, control, and communications (C3), pin-down of ICBMs, and strikes against bomber and naval bases. A final assessment will then be presented.

C3 Disruption

The wisdom of conducting an attack against a superpower's C3 facilities will not be addressed herein. Some would argue such an attack is irrational since it might result in no one to communicate with during a period where war termination was the goal. Nevertheless, there are those who continue to discuss the possibility of such attacks, describing them as "decapitation" implying a loss in political control 2/ and severe degradation of the ability of the U.S. to perform a second strike.

Two distinct possibilities for such attacks are discussed. In the first, only a single warhead may be necessary. This attack involves electromagnetic pulse (EMP) and other disruptive effects to communications which could frustrate U.S. command and control.

EMP effects are not fully understood. One device of several hundred kilotons has been prescribed as capable of disrupting most of the U.S. with a peak of 25,000 volts/meters. 3/ Alternate estimates are for one 10 MT device blanketing the U.S. with 50,000 volts/meters. 4/ In the first case of a modest yield weapon, this is certainly within the capability of known Soviet SLBMs. An SS-N-6 fired from an in-close Yankee would offer the advantage of disruption little or no warning. If a 10 MT device is required, no known Soviet Navy weapon will do.

The second major C3 attack scenario involves individual targeting of facilities that provide command, control, or communications with U.S. strategic nuclear forces. Estimates for such an attack vary from 50-100 warheads and would target all essential links. 5/ This attack includes 10-20 high altitude detonations.

The obvious advantage in conducting a C3 attack using Soviet submarines is that warning time is substantially reduced due to shorter missile flight times. Targets on the U.S. coastlines might be struck within 5 minutes and further inland no later than 15 minutes after launch. Important facilities could be neutralized before the arrival of Soviet ICBMs.

Soviet Yankees on routine patrol off the U.S. coastlines could probably carry out a moderate C3 attack. The bolt from the blue scenario credits Yankees with 56 deliverable warheads or about the minimum number required. The likely mobilization and surge cases increase this number to 90 deliverable warheads making success in a C3 attack more likely but at the expense of using all Yankee capability for this mission.

The attractiveness of a C3 attack by Soviet SLBMs is that success may in fact result in the paralysis of U.S. ICBMs, bombers, and those sea-based systems not assigned to the strategic reserve. SLBMs offer a unique advantage of being able to successfully target the common core for all U.S. systems. The weaknesses in the U.S. C3 have been addressed by the Reagan Administration and partially corrective measures are being funded.

ICBM Pin-Down

Some spokesman have theorized that Soviet Yankee SLBMs would be used against land based missiles by pinning-down U.S. ICBMs forcing them to remain in their silos. Such an attack would need to last only as long as it would take for Soviet ICBMs to arrive, less the flight time it took the SLBMs to arrive, no longer than 15-25 minutes.

A pin-down attack could threaten blast damage to ICBMs as they emerged from silos, and X-ray and EMP damage as they flew along corridors to the USSR, or additional dust/debris damage if surface bursts were used. High-altitude pin-down is not viewed as a logical use of weapons since the primary kill mechanism, X-rays, is dissipated in an extremely short time period, requiring more weapons than a lower altitude attack. The surface burst pin-down might create so much debris that the survivability of incoming Soviet ICBM warheads may be in doubt.

The most logical use of SLBMs in pin-down would be attempting to damage missiles with blast caused by air-burst weapons. Air blast overpressures of 4-10 psi are sufficient to cause complete damage to aircraft.6/ For a 1 MT weapon (carried by the SS-N-6/3 or SS-N-17) the lethal radius would be 2.8-5 miles. For more modern Soviet SLBMs with smaller warheads, the lethal radii are smaller.

During the "dense pack" MX discussions, various estimates were given of the megatonnage necessary to pin down the field of deployed MX missiles. At that time, pin-down estimates ranged from 1 - 10 MT/minute over that small field alone. 7/ Pin-down requirements for MX are considerably higher than for Minuteman since the new MX missile will be hardened and thus more survivable.

The approximate deliverable MT by Yankee is routinely 56 MT/deliverable warheads and in a likely surge or mobilization case 90 MT/deliverable warheads). The U.S. has six Minuteman wings dispersed throughout the Midwest. Each base is of considerable size.

The author feels that the data available in the unclassified arena is insufficient to fully assess the potential for the Yankee fleet to pin-down the entire U.S. Minuteman force. Based upon the limited number of missile warheads available and the limited amount of deliverable megatonnage in Yankee, the author is not optimistic about the ability of the USSR to totally pin-down the Minuteman force given the likelihood that C3 disruption could achieve the same end with less effort, and, attacks on bombers and naval bases may have higher priority. 8/

Attacks on Bombers/Naval Bases

The third category attack would involve SLBMs against U.S. bomber, supporting tanker bases, and certain naval bases. The U.S. air-breathing force is maintained at a small number of bases in peacetime and is theoretically capable of being dispersed in crises to additional bases including those inland. The U.S. Navy is based at a similar small number of bases along the coasts.

To set the boundaries for this third situation, one should assume a Soviet bolt from the blue because it results in a fewer number of aim points. In this case, the U.S. would have not received strategic warning and dispersed its assets. This represents the worst-case (for the U.S.) and is the standard by which bomber survivability is routinely measured.

The Soviets need only target 21 primary Strategic Air Command (SAC) airfields, fields used by SAC and other forces, and SAC headquarters in order to attack all bombers and tankers in the continental U.S. and an additional four or so SAC bases overseas. 9/ In a dispersal to outlying fields the number of airfields rises as high as 45. 10/ In the non-generated alert, the Soviets could easily deliver 2 warheads per base with warheads to spare (80 warheads on routine patrol). By assuming Yankees are quickly able to augment by delaying the off-going submarines, they could raise the number of warheads on patrol to 128 and probably successfully target all bases in a generated alert even with a 70% reliability rating for the missile.

There are a number of variables into an assessment as to how successful an attack against the bombers or tankers would be. These are beyond the scope of this book. The threat should not be viewed through U.S. eyes where, for example, destruction of greater than 95% of an incoming Soviet ICBM force is claimed as necessary to fund an anti-ballistic missile system. Rather, using Soviet Navy standards, 80-90% loss in combat potential is considered "destruction," 70% loss is a "defeat," 50% loss is "doing damage," 30% loss is "substantially weakening," and 10-15% loss is "weakening." 11/

An SLBM attack on bomber bases need not be a destructive or defeating attack. It need only "pin-down" the aircraft long enough until the ICBMs could arrive. One or two ICBM warheads exploding over each bomber/tanker base ought to sufficiently disrupt the planned launch of alert aircraft considering the minimum megatonnage deliverable on each target is 1 MT.

The U.S. Navy maintains only three SSBN bases in the continental U.S. This is generally where the Soviets could find SSBNs preparing for deployment or having just returned. Other submarines can be easily located in a few shipyard locations where they are undergoing overhaul.

Similarly, the U.S. keeps its surface fleet, including aircraft carriers, in a relatively small number of home ports. Although it is possible that the Soviets might catch a U.S. carrier battle group in port, loaded with ammunition and planes, ready to sail, this author does not feel that the use of Yankee SLBMs against surface ships is warranted. An ICBM or long-range SLBM would do.

Unlike the U.S. SSBN, which could in theory fire from its berth and hit the USSR within 30 minutes, the carrier battle group is neither a time-urgent threat nor can its weapons reach the U.S. until the ship sails closer to the Soviet Union. Hence with only a limited number of shorter range SLBMs available it would be a waste to use them against naval targets other than SSBNs or C3 facilities.

A similar question exists for using SLBMs against deployed U.S. Navy forces. There is no reason to use a SLBM to target these forces since Soviet ICBM and intermediate range systems could do the same job.

Counterforce Assessment

It would appear that from the types of Soviet Navy forces and their deployment options that the routine patrols by Yankees are tailored to target bomber, tanker, and submarine bases and conduct a modest but effective C3 attack. A full scale C3 attack or an ICBM pin-down attack may be possible but at the expense of the bomber/tanker/submarine attack. The limiting factor is numbers of warheads.

Soft target counterforce as the primary target set for Yankee appears logical since the SS-N-6 has the unique ability amongst all Soviet strategic nuclear forces to be able to attach time-urgent targets in the U.S.

Assessment of Countervalue Damage to U.S.

Despite the fact that the author views soft target counterforce as the primary class of targets which forward deployed Yankees are committed to, the question remains as to what type of targets longer range SLBMs will be used against. The evidence of the literature strongly suggests that counter-value targeting against cities is <u>not</u> Soviet declaratory policy.

There are those in the West, however, who still feel that targeting cities should be policy for both superpowers, or that the Soviet Union intends to actually do this. Despite the literature evidence to the contrary, this book will assess the possible countervalue damage potential to the U.S. should Soviet declaratory policy not be actual employment policy. In other words, if the Soviets do attack our cities with their SLBMs, what can be expected.

Such an assessment may also give perspective of the limits of civilian/non-military casualties which would be expected even if military targets are the object and collateral damage to colocated civilians occurs. From the static hardware evidence, it was shown that the Soviet SLBM trend is to increase missile accuracy and lower yields. This could be due to an effort to reduce collateral damage.

From the assessment of deliverable warheads and EMT earlier, it is possible to roughly estimate the amount of countervalue damage which the Soviets threatened the U.S. with their SLBMs. There have been a few unclassified attempts to study the effects of a nuclear war on the U.S. and USSR.

Studies involving damage to the U.S. have been criticized in the past for their bias in favor of worst-case assumptions involving high Soviet weapons reliability and survivability. For the purposes of this study, only the impact of weapons actually delivered will be considered. In other words, if the bias has been primarily over how many weapons are deliverable, it is possible to circumvent this problem by sidestepping the issue and using tables herein to input warheads/EMT.

Some of the criticism on nuclear war effects however, concerns the consequences of the explosions themselves. For example, a recently publicized theory suggests that nuclear wars involving 10,400 warheads of 5000 MT would result in a "nuclear winter" has received much much attention despite the unlikelihood of such a massive exchange. The "nuclear winter" prediction was accompanied by a warning that the threshold for a major climatic catastrophe could be as low as 200 warheads. The threshold for major optical and climatic consequences was estimated as low as 1000 small warheads totalling 100 MT. 12/

This book cannot assess the accuracy of studies on the effects of nuclear war but merely cite the conclusions and findings that such studies have presented and assess the political consequences. Two recent studies done for the U.S. government contain data useable herein. These are the Sentate's Economic and Social Consequences of Nuclear Attacks on the United States 13/ and the Office of Technology Assessment's (OTA) The Effects of Nuclear War. 14/

In the bolt from the blue scenario, the Soviets were found to be able to deliver 56 warheads/EMT from close in Yankees and 195 warheads totaling 80.5 EMT from distant Deltas. This is the Soviet Navy minimal delivery threat. If we use the target set from the Senate study of the 71 largest U.S. standard metropolitan areas, we find that a minimal attack (involving 144 EMT) would result in 20-30% population and 25-35% industry destroyed in the U.S. Such an attack assumes all SLBMs are used against cities.

The bolt from the blue, however, would allow the Soviets to use their ICBMs also and perhaps their intercontinental bomber forces. Hence, assuming levels of damage to the U.S. from the submarine fleet alone is highly artificial but is undertaken simply for measurement and analysis.

Submarines cannot target more locations than the total number of individually targetable warheads on missiles allow (unless colocated targets exist). It is possible, but unlikely, that important facilities would be targeted only by one warhead. In the Senate study, cities the size of Milwaukee received hits from at least two 1-MT weapons.

The maximum number of weapons per city would vary with the size of the city and the size of the attack. It is impossible to know how may warheads would be used against any major city. One must not conclude however, that the bolt from the blue threat of 251 total SLBM warheads means that 251 U.S. cities could be destroyed.

A further complication involves MIRV footprints. Simply put, just because the SS-N-18/3 contains 7 individually targetable warheads, the placement of those warheads is constrained. The OTA study contains an excellent descriptive map of a typical Soviet ballistic missile footprint. For example, one missile with 10 MIRV warheads could be used against Los Angeles and as far away as San Diego, or, if aimed at the eastern seaboard, New York and Philadelphia. Warheads from the same missile cannot target both New York and Los Angeles.

At the other end of the spectrum, we found that upon mobilization the Soviets could deploy in home waters alone a force which could deliver 1252 warheads of 508.7 EMT. Such an attack could certainly cover the 71 major urban areas in the U.S. since it would involve over 300 individual deliverable missiles. Using EMT as a guide, the results of such an attack would be around 35% population and 60% industry loss to the U.S.

The Yankee force in the mobilization case could either surge to the U.S. coastline or be withheld in home waters. Using the latter case as more likely, Yankees off the U.S. could deliver an additional 90 warheads/EMT.

The third case discussed was an immediate surge. Here, the Yankee threat to the U.S. is probably the same as in mobilization. The long-range threat would be 804 deliverable warheads on 188 missiles and 320 EMT. Such a force could target all 71 major U.S. urban areas and probably cause 30% population and 45% industrial loss to the U.S.

How much U.S. destruction is perceived by the Soviets as deterring a U.S. nuclear strike? At best, the Soviet day-to-day submarine fleet can threaten destruction of one-fourth to one-third of U.S. population and industry if cities were the targets. This is in contrast to the U.S. goal of keeping a minimal deliverable assured destruction force deployed at sea at all times theoretically capable of destroying one-fifth to one-fourth of Soviet population and one-half industry. In mobilization, the level of U.S. destruction threatened by the USSR might be increased to one-third and one-half industry.

The level of potential U.S. destruction which deters U.S. action is also a function of U.S. decision makers. The Senate study concluded 150 MT delivered on the U.S. was significant. There would certainly be those who would argue that the U.S. should be deterred if the threat were only 1 MT on 1 city. There is no number that we can assign which represents the threat to the U.S. that the Americans say is enough. We can only judge the Soviet view as to how much is enough by measuring their ability to deliver based upon varying scenarios.

It appears that the force of Deltas and Typhoons routinely deployed in Soviet waters is sufficiently powerful to deliver enough damage on the U.S. to make any U.S. decision maker consider the consequences of such an attack. The implications of this conclusion are two.

First, Yankees which could surge in a crisis or be mobilized do not need to deploy off the coast of the U.S. to increase the countervalue threat. Sufficient countervalue capability exists from Deltas and Typhoons. Adding more Yankees or using Yankee against cities is not necessary. Yankee's strong point is the ability to attack time sensitive targets and not cities.

Secondly, the Yankee fleet off the U.S. coastline is ill-suited for destruction of numerous major urban industrial centers since it is limited by deliverable warheads. It would appear to be better suited for destruction of soft military targets where 1-2 warheads/missiles would result in a probable "kill."

NOTES

1. International Institute of Strategic Studies (IISS) Military Balance 1982-1983 (p. 136) gives a reliability rating of 60% to the SS-N-5. Congressional Budget Office (CBO) Counterforce Issues for the U.S. Strategic Nuclear Forces (Washington: U.S. Government Printing Office, January 1978), p. 16, estimates 70% reliability for the SS-N-6/8/17/18. James Dunnigan, How to Make War (New York: William Morrow, 1982) assigns 75% to the SS-N-18. IISS and CBO reliability ratings will be used in this book except for the SS-N-18, where Dunnigan unsubstantiated higher rating will be initially used and later subjected to sensitivity analysis.

2. John Steinbruner, "Nuclear Decapitation," Foreign Policy, Winter 1981-82, pp. 16-28.

3. Office of Technology Assessment (OTA), MX Missile Basing, OTA-ISC-140, (Washington: U.S. Government Printing Office, September 1981), p. 297. See also Hans Neuheuser, "The Nuclear Electromagnetic Pulse," Military Technology, June 1985, p. 98.

4. View of scientists reported in New York Times, June 28, 1983, p. C-1. In July 1962, a 1.5 MT weapon exploding at an altitude of 250 miles caused minor disruptions of electrical power at a distance of 600 miles. See Aviation Week and Space Technology, September 17, 1984, p. 76.

5. Desmond Ball, "Can Nuclear War Be Controlled?", IISS Adelphi Paper 169, Autumn 1981, p. 35.

6. Damage calculations taken from The Effects of Nuclear Weapons, 3rd Ed., Samuel Glasstone and Philip Dolan, Eds. (Washington: U.S. Government Printing Office, 1977).

7. Richard Garwin reportedly estimated that 1 MT would be required and that this would mean, in turn, 2-4 Soviet SLBM warheads/minute. See New York Times, July 21, 1982, p. 15; and Baltimore Sun, December 18, 1982, p. 10. Reports that 5-10 MT/minute would be required against "dense pack" ICBM deployment fields can be found

in *Aviation Week and Space Technology*, May 3, 1982, pp. 18-19; and October 11, 1982, p. 115.

8. Roger Speed, *Strategic Deterrence in the 1980's* (Stanford: Hoover Institution, 1979), p. 159, reports that 200-3000 warheads (size not specified) would be needed to pin-down Minuteman. OTA *MX Missile Basing*, p. 156, reports that hundreds of MT/minute would be neessary to guarantee Minuteman pin-down.

9. "Guide to USAF Bases at Home and Abroad," *Air Force Magazine*, May 1985, pp. 170-179.

10. Speed, *Strategic Deterrence in the 1980's*, p. 46; and Bruce Bennett, *Assessing the Capabilities of Strategic Nuclear Forces: The Limits of Current Methods*, N-1441-NA (Santa Monica: Rand, June 1980), p. 101.

11. CAPT. 1st Rand O. Shul'man, "Wording of Combat Missions," *Morskoy Sbornik*, August 1976, p. 19.

12. Richard Turco, et al., "Nuclear Winter: Global Consequences of Multiple Nuclear Explosians," *Science*, December 23, 1983, pp. 1283-1292; "The Climate Effects of Nuclear War," *Scientific American*, August 1984, pp. 33-43; and Carl Sagan, "Nuclear War and Climate Catastrophe: Some Policy Implications," *Foreign Affairs*, Winter 1983/84, pp. 257-292. Sagan stated that the threshold for nuclear winter would be as low as 500 warheads but apparently revised this estimate downward to 200. See *Washington Post*, July 12, 1984, p. 32.

13. *Economic and Social Consequences of Nuclear Attacks on the United States*, a Study prepared by Dr. Arthur Katz for the Joint Committee on Defense Production and Published by the Committee on Banking, Housing, and Urban Affairs, Senate, 96th Cong., 1st Sess. (Washington: U.S. Government Printing Office, March 1979).

14. OTA, *The Effects of Nuclear War* OTA-NS-89 (Washington: U.S. Government Printing Office, May 1979).

11
Navy Strategic Nuclear Force Issues

There are a number of issues involving the Soviet strategic submarine force that cannot be addressed without consideration of the secondary source literature. In previous analyses, a number of possible interpretations of the data and/or literature has been postulated and needs to be tested against the available evidence.

In the content analysis and hardware analysis sections, findings were based upon the author's reading of the literature or on his assessment of capability. In this chapter, varying hypothesis of interest will be cited and discussed in light of the findings thus far. These issues will be once again raised in the overall findings, conclusions, and implications.

Withholding

There is a general theory that Soviet nuclear ballistic missile submarines (SSBNs) that routinely deploy or could surge or mobilize in home waters will be held as a strategic reserve. Most analysts conclude that those submarines off the U.S. coastline would be used. From the evidence of hardware alone, forward-deployed Yankees are obviously a first-strike weapon. They appear tailored to act as a counterforce against time urgent bomber/tanker and submarine bases. Supporting this view is their lack of survivability against U.S. antisubmarine warfare (ASW).

Soviet Yankees located in home waters could be either withheld or used immediately. Due to the SS-N-6 missile range, they would have to be against theater targets and not the continental U.S. If Yankees attempted to break out into mid-Atlantic or Pacific waters, they might be subject to Western ASW and suffer severe attrition.

The only significant increase in military capability should the Soviets break out additional Yankees to North American waters would be the potential to increase the intercontinental ballistic missile (ICBM) pin-down threat. A successful attack on bomber/tanker/submarine bases and against command, control, and communications (C3) does not appear to need any additional warheads. An increase in submarines off the U.S. shores might be politically desirable as a escalatory statement and as a demonstration of resolve. 1/

From the evidence of the hardware alone, it is impossible to conclude with certainty whether Yankees retained in home waters would be used in theater strikes or as part of a theater or strategic reserve. Some items appear to suggest a theater strike role versus a reserve.

First, there have been reports the Soviets can reload their SSBNs at sea in protected fjords. 2/ This would be beneficial for Yankees in theater actions such as those tasked with submarine launched ballistic missile (SLBM) strikes against forward deployed U.S. Navy assets in ports or concentrated at anchorages. With reloadable launchers, theater-range SLBMs could be used, reloaded, and used again in short order. Thus theater Yankees could be a strategic reserve for the theater. It should be recalled that the Soviet use of the word "strategic" can involve theaters and not only intercontinental missions.

Secondly, the incremental increase available from the Yankee fleet in home waters to Deltas and Typhoon targeted on the U.S. is modest. Under a surge condition, Yankee could contribute only an additional 41 deliverable warheads/equivalent megatons (EMT) to an existing 804 warheads (320/EMT) already from deliverable long-range missiles. In a mobilization, the increase from Yankees would only be 98 warheads/EMT to a deliverable long-range force of 1252 warheads (474.3 EMT) on Delta/Typhoons, etc.

Third, there is the major problem of moving the additional Yankees from Soviet home waters some 4000 n.m. to place them in North American waters. This contingency appears often in both the Soviet and Western literature. The Soviets cannot be assured that their submarines would survive such a transit.

On the other hand, the author is aware of the vast intermediate and shorter range Soviet land systems which make the navy's contribution a mere drop in the bucket. The need for all services to participate in all theaters is probably the only significant theme in the literature evidence that makes Soviet SLBM participation in the Eurasian theaters likely.

Without Yankee in the theater, the nominal navy ballistic missile threat consists of around 5 EMT per theater in a surge and 8 EMT in the mobilization scenario. Thus theater use of these additional 41 or 98 Yankee warheads would vastly increase Soviet Navy theater contribution to "victory".

Long-range missiles aboard Delta and Typhoon submarines have been theorized as part of an intercontinental reserve. From the hardware alone, the evidence supports such a conclusion. Long-range Soviet SLBMs are not capable of hard-target counterforce and suffer the same problems of lack of timeliness as Soviet ICBMs if used against soft counterforce targets. Soviet long-range SLBMs are better suited for strikes against non-hardened targets.

One could certainly theorize that if the Soviets were to employ nuclear weapons against the U.S., both countervalue and counterforce weapons might be used in one spasm. If this were true, why go to all the extra expense of putting relatively inaccurate missiles at sea? Surely the same destruction capability could have been fielded on ICBMs much cheaper than by using navy submarines. ICBM accuracies are generally better than SLBMs meaning that not only could land systems be cheaper but they would be more flexible.

If one spasm response were all that could be expected, survivability, the strong suite of Delta and Typhoon, would not be necessary. A one-shot nuclear force could be constructed by simply proliferating land systems in sufficient numbers that the U.S. could not destroy enough even if the West strikes first (which is presently the case).

Hence the long range of SLBMs and deployment in home waters maximizes submarine survival. Coupled with their lack of accuracy which limits use against hardened targets, this tends to support a reserve vice immediate use role. The one main advantage of Delta/Typhoon is that it further guarantees a Soviet "assured destruction" strike against the U.S. no matter what else happens to other Soviet strategic nuclear forces.

This reserve role does not necessarily mean only for inter- or post-war bargaining or coercion but also as a hedge against the possible but unlikely destruction of Soviet bombers, submarines in port, and ICBMs. No matter what else happens, sufficient capability remains at sea to make a nuclear response. Soviet Deltas and Typhoons appear to constitute a reserve. One *cannot* conclude that they are the only reserve from an analysis of the hardware itself.

Since not all submarines might be capable of getting underway before a potential U.S. strike on Soviet naval bases, units that could survive such a strike would also form a part of the reserve. There have been reports that the Soviet Navy can protect its fleet assets in hardened sea-level tunnels. 3/ Alternatively, they might simply submerge in deeper waters off their home ports. An alternate suggestion for deploying a navy strategic nuclear reserve is to hide submarines in Scandinavian fjords. 4/ The theory is that the U.S. would be reluctant to attack Soviet submarines in neutral waters. SLBMs are "cold launched" and capable of being reloaded from tenders or in bases.

As Soviet submarines become more sophisticated, one must assume they will be quieter. The lack of quiet submarines has been largely negated by the Soviet practices of deployment in home waters. If the Soviet submarines become as quiet as U.S. submarines, would there be any advantage to changing current deployment practices? Deploying SSBNs in greater numbers outside home waters would only increase their possible interdiction by Western forces. Quietness increases can, on the other hand, make a significant contribution to the survival of Soviet SSBNs in home waters. Hence, it does not necessarily follow that newer Typhoons and follow-on classes of SSBNs will be employed in mid-ocean patrols vice in Soviet home waters.

Exercises

Normal hardware analysis would include an assessment of past employment in armed conflict and current employment in exercises. The Soviet Navy has never been involved in a nuclear war, hence this body of experience is simply lacking. With regard to exercises, those few secondary sources which report or analyze exercises contain little reference to Soviet SSBN employment other than to cite SLBMs were fired.

For obvious reasons, official U.S. government discussions of Soviet Navy missile tests are not too revealing. Recognizing that official study conclusions, however, are based upon input of classified inputs, one can speculate on exercise behavior based upon the content of these reports.

Official U.S. government assessments of the expected employment of Soviet SLBMs in war include a first-strike by Yankees off the U.S. coastline, theater strikes by shorter range systems, and a reserve role for Delta/Typhoon. One must assume that Soviet exercises support this official assessment.

Yankee Obsolescence

Yankee I submarines were completed between 1967 and 1974. Since then, a number have been dismantled as SSBNs and converted to other purposes. Depending upon the size of the Delta and Typhoon building program, the status of strategic arms control agreements, and the desire to replace relatively noisy/vulnerable submarines with other systems, the Soviet Union needs to replace Yankee with something else which can provide a similar unique military capability (damage limiting strikes on bomber, tanker and submarine bases, and a modest C3 attack).

A number of options are open to the USSR. First, they can simply deploy Deltas or Tyhpoons off the U.S. shoreline as a replacement for Yankee. Problems with this option include minimum firing distances for the long-range SLBMs (roughly one-third the maximum) and an increased attractiveness of these submarines to U.S. ASW. If the Soviets were to deploy advanced submarines nearer to U.S. shores, the potential payoff in terms of warheads destroyed by the U.S. would make them more likely targets for counter-action.

A new medium-range missile might be developed, and that would once again raise the speculation over depressed trajectory. Depressed trajectory would cut flight time to the target. Although frequently discussed, numerous reports state such a capability has <u>not</u> been tested.

Deploying Deltas or Typhoons near the U.S. might nevertheless be undertaken as a peacetime political statement such as their supposed "matching" of the "new" U.S./NATO capability in theater forces in Europe. As of today, the old Yankee short-range threat is the direct political parallel to "new" U.S./NATO theater forces in Europe. That capability has existed since the late 1960's. There is nothing "new" about the threat posed by submarine systems off the U.S. shores. Yankee is a serious first-strike counterforce weapon whereas making a similar claim for new U.S./NATO systems in Europe is difficult.

A second option is to take nuclear submarine cruise missile carriers (SSGNs) and use these to replace Yankee. Indeed, the press has incorrectly implied that Soviet

SSGNs deployed off the U.S. coastline in early 1984 were supplementing the land-attack mission of Yankee. 5/

Soviet SSGN's off the U.S. coastline are presently carrying missiles designed for anti-ship warfare. New SS-N-21 sea-launched cruise missiles (SLCMs) with nuclear warheads and designed for land attack were expected to become operational in 1984 or 1985. They can be carried by any Soviet submarine and launched through its torpedo tubes. 6/ It is possible that Yankees that have been converted from SSBNs will be used as cruise missile carriers and will return to patrols off the U.S. shores.

Although slower than SLBMs, new SLCMs are small and difficult to detect by radar. It is very possible that due to the difficulty of detecting their presence, an analogous threat to U.S. time-urgent targets might be presented by SLCMs as is currently posed by the SS-N-6. The U.S. is not unaware of this possibility and is taking steps to enhance its warning capability against SLCMs. 7/ Steps will need to be taken to destroy oncoming SLCMs to negate the threat.

A third option is to replace the in-close Yankee threat with SLBMs from Arctic Ocean areas close to the Canadian borders. The potential for Typhoon and perhaps the Delta III to perform this role has received recent attention. 8/ A through-ice capability for Typhoon has been reported by Jane's Fighting Ships 1983-84. Earlier submarines lack the capability to punch through ice areas and ensure proper functioning of missile tube doors and launchers.

The ability of submarines to perform this Arctic mission is theoretically possible, although early press reports stated that the Soviets had not yet been observed practicing it. Missile ranges of Soviet SLBMs allow Canadian or Danish waters to be used for targeting the entire U.S. 9/ Depressed trajectory would cut warning time.

Potential disadvantages include the uncertainty of being able to punch through the ice and using a flight path similar to Soviet ICBMs thus making U.S. warning and tracking easier. Nevertheless, the possibility exists that Soviet under ice capability may be for a current offensive strategy and proof that the Soviets plan to hide submarines held in reserve.

Ballistic Missiles Versus Fleets

The subject of the use of ballistic missiles against naval forces at sea is a topic that comes up from time to time in the secondary source literature. Rear Admiral James Holloway was forced to deal with the issue of ICBMs against aircraft carriers in 1970 hearings before Congress. 10/

A lively debate occurred in the U.S. Naval Institute Proceedings from June 1978 - July 1980 in which it was theorized that Soviet SLBMs could be used as counter battery against U.S. SLBMs 11/ or against carriers. 12/ Other analysts have speculated on Soviet patrols of Golf and Hotel submarines in the 1960's were against naval forces and not for fleet versus shore. 13/

All current official U.S. assessments of Soviet military hardware fail to list surface ships as targets for ballistic missiles. There was one SLBM, the SS-NX-13 which apparently was tested in a role against ships at sea.

Unfortunately, from a hardware analysis point of view, it is entirely possible that an anti-surface ship or even ASW capability exists in Soviet ICBMs or SLBMs and such capability remains classified in the West. The SS-NX-13 may have in fact be shelved, but any multiple independently targeted reentry vehicle (MIRV) or multiple reentry vehicle (MRV) ballistic missile could theoretically be used successfully against surface targets. Testing of this capability would be difficult to prove since no special preparations for the point of impact would be needed although a near circular footprint might be observable.

MIRV/MRV nuclear depth bombs against Western or other submarines are likewise possible. Testing of an actual nuclear depth bomb in the oceans is prohibited by current arms control agreements but development of a depth bomb involves non-nuclear technology, and testing of the warhead can be done underground. Hence, lack of leaks of this capability is not sufficient for the analyst to rule out its possible existence.

The point is that although according to open sources, there is apparently no role for ballistic missiles to be used against naval forces at sea, the lack of such information is not sufficient to make the analyst discount its very real possibility. There is a surplus of land-based missiles in the USSR which can be explained in a number of ways, one of which is planned use against navies.

SSBN Air Defense

Just as publicity that naval forces might be subject to attack by ballistic missiles would not be popular among naval personnel, the ability of submarines to fight back against aircraft would be viewed with alarm by aircrews. Generally, all aircraft involved with ASW operations against SSBNs lack self defense against missiles. This is understandable, given their expected operating environment.

Submarines in previous wars did have an anti-aircraft capability. With the drive for increased speed and decreased noise, externally mounted guns have disappeared. Self-defense was equated with speed and quietness. Surface-to-air missiles on submarines would indicate a major shift in employment philosophy and probably be a serious thorn in the side of ASW flight crews.

Portable anti-aircraft missiles can be fired from any ship including a surfaced submarine. Provisions can be made for a cluster of missiles to be fitted to a submarine sail and fired while the submarine is at periscope depth. 14/

A more favored approach would be a missile capable of being fired while the submarine is submerged and attacking an aircraft without guidance from the submarine itself. The U.S. has been interested in this capability for a number of years.

Reports in the U.S. press have indicated that an attack Soviet submarine was sighted with a dual launcher for a surface to air missile. Citing a leaked intelligence report, the U.S. Navy League reported that the USSR was capable of developing a submarine surface to air defense system. 15/ More recent reports confirm two systems under development. 16/

This is an area to watch, although even if a Soviet air defense system aboard SSBNs becomes operational, the West will be extremely reluctant to discuss the vulnerability of its "defenseless" ASW aircraft. Such a discussion might necessitate (1) costly counter-measures, (2) actively protecting ASW aircraft, (3) admitting to aircrews that the threat exists and nothing will be done, or (4) giving the Soviets a free ride in their operations in vast areas of the ocean.

NOTES

1. The USSR has made use of their SSBNs in such a show of force since January-February 1984 by deploying additional Delta submaries in the mid-Atlantic. See initial reports found in the January 27, 1984 Washington Post, p. 23; and Wall Street Journal, p. 6. The deployment is clearly political according to Party Secretary Brezhnev, Andropov, and Defense Minister Ustinov. It is a case of direct Soviet use of nuclear weapons in time of peace for political purposes.

2. Department of Defense, Soviet Military Power, 2nd Ed. (Washington: U.S. Government Printing Office, March 1983), p. 17; 3rd Ed. (April 1984), p. 22; and 4th Ed. (April 1985), p. 28. The Washington Times, April 20, 1984, p. 1, discusses the reload potential for Soviet submarines in Cuba. If true, then Yankees on forward deployment represent important targets for U.S. ASW even after they have fired their first salvo.

3. Soviet Military Power, 2nd Ed., p. 17; 3rd Ed., p. 21; and Statement on February 21, 1985 of RADM John Butts, Director of Naval Intelligence, contained in Fiscal Year 1986 Defense Department Authorization and Oversight Hearings, Part 3, Seapower and Strategic and Critical Materials Subcommittee, Armed Services Committee, House of Representatives, 99th Cong., 1st Sess. (HASC No. 99-2) (Washington: U.S. Government Printing Office, 1985), p. 4.

4. Roger Barnett, "Soviet Strategic Reserves and the Soviet Navy," The Soviet Union: What Lies Ahead?, K. M. Currie and G. Varhall, Eds., published under the auspices of the U.S. Air Force as Vol. 6 in the Studies in Communist Affairs (Washington: U.S. Government Printing Office, 1985), p. 601; and report of Soviet defector Arkady Shevchenko in the Baltimore Sun, March 1, 1984, p. 2.

5. Washington Post, January 27, 1984, p. 23; and Newsweek, April 2, 1984, p. 41.

6. Soviet Military Power, 3rd Ed., p. 31; 4th Ed., p. 35.

7. Baltimore Sun, November 23, 1983, p. 1; Aviation Week and Space Technology, January 2, 1984, pp. 14-16; and Butts in Fiscal Year 1986 Defense Department Authorization and Oversight Hearings, p. 5.

8. Bulletin (Norwich, Connecticut), November 29, 1981, p. 11; Los Angeles Times, June 26, 1983, p. 1; Aviation Week and Space Technology, December 10, 1984,

pp. 16-17. See also artists depiction in Soviet Military Power, 4th Ed., pp. 90-91.

9. A report of Soviet submarine activities in Baffin Bay including possible visual sightings by residents of Greenland is found in Berlingske Tidende (Copenhagen), December 13, 1983, p. 2.

10. Contained in CVAN-70 Aircraft Carrier, Hearings, before the Joint Armed Services Subcommittee, Armed Services Committees of the House of Representatives and Senate, 91st Cong., 2nd Sess. (Washington: U.S. Government Printing Office, 1970), pp. 18 and 88.

11. Richard Ackley, "The Wartime Role of Soviet SSBNs," U.S. Naval Institute Proceedings, June 1978, pp. 37-39.

12. Carl Clawson, "The Wartime Role of Soviet SSBNs-Round Two," U.S. Naval Institute Proceedings, March 1980, pp. 64-71.

13. Michael MccGwire, "Current Soviet Warship Construction and Naval Weapons Development," pp. 434-435; and Harlan Ullman, "The Counter Polaris Task," pp. 585-600; in Soviet Naval Policy: Objectives and Constraints, Michael MccGwire, Ken Booth, and Johnn McDonnell, Eds. (New York: Praeger, 1975).

14. John Skipper, "Fighting Back," Defense and Foreign Affairs, April 1983, pp. 20-23, reports that the British have developed such a capability.

15. Sea Power, March 1983, p. 44.

16. Statement on February 28, 1984 of RADM John Butts, Director of Naval Intelligence, contained in Fiscal Year 1985 Defense Department Authorization and Oversignt Hearings, Part 3, Seapower and Strategic and Critical Materials Subcommittee, Armed Services Committee, House of Representatives, 98th Cong., 2nd Sess. (HASC No. 98-34) (Washington: U.S. Government Printing Office, 1984), p. 4.

12

Sensitivity Analysis of Navy Strategic Nuclear Forces

One of the more frequent criticisms of any dynamic assessment of military capability is the dependence of conclusions upon crucial and often unstated assumptions. The author has, instead, specified all known assumptions in order to focus attention on the proper creation of a framework for analysis.

Where possible, different approaches were used to derive findings in both content and hardware analysis. For example, the major missions in a nuclear war were derived from multiple themes involving the ability to influence the outcome of war, the major forces of the Soviet military, types of strategic operations, and analysis of means versus ends. Similarly, the assessment of hard-target kill came from the destructive potential of warheads using different measures of effectiveness, demonstrating no matter how the problem was worked, similar findings were reached.

With the dynamic assessment of Soviet naval force disposition, a slightly different form of verification of findings will be used. In this case, major assumptions will be deliberately manipulated to ascertain if findings can significantly change. For example, manipulation of deployment patterns will take place to assess the strength of other findings of the "normal" situation and to see how much the day to day routine would need to change to alter the threat. Such manipulation, termed sensitivity analysis, has been notably absent from previous examinations of the Soviet Navy.

To some degree, this was done in assessing the likely role for additional Yankees being either surged into the deep oceans or mobilized and withheld. By measuring the modest incremental increase additional Yankees would add to submarines already off the U.S. coastline, considering the problems of sending additional units to North America, and by comparing this by the vast increase in theater capability (either as a theater reserve or for immediate use), it was concluded the theater role was more likely.

In this analysis section, major calculations will not be presented as they were previously nor will reference be made to studies, etc., already cited. All calculations and damage assessments remain in the same format and from the same sources.

Strategic Missile MIRVing

The total numbers of ballistic missile submarines (nuclear are SSBNs, diesel powered are SSBs) appear to be a relative certainty as are the numbers of launchers on each submarine. The one submarine launched ballistic missile (SLBM) per launcher rule also appears certain as long as one recognizes the possibility of a reload potential.

The first questionable area in strategic systems is the numbers of SLBMs that have been deployed with multiple independently targetable reentry vehicle (MIRV) warheads. Recent criticism of the Department of Defense (DOD) has included the possibility of deliberate U.S manipulation of the reported MIRV capability of Soviet SLBMs.1/

The specific criticism involves the SS-N-20 aboard Typhoon and Golf V, and the SS-N-18 aboard Delta III. If one assumes a maximum MIRVing of each missile, SS-N-20 and SS-N-18 systems could field 2117 warheads. If one assumes minimal MIRV for the SS-N-20 and single warheads for the SS-N-18, the maximum number of SS-N-18 or SS-N-20 warheads is only 590. The number of warheads used by The Department of Defense (DOD) are virtually identical to the Soviets own figures and appear to have been accepted by the International Institute for Strategic Studies (IISS). 2/

Even if the SS-N-20 or SS-N-18's contained fewer warheads (six and three respectively), the time-urgent threat would not be modified since Typhoons and Deltas do not patrol close to the U.S. shoreline. The only change would occur in the long-range threat.

In the bolt from the blue, the total deliverable number of long-range warheads would be reduced from 195 to 99 and deliverable equivalent megatonnage (EMT) reduced from 80.5 to 47.8. This still leaves enough deliverable warheads to target at least one on each of the 71 major metropolitan areas assumed to be targeted in the Senate study. The amount of deliverable EMT (103.8 including forward-deployed Yankees) would result in significantly less overall damage but sufficient enough to deter those who feel even a modest attack on the U.S. would be unacceptable. Spread out throughout the nation, a 103.8 EMT attack would probably result in less than 20% overall loss in population and industry. When the Office of Technology Assessment described the percentages of population fatalities from a varying attack on the U.S., an 80 EMT attack against 10 urban areas was judged to be capable of killing 1-5 million people.

In the surge scenario, the reduction in the long-range SLBM threat would be from 804 deliverable warheads to 426 and from 320.0 deliverable EMT to 191.6. A surge attack on the U.S. would total 281.6 EMT including only forward-deployed Yankees. Even if the long-range fleet alone was withheld for countervalue attacks or countervalue damage occurred during an attack on military targets, its 191.6 EMT threat gives it around a potential 30% loss in U.S. population and 35% loss in industry.

In the extreme case of mobilization, the long-range threat would be 688 deliverable warheads instead of 1252 and 316.9 deliverable EMT instead of 508.7. Losses from long-range missiles alone would be around 35% of U.S. population and 45% of industry.

The assessment of damage to the U.S. is speculative at best but it appears from this assessment that even if the maximum number of SLBM warheads is significantly less than assumed (1829 instead of 2908), sufficient countervalue capability exists in the surge and mobilization case to deliver what either the Soviets or Americans would consider a powerful attack on the U.S.

In the bolt from the blue the 47.8 EMT deliverable capability in protected bastions in the case of minimal MIRVing is much less. Whether or not it is sufficient to deter U.S. actions is dependent upon the personalities involved and the circumstances at the time. The only scenario that would result in a Soviet response with only the bolt from the blue force in the bastions would be if the West/China pre-empted against the USSR and succeeded in destroying all Soviet land intercontinental ballistic missiles (ICBMs), bombers, SSBNs in port, and forward-deployed Yankees. Otherwise, the bastion does not constitute the only useable strategic nuclear force.

Despite the unlikelihood of this scenario, the Kremlin must account for it in their worst-case assessment of the threat posed to them. It would involve everything going wrong for the USSR. The amount of deliverable force routinely deployed on relatively invulnerable submarines is often described as the minimal acceptable destruction threat that any major nuclear power can deliver. For the U.S., this is around 400 EMT. For the Soviets it is either 47.8 or 80.5 EMT, depending on which version of the MIRV case one accepts.

Since we know that the USSR is still MIRVing its SLBMS, we can conclude either that they are apprehensive about future U.S. anti-ballistic missile defense (hence MIRV is a hedge) or that this minimal response of 47.8 EMT (without maximum MIRVing) is an insufficient "assured destruction" capability. The Soviets can probably both count on strategic warning from the U.S. (hence can at least surge additional submarines and raise the minimal assured response) as well as an inability of the U.S. to successfully eliminate all Soviet ICBMs, 3/ and other strategic nuclear forces.

Hence the Soviet minimal deployment pattern for strategic submarines may not be indicitive of their view of what constitutes an "assured destruction" of the U.S. but rather might demonstrate their not having to routinely deploy, at-sea, an "assured destruction" second strike in time of peace. Soviet confidence in the West's inability to threaten them with a disarming first-strike may mean that they need only deploy sufficient submarines to limit damage to the USSR by attacking bombers/tankers and Western SSBNs in port (as a hedge against uncertainty) and to at least guarantee some nuclear response in the extremely unlikely case that everything else is destroyed.

If this assessment is correct, than the number of warheads on SLBMs being 1829 or 2908 is virtually inconsequential from a political or war-fighting point of view, as are the criticisms that have been raised about possible DOD manipulation of numbers. They may be of interest only to arms controllers or as a symbol of political-military power.

If the Soviets wanted to increase the number of warheads which routinely constituted an assured second-strike, they would only need to increase the numbers of submarines on patrol (from a modest 10-15%) or consider submarines at the pier as on patrol. 4/

Any increase in the number of SSBNs on routine patrol can be viewed as either an attempt at political coercion (if the Soviets already believe they have a satisfactory second-strike routinely deployed) or an indication that they are uncertain of future U.S. actions (and therefore need to deploy their full assured second strike force). Either case can be made as exemplified by recent Soviet statements that both sides already have sufficient nuclear forces to destroy all important targets and that neither side can perform a disarming single strike. 5/

SLBM Reliability

Another major assumption in the strategic nuclear threat assessment was regarding missile reliability. The assignment of a 75% reliability to the SS-N-18/3 is significant since those missiles carry 54% of all SLBM warheads and 39% of all SLBM EMT. Perhaps a 75% reliability rating for Soviet systems is too high? Eighty percent is the maximum rating given to any U.S. "strategic" weapons system.

One of the major issues raised by the defense reform movement and defense critics is that sophisticated weapons systems rarely work as advertised. The actual observed reliability of Soviet SLBMs is probably known in intelligence circles but unavailable to unclassified researchers. Most unclassified analysis done by major government agencies and research institutions, grant the USSR near technological parity with the U.S. in missile reliability. The worst reliability even assigned by a defense critic for a Soviet SLBM is 65%. 6/

There is no question that deliberate manipulation of the reliability factor can affect the ability of the Soviet Navy to deliver warheads or megatonnage. Of the two major types of SLBM strikes, time-urgent and long-range, the former would be more affected.

If we assume in a bolt from the blue that at least 21 Strategic Air Command (SAC) bases in the U.S. need to be attacked, then the absolute minimum number of warheads which need to be delivered is 42 from forward-deployed Yankees (Soviets must assume 1 warhead on each target will not work). With 80 SS-N-6 missiles on routine patrol, firing just over half from the submarine will probably guarantee at least one warhead actually arrives and detonates (50% reliability assumed) on each of 21 targets.

The Soviets might use up to three missiles to attack each SAC base with the assumption that reliability was only 33.3%. The Soviets cannot assess actual warhead performance quickly enough to employ a shoot-look-shoot tactic. Survivability of the submarine is doubtful once the first missile exits the water, hence a total salvo is likely.

There are only three U.S. strategic submarine bases. Assuming that two additional U.S. submarines may be in other locations the Soviets should be able to successfully attack all SSBNs in port (using three missiles per port) and every SAC base even if they assume a missile reliability as low as 33.3%.

Thus even by approaching the problem from the worst possible case to the Soviets (extremely low reliability), it appears that the USSR can at least carry out a bolt from the blue attack against bombers, tankers, and U.S. SSBNs with one functioning warhead likely deliverable per target.

If, on the other hand, a command, control, and communication (C3) attack is higher in priority to the USSR than destruction of bombers, tankers, and submarines and therefore would be undertaken first, then the lack of an unclassified U.S. target set makes mission completion difficult to assess. The minimal requirements for a C3 attack could be as little as one device of several hundred kilotons and as high as 100 warheads. With such a range of uncertainty, unclassified assessment is impossible.

The best one can conclude is that if the Soviets indeed do know more than we do about the effects of high-altitude bursts and their own missile reliability, then they can be reasonably assumed to have at least deployed a Yankee force that can meet their minimum objectives in a war. Either SLBM reliability is lower than 70-75% and the C3 disruption will only take a few missiles, or, the C3 attack would take a higher number of missiles but since missile reliability is high, all time-urgent targets can be expected to be targeted.

A final possibility is that the number of Yankees and the reliability of SLBMs is too low to perform minimal missions (bomber, tanker, submarine, C3) and that the Soviets count on deploying additional submarines off the U.S. shores as a political warning prior to hostilities. This seems unlikely since if off-going submarines are retained (the quickest method of increasing numbers), and the U.S. disperses SAC to outlying fields, Soviet warhead to target ratios are not substantially different.

If the U.S. is in a generated alert posture, the number of bomber and tanker bases could be as high as 45. The maximum number of warheads carried by an augmented surge case Yankee force is 188. To successfully target all SAC and SSBN bases would require 150 warheads even assuming three per air/submarine base. An additional 38 warheads would still be available for C3 or other missions.

The effect of lower SLBM reliability on a long-range missile strike would be to simply reduce the megatonnage and number of warheads delivered. In turn, levels of damage in the U.S. would be less.

The minimal assumed threat from Deltas was 195 deliverable warheads (80.5 EMT). If the reliability of long-range SLBMs was 50% instead of 70-75%, then the minimal assured response would be 132 warheads (55.3 EMT) plus warheads delivered by forward-based Yankees. Would this be enough to respond to a U.S. first-strike? Possibly, but the Soviets can virtually count on strategic warning hence this minimal alert posture probably only represents a hedge against uncertainty. They can also count on the U.S. not destroying all their ICBMs and other strategic nuclear forces, hence the submarine fleet is not responsbile for the entire second-strike.

The more likely occurrence is that the USSR could at least surge deploy additional submarines with long-range missiles. In a surge, even with a 50% reliability on missiles, the threatened response from long-range SLBMs alone is 546 warheads and 218.9 EMT. In a mobilization it would be 854 warheads and 349.6 EMT with 50% missile reliability.

Thus, even with a drastically reduced missile reliability rating, sufficient deliverable megatonnage (MT) and warheads would be available to the USSR in their defended bastions to constitute a substantial response, even if everything went wrong for the USSR and the submarines were all that remained.

MIRV and Reliability

If the assumptions made on SS-N-20 and SS-N-18 MIRVing are incorrect and SLBM reliability is significantly lower (50%), would this impact upon the conclusions of mission capability? The worst-case for the Soviets regarding the close-in threat already has been considered with low reliability alone. The MIRV issue does not effect the SS-N-6.

The impact of lower MIRVing completion and lower reliability would effect the navy's contribution to an assured second-strike from long-range missiles. The minimal strike from the ocean in the ungenerated bolt from the blue would be 68 warheads and 33.6 EMT. In the more likely second-strike response in the surge scenario would be 292 warheads and 132.5 EMT. In a mobilization, even assuming the worst circumstances for the Soviets, their expected response from the navy long-range SLBMs alone would be 474 warheads and 220.4 EMT.

The bolt from the blue scenario only makes sense if the Soviets or the West strikes first with no warning. Even if the unlikely happened (West strikes first), the Soviets will still have forward-based Yankees, undestroyed submarines in port (perhaps in protected tunnels), some ICBMs, and some intercontinental bombers. Hence, even a worst MIRV/worst reliability case for Soviet SLBMs must be viewed in relation to the whole of the strategic nuclear force.

If the USSR strikes first in a bolt from the blue, their massive Strategic Rocket Force makes the navy's long-range contribution insignificant even assuming maximum MIRV/reliability. If the West strikes first in a bolt from the blue, enough strategic nuclear forces would survive to probably ensure a significant retaliation in the minds of the Politburo, even with bad MIRV/reliability assumptions.

In the surge or mobilization scenario, it is likely that all sides are in a generated alert. Even if the USSR was forced to rely on its submarine assets alone, in a surge or mobilization they could still deliver a significant strike even assuming the worst MIRV/reliability case.

SSBN Deployment Areas

A change in deployment areas for Soviet SSBNs or sending all available Yankees to North American waters in a surge or mobilization might impact on the time-urgent counterforce potential of the Soviet Navy. It was assessed that the close-in Yankee threat was already sufficient enough to attack bomber, tanker, and submarine bases with a modest C3 disruption possible but insufficient to constitute a simultaneous major C3 attack and pin-down of ICBMs. If the Soviets were to increase the numbers of close-in warheads, might they be able to increase the counterforce threat?

In past years, it was speculated that the Yankee fleet would in fact deploy to North American waters if surged or mobilized. Although a convincing case can be made that the incremental increase in deliverable weapons/EMT is not worth the risks in time of war, the assumption will now be made that the Soviets do in fact send all Yankees to mid-ocean and that transit safety is assured. Also to be tested will be the assumption that all Deltas and Typhoons also deploy in the Atlantic and Pacific, a possibility hinted at by those who see further quieting of Soviet submarines as a sign that deployment areas will/could shift.

In a bolt from the blue, with only the five Yankees off the U.S. coast, the threat is insufficient to do all potential counterforce missions. If those Yankees were replaced eventually by Deltas, however, the threat would change considerably as would the incentive for the U.S. to quickly neutralize the threat.

With a force of five Delta IIIs equipped with maximum MIRV SLBMs with high reliability, the close in deliverable threat would be 80 missiles, 420 warheads, 143 EMT, 84 MT. If Typhoons were used, then the deliverable threat increases to 100 missiles, 630 warheads, 214.2 EMT, 126 MT. The routine deliverable threat from Yankee is 56 missiles/warheads/EMT/MT.

Thus replacing Yankee in the future with either new and quieter Delta or Typhoons would allow either considerably more capability in deliverable warheads or EMT on the same number of submarines or the ability to reduce the forward-deployed fleet to fewer units. Since survivability of forward deployed SSBNs is questionable, we might expect submarine numbers to remain constant and capability to increase. Replacing routinely patrolling Yankee with newer submarines could threaten the U.S. with more time-urgent warheads than if the entire Yankee fleet was mobilized and succeeded in sailing to North American waters.

If the Soviets were to deploy all their submarines to mid-ocean patrol areas instead of in Soviet home waters, might this improve Soviet capability to perform ICBM pin-down? One could make the case that a peacetime deployment of all available submarines in mid-ocean would so overwhelm Western ASW assets that high submarine survivability is assurred. In a surge, the Soviets could place 25 additional Yankee, Delta, and Typhoon SSBNs in the Atlantic and Pacific. In a mobilization, the increase would be 41 submarines.

The numbers of deliverable time-urgent warheads from Typhoons, Deltas and supplemental Yankees in a surge scenario would be 935 (451 EMT) and 1431 (688.9 EMT) in a mobilization. The minimum range for SS-N-8/18/20 SLBMs (one-third of maximum range) would be a bit of a problem.

In theory, the USSR could deliver a total of 1047.4 MT on time-urgent targets in the U.S. if all of its submarines appeared off the shores of North America. ICBM pin-down has been described as requiring hundreds of MT per <u>minute</u>, hence the entire force could probably not pin-down all U.S. ICBMs for long.

The creation of windows of launch opportunity by irregular arrivals of SLBMs raises additional uncertainies for successful ICBM pin-down. For pin-down to be effective, warheads need to keep arriving with no breaks that can be exploited by the U.S. to shoot through. Window exploitation would be easier with survivable U.S. sensors warning of each new SLBM launch.

Since the Soviets could not count on the absence of sensors nor of guaranteed warhead detonation, their logical action is to use at least two warheads on each target, doubling the requirement. Faced with uncertainties, the limitations of science and hardware, continued U.S. development of new hardened missile systems and dispersion of ICBMs can negate any reasonable threat of total pin-down of American ICBMs by Soviet SLBMs.

This being the case, future massive deployments of all Soviet SSBNs to North American waters seems unlikely. At best, a few ICBM wings might be effected. At worst, the USSR could place its submarine fleet at unnecessary risk. Massive increases in forward-deployed SSBNs also appears inconsistent with declaratory statements emphasizing the need to <u>control</u> strategic nuclear forces and to preclude unwanted launch of weapons.

Yet we may see extra SSBNs deploy in mid-ocean. The USSR has done so since early 1984 when 2-3 Deltas first appeared in the Atlantic. There is no sound military reason to deploy Deltas in this area. Rather it affords Western ASW units an unprecedented opportunity to gain intelligence information. The Soviet action is a clear case of the use of strategic nuclear force to coerce and influence political decisions and actions by NATO member nations.

A mass deployment of SSBNs into the Atlantic or Pacific is allowable under international law. Future repeat surges made as political statements cannot be prevented by existing arms control agreements, nor should any attempt be made to restrict such deployment since it places Soviet SSBNs in areas where they are more accessable to Western ASW action.

If a mass mid-ocean deployment of Deltas, Typhoons, and Yankees did take place, it would probably be designed to send a major political statement rather than shift the military balance. Such a massive surge would not be sustainable since eventually those submarines would need to return for provisions or risk exposing themselves in open-ocean replenishment. A shift to routine mid-ocean deployments instead of bastions would free the general purpose forces of the Soviet Navy from what has been their avowed purpose, protection of those SSBNs under the umbrella of land-based air power.

NOTES

1. William Arkin and Jeffrey Sands, "The Soviet Nuclear Stockpile," Arms Control Today, June 1984, pp. 1 and 4-6.
2. Whence the Threat to Peace, 3rd Ed. (Moscow: Military Publishing House, 1984), p. 6, reports around 2500 Soviet SLBM warheads in 1984, 2000 in 1981, and 724 in 1975. The Department of Defense (DOD) Soviet Military Power 3rd and 4th Eds. (Washington: U.S. Government Printing Office, April 1984 and April 1985) essentially agree, reporting that during those years, the Soviet SLBM totals were 2500, 2250, and slightly over 700. The International Institute for Strategic Studies (IISS) Military Balance 1985-1986, has also essentially accepted the current DOD totals.
3. IISS Military Balance 1985-1986 reports that there are 2118 U.S. ICBM warheads. With a reliability rating of 80% for U.S. ICBMs and the use of two warheads against each of the 1398 known Soviet silos, at best the U.S. could target 847 Soviet silos. Hence a U.S. first-strike using all its ICBMs leaves the U.S. partially disarmed with 0 ICBM warheads (plus SLBMs and air-breathing systems) while the Soviets could retain at least 551 silos for their land-based systems plus reloads, non-SALT accountable systems, SLBMs and air-breathing systems. U.S. SLBMs are incapable of successfully targeting Soviet silos. U.S. air-breathing systems could not arrive in sufficient time to prevent Soviet use.
4. John Collins, U.S.-Soviet Military Balance 1980-1985, Congressional Research Service Report No. 85-89S, p. CRS-100, states that about 25% of Soviet SSBNs are at sea on any given day and another 25% are probably on alert in port. This book has assumed that about 20% of the Soviet SSB/SSBN force (15 submarines) are at sea daily. It is difficult to know how Collins uses the term on alert: as being able to quickly go to sea and fire, or able to fire from the port itself. If he means able to get underway and fire from at-sea locations, then the total of 50% of the full capability of the SSB/SSBN force

is the same as the upper end of my own assessment of the surge case. Firing from the port itself would give the navy the same type of capabilities and vulnerabilities that the land-based ICBMs have.

5. In July 1965, Party Secretary Brezhnev told Military Academy graduates that the USSR had enough rockets to make short work of any aggressor. In July 1974, he told the Polish Sejm that the world already had sufficient stockpiles of weapons to destroy every living thing several times. On August 28, 1982, General V. F. Tolubko, C-in-C of the Strategic Rocket Forces, states in a Moscow radio interview, that it was impossible for either side to bank on carrying out a premptive strike. Marshal of the Soviet Union N. V. Ogarkov, also has used this theme in "On the 40th Anniversary of the Great Victory," Kommunist Vooruzhennykh sil, November 1984, p. 26; and History Teaches Vigilance (Moscow: Military Publishers, 1985), p. 89. One wonders the purpose of continued improvements in Soviet strategic systems.

6. James Dunnigan, How to Make War (New York: William Morrow, 1982), pp. 298-299. Dunnigan gives modern U.S. SLBMs a reliability of 80%.

13

General Purpose Forces

Data Base

For this book, a complete threat assessment of all the general purpose naval forces of the Soviet Union is not possible. Since the purpose of this book is to assess capability for forces involved in a major nuclear war, ships and aircraft whose missions are only or obviously related to peripheral areas (amphibious operations, local border patrol and coastal defense, mine warfare, surveillence, training, research and development, logistics, etc.) will not be considered.

The reason for including general purpose forces at all, is to assess the capability of the Soviet Navy to actively defend its nuclear powered ballistic missile submarines (SSBNs) in bastions close to the USSR. Implicit in such a defensive strategy (which appears to be declaratory policy) is the need for forces to protect the SSBNs that may be withheld as a part of the strategic nuclear reserve.

The forces of interest are active long-range and theater submarines, surface ships (corvettes and larger), and fixed-wing airplanes capable of strikes on major Western surface ships or submarines. As was done for strategic submarines, each of the primary sources in the hardware analysis was consulted to develop an agreed-upon data base of numbers of the various types of ships that exist in the Soviet Navy.

Table 13.1 presents this data in an aggregated manner. For a thorough description of the methodology used in assigning forces to one section or another, etc., reference is made to substantially larger earlier data bases published by the author. 1/ Categories are not fully definitive. For example, antisubmarine warfare (ASW) units are capable of anti-surface warfare and vice versa. By and large, the preponderance of certain types of weapons systems is the criteria for assigning a ship to one group or another.

Table 13.1

General Purpose
Active Navy Forces (1985)

	Jane's	IISS	DIA	Assumed Number
Strike/Attack Submarines				
With cruise missiles	68	66	62	65
Without missiles	212	203	211	209
Surface Strike				
Carriers	4	4	3	4
Cruisers	11	11	11	11
Major destroyer	4	4	5	4
Gun cruiser	11	10	8	10
Surface ASW				
Helicopter carriers	2	2	2	2
Cruisers	17	17	17	17
Major destroyers	5	5	5	5
Surface Escorts				
Missile destroyers	35	35	31	34
Missile frigates	32	33	32	32
Theater Escorts				
Destroyers	28	25	22	25
Frigates/corvettes	154	143	145	147
Airplanes (fixed-wing)				
Bombers	430	345	375	383
ASW	–	195	205	200

Source: Compiled by author.

The next step is to allocate each of these types of forces into the four main fleets of the Soviet Navy with emphasis on the two fleets that might support bastions. Tables 13.2 and 13.3 present the Northern and Pacific fleets, listing the total number of units assumed, the number normally out of area, and the surge and mobilization potential for remaining forces. The methodology and percentages used for the high and low threats are identical to that described in Chapter 9.

Table 13.2
Northern Fleet Surge/Mobilization Threat (1985)

	Assumed Total	Out of Area	Surge Totals		Mobilization Totals	
			Low	High	Low	High
Strike/Attack Submarines						
With cruise missiles	35	7-8	4	11	15	19
Without cruise missiles	88	17-24	5	27	35	49
Surface Strike						
Carriers	1	0	0	1	1	1
Cruisers/major destroyers	6	0	2	3	4	5
Gun cruisers	2	0	1	1	1	2
Surface ASW						
Helicopter carriers	0	0	0	0	0	0
Cruisers/major destroyers	9	0	3	5	5	7
Surface Escorts	19	0-2	4	10	11	14
Theater Escorts	45	0	15	23	30	34
Bombers	54	0	18	27	36	41
ASW Airplanes	58	2-4	15	27	35	42

Source: Compiled by author. Surge/mobilization totals are numbers available in home waters.

Table 13.3
Pacific Fleet Surge/Mobilization Threat (1985)

	Assumed Total	Out of Area	Surge Totals Low	Surge Totals High	Mobilization Totals Low	Mobilization Totals High
Strike/Attack Submarines						
With cruise missiles	24	3-5	3	9	11	15
Without cruise missiles	69	10-12	11	25	34	42
Surface Strike						
Carriers	2	0	1	1	1	2
Cruisers/major destroyers	4	1-2	0	1	1	2
Gun cruisers	3	0	1	2	2	2
Surface ASW						
Helicopter carriers	0	0	0	0	0	0
Cruisers/major destroyers	7	1	1	3	4	4
Surface Escorts	20	6-9	0	4	4	9
Theater Escorts	53	1-2	16	26	33	39
Bombers	176	0	59	88	117	132
ASW Airplanes	70	4	19	31	43	49

Source: Compiled by author. Surge/mobilization totals are numbers available in home waters.

In a Spring 1984 scheduled exercise involving the Northern and Baltic fleets, the Soviets were able to put a significantly large number of ships to sea. The number of ships involved from the Baltic Fleet was 1 cruiser, 4 frigates, 1 cruise missile submarine, 3 attack submarines, and 4 auxiliaries. 2/ According to the Pentagon at the time, the Northern Fleet deployed 135 surface warships, 66 submarines, and 36 auxiliaries. 3/ The 135 surface warships must have included minor classes and amphibious units not tabulated in the tables herein.

Other reports stated the number of major, modern warships deployed along the Greenland - Iceland - United Kingdom (G-I-UK) Gap as 29-30. 4/ Assuming these units were capable of air self-defense, it would confirm the estimate herein of 29 ships in the mobilization, high threat scenario.

The number of submarines reportedly deployed (66) is also comparable to the mobilization high threat scenario (68) for general purpose submarines. Early press reports of the exercise specified a much lower number of 20-30 submarines while later Pentagon reports tabulate a total of 40. 5/ If the later figures of either 40 or 66 submarines was correct, the additional submarines above those reported initially can be explained by at least two major hypotheses.

First, the initial figures could have been in error. Second, the figures reported later by the Pentagon might be correct. In either case, we have to decide if the totals included by cruise missile, strike, or attack submariness or if they include SSBNs. The data presented previously under strategic nuclear forces indicated that the USSR should be able to mobilize and deploy around 24 SSBNs in local Northern Fleet waters. Without access to classified intelligence reports, it is impossible to know how many of what type submarines actually did deploy. It would not have been impossible to mobilize 66 general purpose submarines alone, but a more likely case is a combination of general purpose and SSBNs.

Task Group Baseline

Naval engagements might take place with single units but the preferred method is to aggregate into task groups and task forces. In the Great Patriotic War, Soviet naval forces were organized into task groups including groups of 2-3 submarines. 6/ In the worldwide Okean-75 exercise, the Soviet Navy organized itself into 12 such major task groups. 7/

The International Institute for Strategic Studies (IISS) recognized the need to aggregate naval forces into task groups in their Military Balance 1978-1979. In their attempt to draw up a balance of forces, IISS aggregated the major forces of the Soviet fleet into a total of 16 major task groups.

Any attempt at aggregation will be both speculative and scenario dependent. Units which were never designed to may be forced to operate together. Some ships may be optimized for one major mission but, due to circumstances, perform others. The priority of certain missions may dicate what types of forces are allocated for missions of lesser priority.

From the behavior of the USSR in past crises and by observation of their major fleet exercises over the years, it is possible to construct varying "typical" tasks groups. The task groups listed as "typical" are illustrative of how one could do this and need not be definitive.

The key element in understanding aggregation of forces is to recognize that it includes air, surface, and subsurface forces. For the purposes of this research, a representative set of task forces optimized for the naval tasks most commonly articulated by the USSR. These are: anti-carrier warfare (ACW), antisubmarine warfare (ASW), and surface warfare.

Although not part of this research, amphibious warfare groups need to be accounted for since they will reduce the number of surface ships available for other purposes. A major assumption is that amphibious groups must be formed. It is the author's opinion that if the amphibious ships and craft exist, and the men are routinely exercised in such operations, the Soviets will perform such missions in time of war. Table 13.4 represents "typical" task groups.

Table 13.4

Typical Task Groups

Anti-carrier Warfare Group/Air Supplemented Option

    1 cruiser/major destroyer
    2 escorts
    1 cruise missile submarine
    2 submarines (3 if submarine missiles unavailable)
    (1 carrier or 20 bombers if available)

ASW Group/Air Supplemented Option

    1 cruiser/major destroyer
    2 escorts
    3 submarines
    (1 carrier/helicopter carrier or 5 ASW airplanes
      if available)

Submarine Warfare Group

    3 strike/attack submarines

Surface Warfare Group

    1 carrier, helicopter carrier, cruiser, or major
      destroyer
  3-4 escorts (depending upon availability of above)

Amphibious Group

    1 gun or other cruiser
  3-4 escorts (depending upon availability of above)

Bomber Strike Group

    20 bombers

ASW Air Group

    5 airplanes

Source: Author.

Units have been created with optional air cover. For ASW airplanes, the selected number includes units in transit to/from and operating in one patrol area. For bombers, the strike group is one mass. 8/ By referring to the normal peacetime deployment of the Soviet fleet, we can aggregate forces into baseline cases. Table 13.5 presents a baseline of Northern and Pacific Fleet task groups optimized for support of major combatants.

Table 13.5

Northern/Pacific Fleet Task Group Baseline (1985)

Area	Type	Surge Total	Mobilization Total
Norwegian Barents Sea	Air Sup ACW	1-2	3-4
	Air Sup ASW	1	5-6
	Submarine	0-10	8-12
	Surface	3-7	5-8
Seas of Japan Okhotsk/Bering Sea	Air Sup ACW	1	1-2
	Air Sup ASW	1-2	3-4
	Submarine	2-8	11-12
	Surface	1-2	5-7

In the mobilization case, which represents the most-likely case if bastion defense were to ever be put to the test, (a war of a relatively long enough period to deploy numerous forces), the numbers of anti-carrier task groups in the Northern Fleet matches what the author has been told over the years would be the most likely number of U.S. carrier task groups to be involved. In the Pacific, the shortage of ACW ships is made up for with additional aircraft.

To fully analyze the potential of the Soviet Navy to successfully defend their two major bastions would require an enormous gaming effort that would need to be classified. What this author can conclude from Table 13.5 is that sufficient general-purpose forces can be mobilized to constitute a powerful enough force that the West cannot simply sail its naval assets (especially surface ships) into bastions without considerable risk. It should also be noted that Soviet ASW groups are not deployed either near the home port of U.S. SSBNs nor in the deep Atlantic or Pacific reaches where American SSBNs patrol.

General Purpose Force Issues

A few residual general purpose force issues often raised in the secondary literature will now be addressed herein. First, the number of naval task groups assigned to support the army may not only be a function of the modest amphibious lift and naval infantry capability of the fleet. Western sources have reported for years that Soviet exercises include routine transport of ground forces by ships of the merchant marine. In a recent Soviet book about the Soviet Navy, the editor included pictures of an assault on the beach in which civilian ships are in the background. 9/ The point is that if additional sealift utilizing merchant ships takes place, additional naval force will need to be diverted from the tasks of protecting SSBNs to acccomodate the support of the army.

Second, the numbers of bombers which could act in a maritime strike role supporting bastion defense exceeds the number of units assigned to a Soviet Naval Aviation. Bombers or fighters from the air force can act in a fleet support role. This apparently happened in the Spring 1984 exercises. 10/

Third, the use of the fleet as a first line of defense against bombers and cruise missiles of the Western air forces cannot be ruled out. New SA-N-6 surface-to-air missiles carried aboard surface warships reportedly have an effective ceiling of 100,000 feet and a speed of March 6. This is comparable to the Soviet's land SA-10 surface-to-air missile. <u>Jane's Weapons Systems 1985-86</u> credits the SA-N-6 with an anti-cruise missile capability.

From a hardware perspective alone, there is nothing to prevent Soviet ships with surface-to-air missiles from engaging incoming bombers and cruise missiles. Fleet weapons may not have been developed for this mission but one cannot deny that the capability is there. Thus, bastion defense may not only be to protect the subsurface forces but to add to the layered air defense of the homeland.

Fourth, there is no question that the Soviet fleet has a tactical nuclear capability. Most standard reference works in Soviet hardware list nuclear warheads for their cruise missiles and depth bombs. The presence of nuclear torpedos was confirmed during the 1981 episode of a Whiskey class submarine aground in Swedish waters. The importance of tactical nuclear war at sea is its relationship to possible escalation to global nuclear war.

When a navy ship goes to sea on an operational deployment, it needs to have all of its weapons already on board. It is highly impractical for a forward-deployed ship to return to home bases to load out nuclear weapons and then return to station to fight.

Similarly, there are limits to the amount of weapons that can be carried on any ship. Soviet ships have been notoriously deficient in their lack of re-loads. Even in a non-nuclear war, the longer the conflict, the more conventional ammunition would be used. At some point, a local commander might be faced with the situation of having no conventional weapons but with perfectly useable nuclear ones. 11/ A frequently overlooked point is that naval weapons are frequently dual-use, nuclear or conventional. Will the Soviet Navy commander be authorized to initiate tactical nuclear war on his own in the face of certain destruction?

Fifth, the details of larger theater or world-wide naval exercises have been leaked to some degree. The latest major exercises of this type were the two previously discussed April 1975 Okean, the Spring of 1984, and a July 1985 sea-control exercise. 12/

In Okean-75 the fleet formed into 12 task groups and emphasized world-wide ocean surveillance, ASW, and interdiction of mid-ocean sea lines of communication (SLOCs). Prime targets includes submarines, convoys, carrier and other surface task groups. Attacks against surface ships were executed primarily by aircraft but perhaps coordinated with submarine attacks. "Preliminary" attacks in the North Atlantic appeared designed to attrite "enemy" carriers outside of a defense line along the G-I-UK Gap. Heaviest interactions occurred in the Norwegian Sea. 13/

The Spring 1984 exercise was not world-wide although a greater number of ships was involved. The primary scene of operations was the Norwegian Sea, again with an outer line of defense along the G-I-UK Gap. 14/ Although the increase in air striking range allowed by the new Backfire bomber was widely reported, the "enemy" task group subjected to attack was within the defense perimeter of the G-I-UK Gap. Apparently no attacks occurred south of this line in North Atlantic shipping lanes.

Primary emphasis in this newest exercise appeared to be defense of home waters and denial of the enemy's attempt to penetrate the Norwegian Sea. Ships were deployed in three major task groups including one group of 15 ships (of all types) centered around the new Kirov class cruiser. Undoubtedly this latter group included auxiliaries. Thus, from the perspective of observed behavior in exercises, as well as from the limited number of surface combatants on forward deployment, the theory that the Soviets plan to defend ocean bastions appears to be substantiated. 15/

Sixth, the numbers of task groups of any composition in varying locations may or may not be fully combat capable. Just because a ship has the mobility to get underway does not mean all of its weapons systems are operational. A more normal state of affairs is that operations will occur in which major systems are degraded or inoperable from the start. In strategic systems, this was factored in as reliability rating. With general purpose forces, it would be much more complex and will not be undertaken herein.

Seventh, the ability of the Soviet general purpose fleet to perform strategic ASW against Western and Chinese SSBNs should be addressed. In general, surface and air ASW assets of the Soviet Navy would probably not deploy in a war in areas where U.S./U.K. submarines equipped with long-range Trident missiles can deploy. This is simply due to the lack of survivability of such Soviet forces and no organic sea-based naval air power. The Soviet Navy might be more successful against the few NATO or Chinese submarines equipped with medium range missiles if those submarines chose to enter defended bastions to fire their missiles.

The number of total aim points confronting the Soviet Navy would be at least 22 SSBNs. 16/ It is the author's opinion that with so few quiet nuclear attack submarines (SSNs) in the Soviet inventory (29 newer types), and the concurrent need to use quiet SSNs to protect Soviet SSBNs, the strategic ASW threat to the U.S. is minimal. Not only is there no surplus but there is only enough to put one Soviet submarine (given a maximum of 75% mobilization) in trail of every Western SSBN on patrol. One unit per SSBN would certainly be insufficient. Multiple assets in trial should be considered a minimum requirement.

Eighth, the major assumption in the presentation of a "normal" deployment for general purpose forces in a surge or mobilization was that the first priority of ships in the Northern and Pacific Fleet was to form into task groups maximized to protect ballistic missile submarines in bastions. Task groups were created that would counter Western submarines in Arctic areas and U.S. aircraft carrier task groups attempting to fight in the Norwegian Sea or northwestern Pacific Oceans.

The key questions regarding the general purpose forces are whether or not there exists a surplus of assets above and beyond that necessary for bastion defense. If such a surplus exists, then the West would have to prepare for offensive Soviet naval operations on the high seas.

The limiting factor in offensive general purpose Soviet fleet operations in other than home waters remains, however, the lack of fixed-wing airplanes capable of supporting distant-water naval operations. Thus, even if the primary mission of the general-purpose fleet (bastion defense) were eliminated, the Soviet Navy would still be incapable of sustained, open-ocean, offensive operations against a major maritime enemy.

This assessment could be reversed, however, if Western aircraft carriers and supporting land based aircraft were eliminated. If the West could no longer use crucial air fields in Iceland, Norway, Japan, Alaska, etc. the effect might be decisive in the theater. Lacking opposition from Western air power, even the Soviet Navy might successfully dominate the Norwegian Sea, northern Pacific, and elsewhere.

The Soviets could extend their naval operations if it has use of Western bases in Norway, Iceland, Alaska, etc. Similarly operations would be enhanced when the Soviet Navy has fully-capable aircraft carriers of its own.

Hence, even if the general-purpose fleet were relieved of a mission to protect its own SSBNs, and even if it sent all its surface ships from all four fleets out into mid-ocean, its lack of air power would limit its war-time effectiveness unless Western air power was neutralized.

Ninth, in the Great Patriotic War, the Soviets transferred major surface warships from the Pacific to the Northern Fleet via the Arctic Northern Sea Route. 17/ Submarines were transferred to the Northern Fleet from the Pacific via the Panamal Canal and others arrived from the Caspian Sea and Volga River via inland waters. 18/ There is no question that fleet transfers could happen again in a future war if the Soviets could once again be assured of no major armed struggle in one theater.

Two other inter-fleet transfers are more generally discussed. The first is the exit of naval forces out of the Baltic Sea prior to a war. By looking at the composition of the Baltic Fleet and allies in the Warsaw Pact as well as the geographical considerations of Sweden as a potential threat, and the need to secure Bornholm Island, this author concludes that the Baltic surface and air fleets will probably not exit.

The Baltic fleets appear to be maximized and exercised for amphibious operations and denial of entry by major NATO fleet units. Mine warfare appears logical by all sides. Perhaps a few submarines would successfully exit into the North Sea for local or special operations.

The other widely discussed fleet transfer would involve surface ships out of the Black Sea into the Mediterranean. In order to allow additional units to transit the Turkish Straits, advance notification must be given to Turkey in accordance with the Montreaux Convention. The USSR routinely files contingency notifications which would allow them to reinforce the Mediterranean "Squadron" within a few days. 19/

Although such a scenario cannot be ruled out, it should not necessarily be anticipated. The Black Sea Fleet has few surplus assets above the number necessary to carry out obvious amphibious operations. Removal of anti-air platforms from the sea would degrade air defense against strikes originating in Greece or Turkey or from cruise missiles transiting the Black Sea.

If the Soviets were to strengthen their forces in the Mediterranean, they would have a logistics problem as well as a shortage in supporting air power. Mediterranean geography favors NATO, making Soviet units extremely vulnerable over time.

The seeming surplus of submarines in the Black Sea may in part be explained by their use as training vessels. In any case, Montreaux Convention restrictions and the relative ease of mounting a campaign against submarines transiting from the Black Sea through to the Western Mediterrannean make even this possibility a local threat and unlikely to directly impact operations in the North Atlantic.

Tenth, and finally, the role of German naval forces on forward deployment in both World Wars in similar to that facing the USSR in the future. Soviet naval units on forward deployment are not survivable in the long run. They can either run for home or internment at a neutral port or seek out the enemy and extract the highest possible price for their eventual destruction.

An advantage of their engaging Western forces is that it complicates NATO strategy by diverting attention to possible peripheral areas. From an analysis of Admiral Sergei Gorshkov's views of past wars, it is likely that forward deployed forces will fight no matter now hopeless their strategic predicament.

The Mediterranean "Squadron" is a well formed "fleet" in the Western sense of the word. It seems ideally suited to conduct ACW against the 2-3 U.S./French carriers in that sea. A modest campaign could be conducted against ballistic missile submarines or cruise missile carriers attempting to use the Eastern Mediterranean. The Eastern Mediterranean offers an excellent launch point for a NATO "warning shot" missile against Eastern Europe territory. The Soviets could detect the trajectory or flight path of the missile and see quickly that the intended point of impact was not the USSR.

The importance of the Mediterranean theater in a major war is frequently misunderstood. Despite public statements designed to reassure southern flank allies (Greece and Turkey), the result of emphasizing a Mediterranean maritime campaign and risking loss of NATO carriers could be to place the Atlantic SLOC in jeopardy. This opinion has been voiced at the highest NATO circles. 20/ Thus, a fundamental NATO dilemma is that pre-war political assurances may be at odds with actual wartime necessity.

There has been running controversy over the years between, those who believe that units of the Soviet Navy forward on forward deployment were sent on a political naval diplomacy mission, and, those who have felt that the primary reason was defense against carriers and SSBNs. The reason for the deployment is of only passing concern to this book. The gains that the Soviet Union has obtained by naval diplomacy have been recognized by numerous studies. The benefit of having these units in place would also be obvious if a war were to actually occur and Soviet strategy succeeded.

Should the number of surface units on forward deployment be increased, it might be as a result of total growth of the Soviet Navy or due to improvements in technology making bastion defense possible with fewer assets. The number of units on forward deployment is of interest to this study since such forces must be subtracted from the totals available for bastion defense.

On the other hand, since the Soviets know this also, any unexplained recall of non-vital forward-deployed ships to home waters should be viewed by the West with alarm. Recognizing that the West would be able to observe such an action and might conclude it was strategic warning of a war, the West should not count on such action. Forward-deployed assets are thus probably expendable.

SLOC Mission

Soviet submarine operations would be essentially unhampered by a lack of air power in distant waters. After accounting for those assigned to ballistic missile submarine protection in task groups, there appears to be a "surplus" of attack and strike submarines. In a mobilization, the Northern Fleet might have as many as 49 and the Pacific Fleet around 46 submarines not otherwise employed.

One might posture these "surplus" submarines along a defensive barriers or assigned to directly escort SSBNs. Alternately one could expect them to deploy in distant ocean waters where they could threaten the SLOCs. Either case can be argued. What is significant is that each major oceanic SLOC threat is not <u>hundreds</u> of submarines but under 50 (assuming no extra units exit the Baltic).

In 1968, Robert Herrick attempted to measure the "surplus" in Soviet Northern Fleet submarines in a future war and concluded it was around 100 submarines. [21]/ At that time there were few SSBNs to protect. Even with an assured the 100 submarine threat to the Atlantic, Herrick calculated that the steady state SLOC threat was 20-25 submarines since it would take roughly 4 or 5 Soviet submarines to keep one on station at all times in a long war.

In a short war, all "surplus" submarines would probably deploy. If wartime deployment to the SLOCs are minimal, it might indicate posturing for sustained operations. Assuming a base of 50 would result in as few as 10 submarines routinely along the SLOCs, it is noteworthy to recall German wartime experiences. From 1915 - 1916 the average number of U-boats in the Atlantic was 15. From September 1939 - June 1940, it was 6, from July 1940 - March 1941, it was 10. [22]/

Average monthly shipping losses from those first two periods of World War II were 106,000 and 224,000 gross tons, respectively. Germany started World War II with only 30 serviceable ocean-going U-boats from which to send 6 routinely on patrol. During the initial period of the war, these few U-boats sank an average of 60 ships per month.

The Atlantic Council's Working Group on Securing the Seas (1976) also attempted to measure the surplus Soviet Navy capability in order to quantify the SLOC threat. Michael MccGwire was credited with doing most of the work in a presentation of Soviet naval force allocation. 23/ Their findings were 30-60 submarines for an Atlantic SLOC campaign along with some 50-60 bombers, and 10-30 submarines and 30-60 bombers in the Pacific. In a subsequent attempt to quantify the sealane defense problem, Charles Di Bona and William O'Keefe "conservatively" assumed sixty Soviet submarines against the Atlantic SLOC and thirty in the Pacific. 24/

Estimating the amount of damage a conventional SLOC campaign could do is extremely scenario-dependent. Not only must the numbers of submarines be assumed but whether or not they deploy prior to hostilities, for a long or short war, as well as the allied convoy posture needs to be assessed. One must also consider that if the war has gone nuclear ashore, the SLOC threat is also likely to include tactical nuclear weapons from submarines and Soviet Naval Aviation as well as possible use of ballistic missiles against convoy formations.

The Atlantic Council's assessment of merchant ship attrition is based upon computations performed in a 1976 MIT Master's Thesis 25/ and Alan Enthoven and K. Wayne Smith's logic outlined in their 1971 How Much is Enough? 26/ This author is convinced that these approaches are flawed and that no satisfactory unclassified model exists for a future SLOC campaign (and one that includes the nuclear threat).

Unfortunately this does satisfactorily answer the question of the credibility of a conventional SLOC campaign. Yet for a threat to the SLOCs to be effective, how many submarines actually need be deployed? It is doubtful that NATO would risk the loss of modern merchants used for resupply due to the large size of newer container ships, roll-on/roll-off vessels, and especially tankers, and the fewer number of hulls available. A loss of one ship today is much more serious than the loss a Victory Ship in World War II.

The SLOC problem of sea lane defense only presents itself in an extended war. In short nuclear wars, terminals can be destroyed by ballistic missiles negating the need for a "battle of the Atlantic." Since Soviet declaratory doctrine includes conventional-only operations or a possible extended period of armed struggle it seems logical that a sea lane interdiction threat to the SLOCs remains a required mission for the Soviet Navy. Such a mission is a "strategic" mission and could be undertaken using tactical nuclear weapons to avoid targeting the U.S. itself.

There appears to be no doubt that sufficient surplus exists in the Soviet fleet to at least threaten the SLOCs with 10 submarines for an indefinite period or upwards of 50 if a short conflict is assumed. There also appears to be a surplus in bombers, more pronounced in the Pacific. Additional bombers would be available if the anti-carrier problem had already been solved. No matter what the number of submarines is, if the West perceived a SLOC threat, NATO would probably form convoys and divert substantial naval assets from other missions.

NATO has long recognized this problem and feels that a Western maritime offensive in the Norwegian Sea is the best alternative. The West feels that with naval operations so close to the USSR, most of the Soviet Navy would be kept in home waters defending SSBNs thus making the SLOCs less vulnerable. 27/ The only serious question to this strategy is whether or not the battle for the Norwegian Sea need involve U.S. aircraft carriers or whether or not the same effect can be had by using primarily submarines in Arctic waters.

The SLOC campaign and bastion defense are therefore intertwined. Overall, it appears that even with their minimal surplus submarine and bomber assets and assuming a bastion defense, the USSR can force the West to take a SLOC defensive posture. This, in turn, means that reinforcements and resupply to Europe might be delayed and delivery not guaranteed. On the other hand, the West can probably minimize the SLOC threat by exerting pressure on the bastions.

Elimination of the bastion defense mission does not seriously impact the SLOC threat. For example, if __all__ mobilized submarines were released in the Atlantic from other missions, the SLOC threat merely goes up from 49 to perhaps 79. This could mean a change from as few as 10 to 16 general-purpose submarines routinely on station along the Atlantic SLOC.

Conversely, if the SSBN defense mission requires additional assets and half of the "surplus" is assigned to additional defensive barriers or escorting SSBNs, the Soviets have alternative options to maintain a high SLOC threat. There might be submarines in the Mediterranean of the Baltic that could attempt operations in the Atlantic. Cuba sits astride some of the primary U.S. SLOCs.

Rather than using torpedos or cruise missiles as the primary weapon, mines can also cut the SLOCs and could be placed by submarines or Soviet merchant or fishing ships. The conclusion must be that sufficient and varied conventional capability exists in the Soviet fleet to make a SLOC campaign even possible without the use of nuclear weapons on U.S terminals and despite the need to provide protection for SSBNs.

NOTES

1. "Soviet Navy Data Base: 1982-83," P-6859 (Santa Monica: Rand, April 1983); and "The Strategic Employent of the Soviet Navy in a Nuclear War," unpublished Ph.D. dissertation at the University of Southern California, December 1984.
2. Report of Danish authorities found in the Los Angeles Times, April 4, 1984, Part I, p. 1.
3. Figures based on Pentagon release according to Newsweek, April 16, 1984, p. 46.
4. See April 4, 1984 New York Times, p. 4, and Philadelphia Inquirer, p. 2.
5. April 4, 1984 New York Times, p. 4, and Philadelphia Inquirer, p. 2; Wall Street Journal, April 9, 1984, p. 38; and Office of the Chief of Naval Operations, Understandng Soviet Naval Developments, 5th Ed. (Washington: U.S. Government Printing Office, April 1985), p. 31.
6. V. I. Achkasov and N. B. Pavlovich, Soviet Naval Operations in the Great Patriotic War 1941-1945 (Annapolis: Naval Institute, 1981) translation of the 1973 Russian edition, p. 205.
7. Bruce Watson and Margurite Walton, "Okean-75," U.S. Naval Institute Procedings, July 1976, p. 94.
8. Achkasov and Pavlovich, Soviet Naval Operations in the Great Patriotic War 1941-1945, p. 207, state this was a Soviet practice in that war.
9. The Navy of the USSR, ADM A. I. Sorokin, Ed. (Moscow: Planet Publishing, 1982), pp. 178-179. It is not clear if the exercise in this photograph was Zapad-81 but a December 8, 1981 NATO press release specifically pointed out that Soviet ground forces were embarked in merchant ships during that exercise.
10. Understanding Soviet Naval Developments, 5th Ed., p. 31.
11. Elmo Zumwalt and Worth Bagley raise this issue in Navy Times, December 28, 1981, p. 19.

12. Washington Post, July 18, 1985, p. 2; Philadelphia Inquirer, July 24, 1985, p. 15; and Jane's Defence Weekly, July 27, 1985, p. 155.
13. Donald Daniel, "Trends and Patterns in Major Soviet Naval Exercises," Naval War College Review, Spring 1978, p. 37.
14. The G-I-UK gap refers to a line drawn from Greenland to Iceland, thence to the United Kingdom. This is similar to behavior reported in the Okean-70 exercise where the G-I-UK gap was the outer defense line and enemy units that crossed it were subject to heavy attacks.
15. Springex 1984 was described in a statement on February 21, 1985 of RADM John Butts, Director of Naval Intelligence, contained in Fiscal Year 1986 Defense Department Authorization and Oversight Hearings, Part 3, Seapower and Strategic and Critical Materials Subcommittee, Armed Services Committee, House of Representatives, 99th Cong., 1st Sess. (HASC No. 99-2) (Washington: U.S. Government Printing Office, 1985), p. 4, as including the control of the seaward approaches to the USSR and the protection of Soviet SSBNs.
16. Assumes that 55% of U.S. SSBNs are on patrol and at least 1 British and 1 French submarine.
17. ADM Arseni Golovko, With the Red Fleet (London: Putnam, 1965) translation of 1960 Russian edition, pp. 117 and 131.
18. Golovko, With the Red Fleet, pp. 148-149; RADM I. Kolyshkin, Submarines in Arctic Waters (Moscow: Progress Publishers, 1966), pp. 183-186; and MG S. A. Tyushkevich, The Soviet Armed Forces: A History of Their Organizational Development (Moscow: 1978), English translation authorized by the USSR and published by the U.S. Air Force as Vol. 19 of the Soviet Military Thought Series, p. 324.
19. Jesse Lewis, The Strategic Balance in the Mediterranean (Washington: American Enterprise Institute for Public Policy Research, 1976) p. 72.
20. NATO Anti-submarine Warfare: Strategy, Requirements, and the Need for Cooperation (North Atlantic Assembly Papers, 1982), pp. 26-27, words the discussion very diplomatically . . . . "Given present naval force levels, however, offensive operations in the Norwegian Sea would have to come about at the cost of maintaining adequate forces in the Southern Flank."
21. Robert Herrick, Soviet Naval Strategy: Fifty Years of Theory and Practice (Annapolis: Naval Institute, 1968), pp. 79 and 133.

22. Charles Sternhell and Alan Thorndike, <u>Anti-submarine Warfare in World War II</u>, OER 51 (Arlington: Center for Naval Analyses), pp. 1, 6, 14, and 83-84. All references to U-boat operations are from this study.

23. Paul Nitze, Leonard Sullivan, and the Atlantic Council Working Group on Securing the Seas, <u>Securing the Seas: The Soviet Naval Challenge and Western Alliance Options</u> (Boulder: Westview, 1979), pp. 111 and 114.

24. Nitze, et al., <u>Securing the Seas: The Soviet Naval Challenge and Western Alliance Options</u>, pp. 351-352.

25. Christopher Wright, "Developing Maritime Force Structure Options for the U.S. Defense Program," unpublished Master's thesis at the Massachusetts Institute of Technology, May 1976, pp. 164-165.

26. Alain Enthoven and K. Wayne Smith,, <u>How Much is Enough?: Shaping the Defense Program 1961-1969</u> (New York: Colophon, 1971), pp. 225-234.

27. <u>NATO Anti-submarine Warfare: Strategy, Requirements, and the Need for Cooperation</u>, p. 25. SACLANT apparently listed his requirement as 4 aircraft carriers to perform this mission.

PART THREE

Findings and Conclusions

14

Findings

The evidence of the content and hardware analysis has been presented previously and subjected to sensitivity analysis. This chapter will summarize overall findings. Findings blend the evidence from all types of analysis and consider policy/capability match or mismatch and whether the probable employment of the Soviet Navy in a strategic nuclear war (and nuclear deterrence) has been determined. In each section, a summation will be given on whether it was the content or hardware analysis that drove the author's findings.

In specifying whether it was primarily the content analysis or the hardware analysis that drove the findings, the author will in a sense be conducting a final sensitivity analysis. If a major finding is based upon one or the other but not both, the level of certainty of that particular finding is different than if both analyses agreed.

By specifying the driving factors in reaching conclusions, the author is further subjecting himself to scrutiny by the informed reader. Too often the basis for reaching conclusions/findings is not specified by analysts making independent oversight and/or review difficult. The follow-on conclusions chapter will then take the author's findings of the probable employment of the Soviet Navy and present conclusions, implications for the West, and policy recommendations.

Navy Strategic Nuclear Forces

The obvious starting place is to define what navy forces are included in the triad of Soviet strategic nuclear forces. From both the content and hardware analysis, the finding is that nuclear powered ballistic missile submarines (SSBNs) and diesel powered submarines (SSBs) carrying submarine-launched ballistic missiles (SLBMs) are a part of the Soviet strategic nuclear triad.

Older, even obsolete SSBNs and SSBs are not normally considered part of the "strategic" nuclear forces by most Western analysts and the media but this distinction is probably not valid from a Soviet prospective. In the first place, the Soviets use the term "strategic" in a completely different context than does the West.

Second, some SSBs and old SSBNs carry SLBMs that are capable of reaching North America. Thirdly, it ignores the strategic importance of theater strikes including strikes against U.S. territory (Alaska, etc.) or U.S. forces on forward deployment, including the Strategic Air Command (SAC).

Although the Soviet Navy has the largest naval cruise missile capability in the world, and at one time did have submarine sea-launched cruise missiles (SLCMs) capable of shore bombardment, these forces were not part of the strategic nuclear triad at the end of 1985. New developments in SLCMs seem likely to change this in the near future. We can anticipate shore bombardment SLCMs being added in the future to the Soviet strategic nuclear forces.

Navy strategic nuclear forces are capable and tasked with executing certain types of missions controlled and directed by the ruling political-military leadership of the USSR. Their use is not authorized by the individual services. Navy strategic nuclear forces are a part of a triad consisting of land-based missiles of the Strategic Rocket Forces (SRF) and Strategic Aviation units subordinate to the Supreme High Command.

Not all Soviet Navy strategic missions are performed by navy strategic nuclear forces nor could these forces perform all strategic missions even if tasked. There are other navy strategic missions that are normally associated with general purpose naval forces (such as defense of the borders and destruction of enemy nuclear forces at sea), that might include the involvement of tactical nuclear or conventional weapons. The strategic nuclear mission associated with the Soviet Navy is participation in nuclear strikes on the enemy shore in order to crush/undermine his military-economic potential which is a strategic goal capable of influencing the outcome of a war.

Forward-Based Systems

A clear distinction must be made in considering Soviet SSBNs due to their deployment area. Those units deployed near the U.S. shores carrying medium-range missiles are forward-based systems whose first-strike function is certain from the available evidence.

In the content analysis, both from manifest themes and latent themes, the Soviets emphasize the initial period of war, especially the initial period of a nuclear war. Specific targeting objectives of these Soviet SLBMs include military bases, especially bases that can be considered a springboard for attacks against the USSR. The literature does not specify what constitutes such bases.

Prevention of strikes by an enemy against the territory of the USSR is a frequent theme in speeches and the literature. Frustration of enemy strikes (active damage limitation) is a major mission of all the Soviet armed forces. From the evidence of the hardware analysis and certain statements in the literature, success need not be total. Each segment in layered defense has a role in weakening the attack as best possible.

Another important theme in the literature is the need to ensure command and control of strategic nuclear forces. Implicit in this theme is the recognition that disruption of communication can have the same effect as destruction of the force itself.

The Soviet literature downplays certain innovative hardware contributions. In fact, the USSR pioneered submarines with ballistic missiles (in 1955), years before Polaris. This early surface-launch system may not have been technologically as advanced as Polaris but it demonstrates a Soviet willingness to experiment with innovative techniques.

Comparison of the content analysis evidence with the hardware reveals that actual force capability parallels declaratory policy. The Soviets have, in fact, deployed SSBNs off the U.S. shores since 1969. By considering the capability of the missiles and the lack of survivability of forward-deployed submarines once a war begins, it is possible to assess the most likely military use for these systems: first-strike damage limitation.

Soviet SSBNs in North American waters can successfully strike U.S. Air Force bomber and tanker bases, U.S. Navy SSBN ports, and the command, control, and communications (C3) infrastructure that controls the triad of

U.S. strategic nuclear forces. Whether or not such an attack would succeed is beyond the scope of this research effort. At worst, a one megaton warhead would explode over each bomber airfield. At best, three one megaton warheads would arrive at each airfield. Damage to all non-alert aircraft is virtually certain. Damage to alert aircraft which may have been already launched is extremely scenario dependent.

The forward-based Yankee class SSBN is not the only threat to the U.S. bomber force. Those alert aircraft surviving the initial submarine attack must successfully refuel, perhaps be subjected to intercontinental ballistic missile (ICBM) barrage attacks along the flight path, and penetrate the world's most sophisticated air defenses. If the Yankee mission was to <u>totally</u> neutralize the U.S. bomber force, the number of deployed submarines would have to be higher.

By deploying missiles at sea along the U.S. shores, U.S. warning systems (with nonexistent active missile defenses) are degraded and bombers/tankers forced into a launch-on-warning posture. Fortunately, airplanes may be launched-on-warning and recalled if in error. The close-in SLBM is a credible threat to C3 resulting in frequent academic and press consideration of launch-on-warning as an option for ICBMs. The credibility of the direct SLBM pin-down threat to ICBMs appears low but it is recognized that the same result can be achieved by C3 disruption.

The findings on the use of forward-based systems are based upon the evidence of statements and the literature in which generally, a distinction is not made between submarines on forward deployment and those found in Soviet home waters. Therefore, the major driving factor in assessing the probable missions for the forward-based systems is the hardware and deployment analysis for which there is parallel supporting evidence in the literature.

Long-Range Systems in Soviet Waters

The other major type of Soviet SSBN operations are patrols and deployment in home waters adjacent to the USSR. In these home waters, the Soviet Navy deploys both submarines with long-range missiles capable of reaching the U.S. as well as medium- and short-range SLBMs capable of theater strikes. Each type must be considered individually.

Targeting for navy strategic missiles, according to the literature, includes political-administrative centers, military-industrial centers, military bases, and terminals for the sea lines of communication (SLOCs). Targeting is designed so that the strikes by nuclear forces would result in the strategic goal of undermining the military-economic potential of an enemy which can affect the outcome of a war.

The targeting of SLOC terminals by ballistic missile is a result of both the increased capability of military hardware and the recognition that what happens at sea can have a direct influence on operations ashore even in a continental war. Admiral Sergei Gorshkov has described SLOC disruption as part of the overall effort to undermine the military-economic potential of an enemy (a strategic goal).

The distinction between targets for long-range SLBMs and those aboard forward-based systems is time urgency. The overwhelming advantage of forward-based systems is their ability to frustrate an immediate U.S. attack on the USSR. No such time requirement exists for long-range missile targets nor can long-range SLBMs offer any striking potential which is superior to that already contained in the SRF.

Hence the underlying question of why the Soviets put long-range missiles on submarines instead of only on the land must be viewed in relationship to missile survivability. The literature reveals that the Soviets are not completely assured that their land-based systems are fully survivable. From the manifest evidence (the need to perform the strategic nuclear strike no matter what) happens and the latent evidence (the need for a strategic reserve), we can conclude that the major advantage and reason for deployment of long-range missiles aboard submarines is to ensure there is a survivable nuclear reserve that can carry out the nuclear strike/or threatened strike no matter what else happens.

It is the author's opinion that the literature evidence does _not_ point to the navy as the _only_ strategic nuclear reserve. That would be contrary to the need for all services to participate in victory. The author rejects previous findings that the latent evidence in the literature supports a conclusion that the navy's major or only contribution would be to provide the strategic nuclear reserve for inter- or post-war negotiations or bargaining. A strategic reserve might be used for this purpose but to simply assign it to one service is not consistent with Soviet declaratory policies.

The author recognizes the large amount of previous analyses that demonstrate the use of latent historical surrogates that explain how navies have won wars, can influence the outcome of wars, and can be used for political coercion. This author found additional evidence to support the view that navy missiles are a hedge against a successful attack on the USSR in which their land systems were neutralized. By considering the hardware and deployment patterns evidence, a similar pattern emerges. By deploying submarines in home waters, survivability is maximized and closer control is maintained over weapons of mass destruction. Maintenance of command and control over strategic nuclear forces is a strong theme in the Soviet literature.

Very few SSBNs are actually at sea on routine patrol. Yet the potential exists to rapidly increase the SSBN force in local waters and threaten North America. Hence the fleet in port is the real fleet-in-being. The targeting possible by long-range SLBMs does not include time-urgent targets nor hard-target counterforce, yet would include targets identified in the content analysis. Hence, it appears that Admiral Gorshkov, whose targeting statements were more explicit then those of his seniors, was the authorized spokesman for this matter.

An unresolved issue from the content analysis section was if cities were not targets, per se, then was non-combatant collateral damage unfortunate, something to avoid, or a bonus. The continued decrease in yields and increase accuracy in Soviet Navy SLBMs over the years supports a finding that civilian collateral damage avoidance must be a goal although one that has not yet been achieved. If cities were the target, yields would remain high and accuracy need not be increased.

Increasing accuracy alone can be explained as a goal in order to achieve hard target kill. Increasing accuracy <u>and</u> decreasing yield however, may be required in order to further increase missile accuracy by carrying more internal merchanisms. Since it was shown that Soviet hard-target kill capability is <u>not</u> increasing with newer SLBMs, it must be concluded that decreasing yields and increasing accuracies may be an effort to minimize collateral damage.

If collateral damage avoidance is a goal of Soviet Navy strategic nuclear forces, this supports a finding that targeting cities and civilians is not military strategy. Navy nuclear weapons appear <u>not</u> to be consciously designed in support of the Western concept of an "assured destruction."

A related finding is that the Soviets pioneered the development of long-range SLBMs. The SS-N-8 and SS-N-18 appeared years before comparable long-range missiles in the U.S. Reference to action/reaction to the U.S. development of long-range missiles alone is incorrect. If any action/reaction is justified, it would be a Soviet reaction to U.S. antisubmarine warfare (ASW) capability necessitating survivability by changing deployment area.

From hardware sensitivity analysis of the minimum possible amount of deliverable warheads or megatonnage, it was shown that the long-range SLBM threat is not overwhelming but is still respectable. It was also shown that the Soviet land forces survivability problem was also not overwhelming, i.e., the West cannot perform a disarming first-strike on the USSR. Hence, the Soviet Navy would never have to act as the total strategic nuclear reserve.

The fact that the USSR routinely deploys such a minimal assured retaliatory strike by long-range SLBMs is probably indicative of their recognition that their land-based systems are actually not in serious jeopardy and that they can count on strategic warning from the West. Long-range SLBMs are currently maximized as second-strike weapons but are not capable of hard-target or prompt counterforce.

As was the case with forward-based systems, findings for long-range force utility is driven by the hardware and deployment analysis supplemented by strong supporting evidence from the literature. The findings include the Soviet Navy constitutes only a part of the strategic nuclear reserve. This finding is based upon the content analysis herein and on supporting hardware evidence.

Theater Systems

Those submarines that deploy near the USSR but carry missiles incapable of reaching the continental U.S. have been the subject of much debate by Western analysts. The literature evidence is extremely thin since as was mentioned before, distinction between varying submarine systems is rarely made.

The literature evidence does contain reference to strikes against naval bases in the European Theater and against springboards for attacks against the USSR. Related themes are the need for all services to participate in operations resulting in victory and the need for reserves.

From the hardware, deployment, and sensitivity analysis, it was concluded that the most logical use of submarines carrying medium-range systems in nearby waters was to participate in theater attacks. This author found the incremental increase in strike potential against the U.S. neither timely nor sufficient to warrant sailing these submarines through choke points in order to reach North American waters.

Hence, this book rejects the credibility of a mass deployment of submarines in mid-ocean waters for military purposes. However, exactly such a limited deployment has already taken place and probably will in the future but for <u>political</u> and <u>not</u> sound <u>military</u> reasons.

The most logical use of theater submarines is against SAC, naval bases, ships in ports, at anchorages. One problem with this idea is that all these missions could be performed by land missiles. Perhaps the submarines are solely for a theater reserve. The evidence is inconclusive regarding these systems to make a definitive stand, although use and reload seems more likely.

<u>Miscellaneous Nuclear Issues</u>

<u>Ballistic Missiles Versus Fleets at Sea</u>

The possibility that Soviet ballistic missiles will be used against naval forces at sea has not been cleared up by this research effort. The literature evidence is contradictory, elusive, and slim. Gorshkov made one reference that the views of the Khrushchev-era thinking that land-based missiles could be used against surface ships and submarines were incorrect.

Marshal Grechko, on the other hand, made a subsequent direct statement that the SRF was tasked with attacking naval forces in the theater. Did he mean in European ports and anchorages or at sea? A few years later Gorshkov discussed Soviet SSBNs as a counter-balance against Western systems. Is this counter-battery or deterrence?

The hardware evidence is equally thin, although better data is probably available within the intelligence community. In theory, land-based missile systems could be developed for use against naval forces, including submarines, at sea.

There is no doubt that ballistic missiles can already be used against known concentrations of fleet units at anchorages or in ports or against mass concentrations of ships in convoys. Targeting these forces could appear to be relatively easy since the Soviet Navy routinely shadows Western high-value units and could identify large convoys using a variety of intelligence platforms.

The issue remains unresolved, and the author suspects that there would be a built-in bias in the West against releasing a finding of an ICBM capability against ships even if it existed. Key indicators to look for would be surplus capability in land systems, deployment of medium range systems in an area where no land targets exist, deployment of space systems capable of more than simple radar contacts (such that identification is possible using other electronics sensors), and obviously testing of land-based missiles against sea targets.

Limited Nuclear War/Tactical Nuclear War at Sea

From the content analysis, the initiation of the nuclear phase of a future armed struggle was generally referred to as inevitable but not automatic. The need for conventional operations as an alternative or as a complement to a spasm nuclear response in war is a constant and recurring theme. There appears to be strong support for avoiding a nuclear war but if one were to be fought then obviously the Soviets feel it should be terminated on terms favorable to the USSR. Nuclear superiority allows escalation domination. Parity prevents domination by an opponent.

The literature analyzed in this study suggests that if a war were to occur, Soviet strategy would be to routinely utilize nuclear strikes when it made military sense. In other words, if the political decision is made to initiate armed conflict, then we should expect Soviet use of nuclear weapons based upon the military advantages of doing so. If U.S.-based systems were to initiate nuclear warfare, the declaratory policy appears to be a massive response on the U.S. This is not to say the Soviets would not absorb a modest warning shot.

When release is authorized, Soviet nuclear weapons will be utilized to terminate the war quickly. The question remains, however, of an armed conflict in which the Soviets would make the first moves. From the author's reading of literature outside the scope of this study, he concludes that Soviet nuclear use ashore may be expected in the European theater if they detect NATO shifting to a nuclear defense. If this is the case, there would be no reason to assume restraint on nuclear weapons at sea.

An issue that remains inconclusive is the potential for a tactical nuclear war only at sea. The obvious advantages of tactical use at sea are that collateral damage to non-combatants may be nil, and residual damage to the environment is minimal. A nuclear winter could not result from an nuclear war at sea. Furthermore, uncertainties against poor weapons performance can be compensated for if just one warhead is needed to destroy a target.

The Soviet Navy says it is prepared to go nuclear at sea but the evidence of the political-military leadership literature analyzed in this study includes rejection of limited nuclear war or war by pre-arranged rules. The author therefore cannot conclude that a nuclear war would be fought only at sea.

The major issue of a limited nuclear war (whose emphasis is a European land campaign) being limited to that theater and not involving U.S. soil is outside the scope of this study. A case can be made for the Soviets contemplating theater-only use as well as a case for any European theater use requiring a simultaneous attack on the U.S. The author's concern was simply to analyze the literature to ascertain if the war were nuclear ashore would it be nuclear at sea (yes) and would it be initiated at and limited to the sea (inconclusive).

From the evidence of hardware, we find a match in Soviet Navy capability to actually fight a nuclear war at sea. The USSR does have tactical nuclear weapons at sea. Detailed evidence from exercise observations could tell us if Soviet delivery crews routinely practice the special procedures which would need to be followed if the weapon produced fallout or a base surge. Ships and aircraft would maneuver around temporarily contaminated areas.

A navy must deploy with all of its weapons already on board. The nuclear torpedo on the Whiskey aground in Swedish waters should have surprised no one. Yet capability does not equate to intent, unless forces have been developed which are nuclear only (not dual-capable). Most Soviet weapons which could be nuclear are also capable of conventional warheads.

It is the political leadership, not navy officers, that should be watched for future evidence in public statements. A tendency to continually practice nuclear delivery at the expense of conventional or the deployment of systems which are nuclear only would be an alarming situation. The Soviet Navy is obviously prepared for tactical nuclear war at sea and the West must prepare for it.

General Purpose Forces

Not all forces of the Soviet Navy associated with the term "strategic" are armed with nuclear nor ballistic missiles. To the Soviets, strategic goals, such as undermining the military-economic potential of the enemy and defending the state from attacks, are requirements for its armed forces in conditions of either conventional or nuclear war. Strategic goals and missions have nothing to do with the type of weapon involved. The participation of the navy in nuclear strikes (a major strategic mission) directly involves the success of the general purpose forces missions in protecting the SSBN fleet.

Bastion Defense

From both the manifest and latent evidence uncovered by content analysis, there is no doubt that the Soviets say they are going to actively defend SSBNs from attack. According to their literature, many of the surface and air forces will perform defensive missions supporting SSBNs implying the need to withhold some for a reserve role.
Cross-checking with hardware reveals that the Soviet surface navy is comprised of forces that make open-ocean distant-water operations unlikely. The limiting factor is the lack of air power. Should Western air power be eliminated or neutralized, then the Soviet surface fleet would be capable of distant-water operations. Soviet use of Third World airfields probably is a plan to compensate for the lack of sea-based airpower.
Most major Soviet naval surface forces can be viewed as anti-carrier, ASW, or for amphibious support. They are routinely deployed in such a manner that priority seems to be given to bastion defense of home waters specifically against aircraft carrier supported task forces and Western submarines attempting to sail in Soviet home waters and threaten Soviet SSBNs.
The Soviets probably believe they could succeed in their defense of bastions. Their literature indicates their strategy appears to ensure survivability of sufficient numbers of SSBNs (to constitute a portion of a reserve), preclude attacks by Western carrier forces against the

Soviet maritime flanks, and contribute to homeland defense against strategic bombers and cruise missiles.

If bastion defense were the sole mission for Soviet general purpose forces, there would not need to be the current surplus of submarines that exceed any logical possible defense requirement. There is a similar policy/force mismatch regarding the few deep-water amphibious, hospital, logistics ships, and aircraft carriers. These units do not belong in a "defensive" navy as that term is understood in the West. The Soviet concept of defense, however, includes offensive first-strikes on enemy forces capable of striking the USSR or its SSBN assets.

A bastion defense strategy is strongly supported in the literature and hardware. Neither drives the analysis, which is why the West appears so certain that this will be the actual employment of general purpose forces in a major war. Bastion defense baits the West to fight on Soviet turf and terms.

Anti-Carrier Warfare

Implicit in the bastion defense literature and hardware evidence is the Soviet strategy for anti-carrier warfare (ACW). The literature describes such attacks as part of fleet-versus-fleet operations. The Soviets do not appear to view the Western carrier as a major threat against the Soviet homeland.

ACW is routinely practiced by the Soviet Navy and deployment patterns suggest that carriers would be amongst the first units to be targeted if armed conflict arose. Forward-deployed ACW forces are essentially throw-away assets.

The Western carrier is viewed in the West as a major force frustrating any Soviet Navy plan to exit home waters. Carriers may also be crucial to NATO success on the Atlantic SLOC and can be used in a campaign against Soviet SSBNs. Carriers also have the capability of attempting to launch conventional strikes against the Soviet maritime flanks, or conducting nuclear attacks on Soviet soil. The Soviets devote much less attention to these latter two missions in the literature. Carrier survivability is crucial for the U.S. in support of post-war foreign policy.

The evidence in both the content analysis and the hardware analysis was overwhelming that ACW is something on which the West can count if war were to occur. All the evidence is strong, and neither methodology drives the analysis. The Soviet plan of attack will probably be overwhelming numbers of all available types of forces against deployed units and ballistic missile strikes against units in port or at anchor.

Strategic ASW

Content analysis supports the contention that the USSR will attempt an ASW campaign against enemy SSBNs in a future war. Prevention of attacks on the USSR is a mission for all Soviet armed services. The potential payoff in terms of warheads destroyed if the Soviets were to neutralize a U.S. OHIO class submarine is so high, that this mission likely to increase in importance the future.

Despite the priority in declaratory policy, there is a distinct mismatch in surface ship, submarine, or air, open-ocean, distant-water, ASW by the Soviet Navy. The Soviets do have methods to combat Western submarine systems but these methods do not parallel similar Western plans. Mirror-imaging Soviet strategic ASW operations to Western methods is just as dangerous as mirror-imaging overall strategy or doctrine.

There are two major problems for the Soviets conducting distant-water ASW in areas patrolled by U.S. submarines equipped with Poseidon or Trident missiles. The first is that Soviet surface and air ASW forces would not be survivable to U.S. naval or land-based forces given the lack of sea-based air power. The second is that there are insufficient numbers of quiet ASW submarines both to protect Soviet SSBNs and successfully trail all Western SSBNs on routine patrol.

Nevertheless, there are other capabilities that may be employed. Conventional anti-satellite measures can be taken to decrease U.S. SLBM accuracy and frustrate communications. Surplus submarines in the Soviet Northern and Pacific Fleets could attempt to destroy even one or two Western SSBNs. The potential pay-off is high enough to make this a worthwhile mission. Such actions might be conventional and not require nuclear release authority.

Should the war involve the U.S., Soviet ballistic missile strikes on bases can be expected to destroy or damage SSBNs in port, eliminating their later use or in the next inter-war period. A bonus would be destruction of missile re-load facilities. A C3 attack might succeed in severing the links between the U.S. national command authorities and the SSBNs themselves.

Should the West choose to use SSBNs to fire warning shots or otherwise participate in a limited nuclear option, there is the risk that by revealing their presence they will be subject to effective Soviet ASW counteraction. Once SLBMs have been fired they are then subject to active anti-ballistic missile (including surface-to-air missiles) and passive civil defenses.

If the U.S. plans to withhold a significant portion of its SLBMs as a strategic nuclear reserve for inter- or post-war bargaining and war termination, it can no longer expect to dominate the talks from a position of unmatched strength. The strategic reserves of the USSR, including some of their SSBNs, allow the Soviets a similar card to play.

In short, the doctrine/capability mismatch found regarding strategic ASW as it is practiced by the West is compensated for by the potential to achieve similar results via different methods. Due to the emphasis on this mission in the literature, we should expect continued Soviet research and deployment in this area. The total Soviet system of defenses against Western SSBNs or missiles is currently not capable of undermining our second-strike capability.

SLOCs

Finally, interruption of SLOCs receives much more attention in the Soviet literature than many Western politicians care to admit. There is no question from the manifest and extremely strong latent evidence that the SLOC mission exists no matter the conditions of war (nuclear or conventional). What was unclear from the content analysis was if Gorshkov was arguing for the mission or announcing it.

As was mentioned earlier, the SLOCs can be cut at the terminal ends using ballistic missiles. During a nuclear war involving strikes ashore, this would appear to be the logical method. Such an attack is likely to destroy ships and the unique facilities used for loading and unloading.

The Soviet Navy has a distinct surplus of submarines which can be used to interdict the mid-ocean SLOCs. A surplus capability in bombers is less evident, however, if bombers did not need to be used against Western aircraft carrier task groups, they would be available for a SLOC campaign. This author concludes that Admiral Gorshkov announces this mission since the USSR has the capability to successfully interdict the SLOCs by other than ballistic missile strikes.

A SLOC campaign would obviously not be crucial in a short war or one in which ballistic missiles would be used on the U.S. If the political decision were made, however, to attempt to confine the land warfare to Europe, the Soviet Navy must still have the capability to sever the SLOCs by means other than ballistic missile strikes. The means exist in the form of submarines (primarily) armed with mines, cruise missiles, and torpedoes with conventional or nuclear warheads.

The evidence most supporting this mission is the content analysis. Capability cannot solely determine intent. Multi-purpose submarines and bombers can be used in a variety of ways. From the hardware alone, one cannot say for certain what wartime missions would be. The capability is there for a SLOC campaign, and this is what the Soviets say they are going to do. One should expect it.

Soviet Military Strategy for Deterrence

The author finds that deterrence of a major (especially nuclear) war with the U.S. is an objective of Soviet military doctrine. The military strategy associated with attaining that objective appears to be to have the capability to use nuclear forces in a manner in which the potential aggressor cannot achieve his aims and the USSR maximizes its opportunities to conclude a war on favorable terms.

Soviet military strategy for deterrence is based upon preventing damage to the homeland and ensuring survival of essential assets. It recognizes both the possibility of a short war or a long war. Although a land war might be "enhanced" by quick nuclear use, the option of _not_ going nuclear immediately appears to be a more recent theme in the literature.

The Soviet Navy strategic nuclear forces appear to be designed for a purpose and that purpose does not seem to be "punishment" of an aggressor if deterrence were to fail. Forces are capable of sound military missions which can attempt to prevent Western war aims. There does not appear to be a distinction between deterrence and the capability to fight a war.

Under the concept of assured destruction (AD), a superpower should be able to absorb a surprise first-strike and still respond with an "unacceptable" amount of damage to the other. Western advocates of AD argue that holding Soviet cities as hostage is a sufficient enough threat of punishment to deter nuclear war. AD advocates generally then take the next step to claiming that a unilateral AD posture (significantly less capability than war-fighting) by the U.S. would convince the Soviets that their following our lead would result in a <u>mutual</u> assured destruction (MAD) state of the world in which strategic stability (neither side need fear nuclear attack) will be ensured. MAD pre-supposes each superpower will leave its cities open to attack by the other.

In reviewing the findings presented in this chapter and the previous analysis, one cannot help but notice a number of Soviet inconsistencies with the AD concept. In other words, the Soviets have made statements and deployed forces that are not compatable with an assured destruction concept of deterrence.

In the first place, content and hardware analysis supports a finding that military and related industrial targeting can be expected from Soviet Navy strategic nuclear forces. If the SSBNs withheld in bastions protected by general purpose forces as a part of the strategic nuclear reserve were to only constitute an assured second strike on cities, yields would not be lower in newer missiles nor would accuracies continue to be increased.

The Soviet literature does not support targeting cities nor did the author find any themes which support leaving Soviet cities open to a Western assured second-strike. On the contrary, active defense of the homeland is an extremely strong theme in the literature. Active defense of withheld SSBNs is not incompatable with MAD nor strategic stability since it ensures a survivable second strike.

The hardware analysis concludes that successful active defense of most Soviet SSBNs in bastions can probably be achieved. However, other Soviet Navy forces have been designed to defend the Soviet homeland. The forward-deployed Yankee system is maximized to prompt counterforce against the U.S. which inhibits the U.S. assured second-strike. This is incompatible with leaving one's cities hostage.

Since the U.S. maintains most of its strategic nuclear reserve capable of delivering an AD response on its SSBNs at sea, the continued efforts of the USSR to improve strategic ASW might actually be considered so contrary to the essence of MAD that strategic stability might be upset <u>if</u> the Soviets could succeed. Fortunately, this is not the case yet, although if we take the Soviets

at their word, they are giving high priority to strategic
ASW. Strategic stability has not been upset due to the
lack of a Soviet open-ocean ASW capability and current
U.S. deployment practices.

The pattern of Soviet words and deeds is not indicative of a nation which supports MAD. If anything,
the finding must be that the minimal amount of forces
necessary for an AD response on U.S. cities has been
fielded by the USSR and then exceeded. Their active
defense damage limitation program is not compatible
with MAD.

15

Conclusions and Implications

This final chapter will present the author's conclusions based on the evidence developed by this research and the findings outlined in the previous chapter. Implications for the West will then follow, and an end note contains final thoughts about the methodology.

The distinction between this chapter and the previous is that findings are tied directly to the evidence of the research effort. Conclusions and implications draw upon those findings and present opinions of the author based upon his knowledge of issues broader than what has been addressed directly herein.

Soviet Political-Military Doctrine

1. <u>The Soviet Union deters nuclear war with the U.S. by having the capability to fight one.</u>

 This conclusion appears valid over the long term (two years plus). There is no Soviet declaratory policy to initiate a major war but rather to "deter" war as that term is understood in the West. Military forces appear to be designed to support deterrence although through different methods than generally accepted by many politicians in the West.

 Should a nuclear war come about, there is a strong doctrinal tendency to conclude the war on terms favorable to the USSR. If anyone is to blame for initiating the phrase "winning" a nuclear war, it is the Soviets themselves. Their literature abounds with rejection of any notion that such weapons are "absolute" or not useable to obtain the political goal of ending war in their favor. A nuclear war may or may not be "winnable," but it was the

Soviets who openly used such themes for years, until they finally realized how it was being viewed in the West. Since then, they have taken the stand that a nuclear war is not "winnable" but still say that they will conclude a war on terms favorable to themselves.

The oft used bolt from the blue surprise attack by the USSR on United States strategic forces without strategic warning is one which <u>must</u> continue to be used by analysts. It represents the worst-case (for us) if the Soviets provide no strategic warning. Hence, it is a baseline against which further analyses can be measured.

First-strikes must be separated into nuclear and conventional surprise attacks. The Soviet literature abounds with the recognition of the tactical advantages of striking first. One should realize, however, that most of the Soviet literature evidence of the advantage of striking first involves <u>tactical</u> surprise.

If the Soviets have confused the West by their continued references to surprise being interpreted as their intent to initiate a nuclear war without warning, again they have no one to blame but themselves. One <u>can</u> interpret the literature evidence this way.

The discussions on conventional war-fighting in the literature reviewed in this study and in actual force development supports the conclusion that a future war at sea <u>may</u> start with or without the use of nuclear weapons. If the war were immediately to go nuclear, the Soviets appear to be in a position to do so with their strategic nuclear systems targeted on the U.S. Yankee submarines are routinely deployed in areas where their first nuclear strike potential is maximized.

The Soviets are not adverse in using nuclear weapons for peacetime coercion as witnessed by their deployment of nuclear powered ballistic missile submarines (SSBNs) as a "counter" against U.S./NATO theater systems since early 1984. This deployment served no significant military purpose and was clearly a case of using nuclear weapons to coerce the West. Having the existing forces in their navy allowed the USSR to make a political statement that was otherwise virtually impossible to do.

2. <u>Should a nuclear war come about, the Soviet objective will be to terminate it quickly</u>.

Implicit in this conclusion is the realization that nuclear weapons must have a political utility. This utility may only be quick war termination on favor-

able terms, but nevertheless it is there. Soviet Navy
strategic nuclear forces appear to have been designed with
the possibility that a nuclear war might actually be
fought. Soviet naval nuclear weapons have distinct
military utility and serve the political purposes of
quickly ending war favorably and minimizing damage to the
homeland.

Of interest is the general absence of doctrinal/
force mismatch. The Soviets have the types of forces
necessary to carry out the missions that they advertise.
This would indicate a high probability that the decisions
were reached some time ago and objectives were slowly
achieved. This is also indicative of strong resolve.
This is in sharp contrast to the U.S., which has a marked
mismatch in strategy (countervailing) and deliverable
forces (probably no better than assured destruction).
U.S. doctrine and strategy have not remained static
but rather have been evolving over the years.

The Soviet Navy appears ready to contribute
to the deterrence of war in peacetime as well as nuclear
deterrence during the initial phases of a conventional
war. Should deterrence fail, the Soviet Navy can perform
militarily significant functions. The USSR obviously
takes nuclear war quite seriously and does not subscribe
to the Western tendency to consider politics and nuclear
force as mutually exclusive. This conclusion also appears
to be valid over the long term.

3.   The Soviet Union has not accepted Mutual
     Assured Destruction (MAD).

Overwhelming evidence exists to demonstrate
the Soviet view that defense of the homeland and damage
limitation/avoidance are not only good ideas but an
integral part of deterrence. Rejection of MAD does not
does not imply a rejection of deterrence, only the
method of achieving it.

Rather than base all of their hopes for deterrence upon offensive weapons that threaten an assured
second-strike, the Soviet Union includes weapons usable
specifically in a first-strike. They further appear to
accept defense against first, second, and additional
nuclear strikes from her enemies as an integral part of
deterrence. Efforts to counter Western SSBNs, which might
be held in reserve or aircraft carriers, which could only
strike the USSR in a long war, indicate a preparation for
a long war, although preference is for a quick resolution.

The Soviet concept of deterrence of war is not based upon the threat to punish an agressor but rather the ability to deny an aggressor's attempt to achieve war aims, to use weapons including nuclear weapons to achieve its own aims, and if all else fails, then to punish. These concepts are traditional methods of warfighting.

Leaving the homeland or its military forces open to attack by an enemy is simply not in observed Soviet behavior or in their literature. Active defense of the homeland is seconded by hardware capability and deployment patterns. This does not preclude the USSR from being converted to MAD, but one must remember that their "education" to MAD began before SALT I. If the Soviets are swinging around to MAD, it is not obvious.

If minimal numbers of offensive nuclear forces are implicit in MAD, then obviously the USSR has built up through this level and beyond. Their submarine force alone can field what many Americans would feel is the necessary amount of deliverable damage to constitute an assured destruction of the U.S.

Building beyond the assured destruction level allows the ruling circles in Moscow greater flexibility and increased options. Those SSBNs used for coercion since early 1984 in "response" to new U.S./NATO systems in Europe were a mere drop in the bucket of total capability. They could afford to be risked to make a political statement.

4. The USSR has given priority to its America problem.

In order to build the forces now on hand in the Soviet Navy and in the other military services, the Communist Party of the Soviet Union (CPSU) must have decided its American problem was great enough to warrant a major committment of resources over a long period of time. The Soviet Navy is not maximized for distant water operations against the Third World. It is maximized against the U.S. (and NATO) which represent the principal threat to the CPSU and any further plans it might have.

This is not to say that the fleet is not usable in the waters of the Third World or that it has not already been successfully used there. Rather, the author accepts the conclusions in numerous previous studies which show how the USSR has used their fleet for coercive or influencing naval diplomacy.

One limiting factor in such Third World use, however, has been the preoccupation with the U.S. As the Soviet Navy has had its direction focused on the main enemy, it has not been afforded the opportunities nor resources possible if not so constrained. One can only speculate on the possible composition of the Soviet Navy if it were maximized for distant-water offensive operations in the Third World.

As long as resources made available for the Soviet Navy remain relatively constant, the Soviets are vulnerable to manipulation that limits the utility of their fleet for Third World missions. A strong U.S. Navy which can threaten the Soviet SSBN fleet will probably continue to result in Soviet concentration on defended bastions. The more the Soviets devote to this mission, the less is available for distant-water adventurism. If Soviet submarine technology were developed to a point that their preoccupation with the bastion defense would change, their surface fleet would be a surplus asset whose loss would be more able to be risked in time of peace.

5. **The CPSU feels its America problem can be solved.**

The lack of an overwhelming nuclear strike capability on routine deployment strongly suggests that despite the unpredictability of American politics, the West is not expected to launch a surprise attack on the USSR. As a hedge, however, the nuclear strike potential of the Soviet Navy can be very quickly supplemented by additional submarines in defended home waters.

Thus the worst-case for the Soviets (a first-strike against them) has been managed with a backup. Their confidence in the West not striking first is typified by continued deployment of only a few relatively vulnerable Yankee submarines off the U.S. shoreline. The low number of these systems with a high payoff for preemption makes them, in theory, especially inviting to a surprise attack by the U.S. Such an attack by the U.S. can be done using only conventional weapons.

If the Soviets were so confident as to deploy Yankees in the early 1970's in such a manner when they had strategic nuclear inferiority, one can only wonder what their behavior will be in an era of overall strategic nuclear parity or superiority. We know it will at least include the use of SSBNs for political coercion even at the price of placing them at higher risk and exposing them to greater intelligence collection efforts.

6. <u>The CPSU will solve its America problems in ways unique to the Soviet Union.</u>

The Soviet approach to managing the U.S. is not at all similar to the American approach of managing its Soviet problem. The Soviet interrelationship between military force and politics has been widely commented on by others. The Soviet style of deterrence appears to reject the non-zero sum game in which both can win and instead appears to be developed using a zero-sum game concept in which the Soviets will try to win regardless of impact on the U.S.

The author finds a pattern of three "responses" to perceived "threats from imperialism." The first response is military programs. Programs are always cast in the light of action/reaction but we have seen it was the Soviets who initiated both new submarine and missile programs. The Soviets appear willing to invest inordinate amounts of time and assets to research to a multiplicity of military solutions despite the potential of only limited gains.

For example, the strategic ASW threat by the Soviet Navy attack submarines is not overwhelming. If trailing U.S. SSBNs by Soviet submarines were a <u>major</u> goal, the Soviets would have needed to build more quiet submarines. Instead we have seen the USSR attempt to find alternative solutions, none of which have apparently yet provided them with a simultaneous disarming threat to our SSBNs on patrol, but all in combination cannot be ignored.

Similarly, rather than having an overwhelming capability and massive deployments that can crush an opponent, Soviet Navy forward-based systems appear to be less than awesome. The routine Yankee threat is sufficient to do a modest attack on command, control, and communications (C3) facilities and attempt destruction of all U.S. bombers, tankers, and SSBNs in port. A crushing time-urgent capability to include ICBM pin-down additionally could have been deployed in North American waters but at the expense of more rubles and decreased control. The author's reading of Western analyses of the Soviet ground and Strategic Rocket Forces (SRF) has led him to believe that those services deploy overwhelming and considerable surplus capability. This pattern is not repeated in the Soviet Navy except in general purpose submarines.

The second major solution to "threats from imperialism" is talk. Soviet literature is filled with numerous examples of Western military threats and how easily they can be countered. Many references by authoritative Western spokesman which stress the ease of destruction of naval ships at sea sound like they could have been taken from Soviet literature. Perhaps the West can simply be talked out of building a weapons system. Is this not what happened to the initial deployment of the enhanced radiation/"neutron" bomb?

A good follow-on study would be of the relationship between cancelled or postponed Western military programs and Soviet propaganda/manipulation of arms control. For example, in mid 1984, the Soviets were placed in a position to postpone the U.S. MX program merely by engaging in arms control negotiations.

The third solution to a "threat from imperialism" is arms control itself. The Soviet Union cannot simultaneously destroy all U.S. SSBNs in part because they operate extremely quietly in unknown areas of the vast deep ocean expanses. The USSR keeps only a few SSBNs in relatively known areas and achieves survivability (of some) by defense. The Soviets are attempting to regulate SSBN deployments to known areas, and to regulate strategic antisubmarine warfare (ASW). Such limitations would decrease U.S. force survivability or would force the U.S. to defend its submarines. If we defend, we limit our ability to attack in wartime and to use our general purpose fleet for naval diplomacy in peacetime.

The Soviets have been successful in limiting the U.S. through arms control in the past. We agreed in SALT I not to build more than 44 SSBNs with President Nixon's private assurance not to exceed 41. The Soviets were allowed superiority in numbers of submarines (41% more submarines) and missile launchers (34% more launchers). Yet the USSR knew its SS-N-8 long range missiles would invalidate this "need" since they could target the U.S. from Arctic waters using this new misile. Furthermore, the Soviets totally excluded theater submarine systems from regulation.

Soviet naval arms control is a tool to limit the U.S. building of weapons in areas where the Soviets cannot compete and feel threatened. It is not surprising that their latest proposals would limit U.S. aircraft carriers, ASW forces, naval bases in foreign territories, and forward deployment. These are all areas where the U.S. is strong and a condition of parity or equality would only result in a reduction in capability and flexibility for the U.S. Based upon past success, we should expect the Soviets to continue to attempt to use arms control as a vehicle to participate in U.S. military decision-making over the long-term.

Soviet Military Strategy

Conclusions regarding the strategic employment of the Soviet Navy properly fall under military strategy. The lack of the term "naval" or "navy" is intentional. There is only one strategy for the employment of nuclear and non-nuclear weapons and the conduct of operations in a major war -- military strategy.

7. <u>Military doctrine is the basis for military strategy which in turn is a determinant of forces actually procured. However, the capabilities of those forces in turn influence doctrine and strategy.</u>

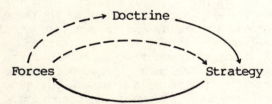

Despite the logical progression of doctrine to strategy to forces, we have to conclude that strategy is only one of many determinats of force procurement. The inertia caused by existing bureaucracies and weapons is a significant factor. This author is convinced that we simply do not know enough about the internal dynamics of previous decisions to know why certain weapons were built. For this reason, he has avoided speculating about past decisions.

A nation is limited in actual strategy by the forces it has on hand. For the USSR, there appears to be a good match between declaratory strategy and force capability. In the U.S., the mismatch is dramatic.

Similarly, the actual weapons on hand have an influence on doctrine. Having invested in an active defense force in order to support its own concept of deterrence, it would appear highly unlikely that this unique Soviet deterrence doctrine would be abandoned. The U.S. dismantling of its one anti-ballistic missile

(ABM) site a month after it was completed demonstrates the difference in American attitudes.

      Not only are the weapons themselves an investment that would be difficult to abandon, but the bureaucracy and resultant military manpower create a built in bias in favor of continuation of existing programs. Furthermore, the CPSU will probably never forget that the mere failure of the Czarist military to support the Kerensky regime was a significant enough non-action to allow the Communist October Revolution to succeed. We should not expect any long-term changes in the attitudes of the CPSU towards major support for its military and to continue to provide them all that they "need."

8.   <u>The Soviet Navy can perform a variety of significant missions during a nuclear or conventional war with the U.S.</u>

      The dramatic shift over the years of the Soviet Navy from a mere coastal defense force to one of the world's two major navies is best exemplified by the capability of its hardware. The USSR can now call on its fleet to perform numerous missions which exceed any Russian fleet in the past. This is not to say that the Soviet Navy can sail at will into harms way; it cannot, but it can perform missions which the West cannot ignore and must take measures to prevent.

      The Soviet Navy is not restricted to an all-nuclear capability. The use of nuclear weapons is an eventuality that has been accounted for, but some major missions against NATO can be executed without their use. The notable exception has been attacks on the continental U.S., which, up until present, required the use of nuclear weapons.

      The Soviet drive for a balanced navy, capable of escalating through varying levels of conflict up to nuclear war, has occurred over the past 25 or so years. The USSR does <u>not</u> have to go nuclear right away, but its Navy allows them some distinct advantages if nuclear war was to occur. The essential point is that the Party now has options. Strategic missions still have to be performed whether or not nuclear release has been granted.

      The massive investment in conventional war-fighting forces must be indicative of the resistance of the military to place all its hopes on nuclear and short wars. The sole nuclear option must have appeared as incredible to them as it did us. Yet if the decision is made to immediately go nuclear, the navy can participate.

There are certain missions that will undoubtedly exist in the long-term future. Anti-carrier warfare (ACW) is one of those in which doctrine and present capability match. The U.S. must and does take the ACW threat seriously since it is credible. Emphasis on ACW implies the possibility that the war will be long, can be used to redress the current disparity between the U.S. and Soviet fleets, and if operations are successful, may make the post-war era more palatable.

Strategic ASW is another mission that we can expect to receive emphasis over the long-term. In terms of payoff, the destruction of a single OHIO class SSBN, would have a greater reward than the destruction of a single Polaris submarine, a bomber base, or missile silo. Fortunately survival of the OHIO class has been maximized. The current Soviet doctrinal/force mismatch should be a signal alarm to look for non-traditional methods. The Soviets might be more successful in operations against NATO or Chinese SSBNs due to their more limited missile ranges making missile firing positions closer to Soviet defense perimeters.

9. Only the Soviet Navy can perform certain strategic missions in the event of a war with the U.S.

One of the frequent conclusions in studies about Soviet naval diplomacy has been that Admiral Gorshkov has been stressing the unique abilities of a fleet. There is no question that navies can perform certain political tasks easier than other military forces.

This conclusion is also valid for Soviet strategic missions in war, including a non-nuclear war. With a navy, certain strategies are possible or at least made easier. The most dramatic strategic nuclear mission is damage limitation by the use of forward-based systems.

Deployment of Yankee submarines in North American waters allows the USSR to threaten the U.S. with a debilitating direct nuclear attack on its C3 systems much more quickly than could be delivered by intercontinental ballistic missiles (ICBMs). Success in such an attack would affect all U.S. strategic forces. Yankee deployments also allow direct attack on time-urgent military forces which could otherwise quickly strike the USSR.

Damage limiting conterforce attacks on bombers/tankers and SSBNs might not totally destroy all U.S. forces on generated alert. The Yankee systems do allow the SRF rockets to arrive with conditions made more favorable. The navy's role appears to be to contribute as much as they can in the layered defense system and to attempt a "cheap shot" disruption of the U.S. C3 structure.

It is the author's conclusion that the contribution of the navy is so significant that the CPSU allows nuclear weapons to be deployed in a situation where routine tight Party control is less assured. Perhaps large KGB contingents are aboard forward-deployed Yankees.

There seems to be little doubt that the present Yankee threat will be replaced in the long term. A Typhoon through-ice replacement is a possibility but seems not as likely as continued use of deployment areas off the U.S. coastline.

The quick fix will probably be a sea launched cruise missile (SLCM). Not only might the military threat be virtually the same as from the SS-N-6 submarine-launched ballistic missile (SLBM) but the Soviets would be making a major political statement to the U.S. and NATO. Since the USSR is supposedly denied the use of Cuba as a platform for "theater" systems, the Soviets will justify new SLCMs as the analagous threat of "new" U.S. missiles in Europe, and then blame the U.S. for another round in the arms race. The Soviets naturally ignore the upset in the balance _they_ caused by their SS-20 deployments.

The long-term solution will be a replacement for the Yankee hull perhaps using a derivation of the Delta or Typhoon. The Soviets would probably risk larger SSBNs for forward deployment since it is unlikely that the U.S. will preempt with a surprise first-strike on these "magnets." The problem of minimum missile ranges for North American patrols will drive the Soviets to develop a new medium-range system. We must be alert for testing depressed trajectory and multiple independently targetable reentry vehicles (MIRVs) on any new missiles which would result in greater capability to disrupt a U.S. second-strike.

There will probably be no Soviet desire in an arms control agreement to actually reduce forward-deployed units within range of the continental U.S. to zero. If, on the other hand, the Soviets were to actually restrict submarine deployments to well outside the range of their forward-deployed missile systems, this would be indicative of a shift in doctrine towards MAD. Official Washington can only decide if the U.S. can accept a similar restriction based upon the intended use of U.S. and NATO SSBNs and cruise missile equipped submarines.

Another unique contribution of the fleet is its future ability to deliver strategic attacks on the U.S. shores in conventional war. New SLCMs with conventional warheads would be capable of sending a major political message to the American public and President that America will not be spared damage, even if modest. Current conventional systems (torpedos and mines) suffer the problem of naval warfare's lack of visibility. More militarily significant damage might be achieved by mining and torpedoing, but a few even conventional missiles exploding in New York or Los Angeles would certainly get everyone's attention.

A conventional campaign against the sea lines of communication (SLOCs) is best performed by the Soviet Navy although it may not necessarily only limited to that service. Soviet Air Force assets can be used in a SLOC campaign but may very well be otherwise involved with land operations. Thus, it will probably be the navy which will have to perform this strategic mission.

We should be on guard for Soviet Navy willingness to commit large numbers of assets to a SLOC campaign. We know from reviewing the Soviet literature that surprise, innovation (when successful), maximum use of available assets, and heroic self-sacrifice are all traits stressed by the military. We should anticipate the unexpected from surplus Soviet submarine units. The SLOC mission remains high in priority and is a valid fleet requirement even in an all-conventional war or one in which attacks on the U.S. have not taken place.

Perhaps major portions of submarine fleet will be employed en-masse in order to preclude the U.S./NATO long war option. If survivability of those forces is not a consideration, the SLOC threat would be considerably higher than depicted herein. Perhaps the loss of a hundred submarines is worth precluding the long war. The Soviets could succeed in destruction of the few irreplaceable NATO strategic lift hulls and present the West with a short war fait d'accompli.

10. <u>The Soviet Navy is not a "defensive" navy.</u>

There is no question that bastions and reserves of certain SSBNs are defensive concepts. There is also no question that forward-deployed Yankees employed for damage limitation are offensive systems, although the Soviet official perception is that first-strikes for damage limitation are a form of defense.

The surplus of Soviet general purpose submarines certainly exceeds that necessary by any logical standard for pure bastion or homeland defense. Aircraft carriers are not <u>needed</u> for defense nor are large deep-water amphibious ships, open-ocean underway replenishment ships, and hospital ships.

Sufficient surplus does not yet exist to conclude the USSR can carry out distant-water maritime operations against a major Second or Third World power. The landing of Soviet troops can be performed, however, in a benign environment using merchant ships. Soviet growth has been incremental but steady.

To conclude that the Soviet Navy is defensive-only is to ignore the body of evidence contained in the Soviet literature. In the literature, all operations stress the offensive. A defensive strategy such as bastions can and probably would involve offensive tactics. The employment of forward-deployed forces is likely to be also based upon the tactical offensive and represents a strategy of striking exposed enemy positions in an attempt to trade a few non-vital naval assets for destruction of crucial Western bombers, SSBNs and aircraft carriers.

The bastion defense strategy allows the CPSU to maintain closer control over navy nuclear missiles and costs to be reduced. Bastion defense also results in more American military resources being devoted to the navy if the U.S. government approves a policy to conduct a strategic ASW campaign. We can anticipate the SLBM MIRVing to continue and SSBN building to replace older more vulnerable hulls.

Technology has allowed the Soviets to occupy more effectively the ocean spaces that comprise their bastions. However, there is a limit to the ability of any nation to occupy ocean space. Presently the Soviets are incapable of keeping out Western platforms in time of peace (unless they succeed through arms control), and they probably could not keep out all Western submarines in time of war.

Implications for the West

Implications contained herein are based upon the author's conclusions and his broader knowledge of U.S. and Western defense issues. They represent his policy recommendations for the U.S. defense doctrine and strategy.

1. **The West must develop strategies based upon the lack of Soviet adherence to MAD.**

   The U.S. has been attempting to "educate" the CPSU for years about to the "advantages" of leaving one's nation open to a nuclear attack. Having failed in this endeavor, the U.S. government must provide for the defense of its citizens based upon what **is**, and not what could or should be. If we cannot change Russian political-cultural attitudes, we can change their cost-benefit calculations, upset their pre-war planning, and keep the nuclear threshold high.

   The West needs forces that both deter war and that are usable if deterrence fails. Soviet Navy strategic nuclear forces are not designed for senseless punishment of an agressor but have been clearly designed as a part of an overall system that will try to prevent the U.S. from using its forces successfully. Soviet forces are also more usable for peacetime coercion because the West would know that its own threat to use nuclear weapons lacked the same credibility.

   Taking a page from the Soviet book and building defensive forces would direct resources to military systems that kill weapons and not people. It would also result in a force which the President would find useful if Soviet Navy strategic weapons were to actually fly. Building a leak-proof defensive system is not necessary. If even 50% of Yankee SLBMs could be destroyed, the Soviets would be faced with a much higher degree of uncertainty in their ability to carry out missions **they** obviously think are important.

   The object is to deter war and especially nuclear war. Most navies believe that the best deterrent against the use of force against their ships at sea is a combination of passive measures and active defense. The weapons carrier is the initial target, preferably as far away from one's own shores as possible. Incoming ordnance is dealt with as required. If all else fails, damage control has saved many a ship. Layered defenses are the norm in naval warfare. Are the concepts of war at sea so different as to invalidate utility for defense of our nation?

Naturally a shift in doctrine to include active and passive defense of the nation would require a fundamental shift in U.S. military and arms control policies. The deployment of long-range Soviet Navy SLBMs alone constitutes a fundamental strategic imbalance that justifies the U.S. ceasing to adhere to the expired SALT I Interim Agreement. There is simply no reason to continue to grant the USSR superiority in submarine systems (hulls and launchers) and total freedom in theater-range systems.

Similarly, the specific conditions for withdrawal from the ABM Treaty have already been met, yet the Treaty remains in force. U.S. ABM systems located near Soviet SSBN patrol areas (especially in the Aleutian Islands) would be a significant problem for the USSR. If we cannot destroy the SSBN before it launches most of its missiles, the destruction of those missiles should be the object. An at-sea ABM capability might be usable against SLBMs in other patrol areas, against land-based systems, and missiles directed at Western ships.

2. <u>We should attempt to push Soviet strategic nuclear forces to sea.</u>

Implicit in the START negotiation has been a U.S. attempt to reduce the number of land-based Soviet ICBMs and a willingness to accept more Soviet capability at sea. This push is not without risks. The sudden interest in naval systems might cause spill-over arms control regulation in areas not in the best interests of the U.S. It would also undoubtedly involve internal resistance within the Soviet military service with the most to lose--the SRF. Emphasis on submarine systems might result in opening up ASW to more Soviet scrutiny and making more resources available.

Whether or not the CPSU would allow the U.S. to enter Soviet political-military decision-making structure (as the USSR has in the U.S.), is unanswerable. The potential benefits include: forced expenditure of resources and dismantling of usable systems, immediate reduction in the hard-target counterforce threat to U.S. ICBMs, a somewhat simpler verification problem for the intelligence community, and increased vulnerability of the strategic Soviet arsenal to U.S. conventional warfare action. Any actions taken that reinforce the Soviet bastion defense problem will probably serve to limit the numbers of Soviet Navy assets available for naval diplomacy and direct additional Soviet resources for defensive-only systems.

Bastion defense by the Soviets is a strategy that the U.S. should therefore encourage. At best, it will keep Soviet Navy resources directed to systems deployed in home waters and open up new avenues of U.S. attack in the event of war. Allowing a conventional campaign against strategic forces is adding a major rung in the escalation "ladder" (as perceived in the West) and, therefore, raises the nuclear threshold and does not necessarily upset strategic stability.

Bastion defense will probably result in a continuation of a Soviet assured second-strike capability. It is doubtful that the West could ever procure sufficient forces to mount such a successful strategic ASW campaign against Soviet SSBNs that their wholesale destruction would be an issue.

3. <u>Extended deterrence extends to naval forces</u>.

In sizing U.S. strategic nuclear forces, one of the criteria has been that deterrence must be extended over our allies, notably Europe. An attack on NATO is deterred partially by the threat to respond with U.S. strategic forces. Has the West accounted for the need to extend deterrence to its naval forces?

There is little preventing the tactical use of nuclear weapons against major naval forces, such as aircraft carriers in international waters. To deter the tactical use of nuclear weapons against our vital major naval forces, concealment, passive defense, and active defense are all used. The ultimate deterrent against tactical nuclear war at sea is the U.S. strategic forces that threaten escalation and retaliation.

A set of limited responses must be thought through and communicated so that a credible threat is made to destroy something the Soviets value as much as we do our aircraft carriers, SSBNs, or other major naval forces. Attacks on forward-deployed Yankees or major Soviet surface ships on forward deployment seem to be the best targets for tit-for-tat response. Such attacks need not be nuclear if escalation control were the goal. On the other hand, a limited nuclear strike on Soviet territory should not be ruled out to signal the importance we give to deterrence of tactical nuclear war at sea.

4. <u>Uncertainty can be dealt with.</u>

Analysts must calculate the most optimistic case and the worst-case in order to set the parameters for scenarios and analysis. Statistical probabilities and the intuitive knowledge of the area specialist can be applied to derive a set of most likely cases. If fundings were not constrained, the proper response to a perceived threat would be to tailor one's response to the worst-case. As was mentioned in the analysis, the U.S. has historically adopted worst-case threat assumptions to its strategic nuclear forces.

In the real world of fiscal and similar restraints on other resources and capabilities, elected and appointed political decision-makers (who rank senior to the analyst) will prioritize military and other needs. To do this job properly, they do need the best possible information. Decisions must be made despite the quality of the information fed to the decision-maker. If the analyst can present the most accurate version possible, he will minimize the risks of adverse consequences should the decision-maker accept a version of a more optimistic threat than the worst-case. The role of the analyst is to have the strongest possible support for his studies in order to reduce the uncertainty about the evidence and support his view of the likely cases.

5. <u>The U.S. Navy cannot disrupt the Soviet strategy for employing their navy in a nuclear war but corrections are moving us in the right direction.</u>

The U.S. can do little to prevent a signaled Soviet nuclear first-strike or one out of the blue. We must always be alert when "exercises" are held by the Soviets since in reality this generates their forces to a higher level of readiness.

The U.S. Navy has been allowed to erode from a position of clear superiority over any other Navy at the end of World War II, to a level that now <u>allies are needed</u>, operations must be planned sequentially, and only selected areas of the oceans will be contested. The Soviet Navy can deny our strategy by their anti-SLOC capability, making long war reinforcements and resupplies difficult at best.

Can the West upset Soviet conventional or nuclear war strategy? No one can answer that for sure, but this author thinks not. Can the West prevent Yankee SSBNs from firing first? No, we can only threaten to punish if this happens. At best, with high cost, we can fight in the bastions (if a war lasts that long) and perhaps reduce the numbers of SSBNs.

The need to defend the nation from Soviet Navy weapons and not simply threaten reprisals, needs to be further understood by the American public, who ultimately pass judgment on defense and foreign policies. Deterrence need not be upset by defense and proliferation of offensive systems. If the number of aim points is increased, this can be a stabilizing factor. Hence, more might actually be good for strategic stability.

To meet the Yankee threat, we need to improve C3 redundency and survivability. We also must be prepared to deploy bombers to outlying airfields for lengthy periods and to launch them on warning. Has the U.S. thought through defense against new Soviet SLCMs? We must also attempt to use arms control to minimize the increased threat when Yankee is replaced by a new SSBN.

The West must think through the conventional campaign against Yankee and in the bastions which might occur prior to the nuclear phase of a war. Will the Soviets view the loss of SSBNs as a continuation of the conventional war or will they regard it as initiation of nuclear warfare? This author did not uncover any themes that he felt would help answer this question, hence the decision may have to be made on very incomplete supporting analysis unless classified data can illuminate Soviet thinking. Perhaps the loss of a Yankee could serve as the warning shot prior to actual initiation of nuclear warfare.

The West must likewise anticipate a conventional war period in which Western SSBNs are the target. Has NATO prepared for this possibility with its deployments in the vast deep oceans or do we need to be more innovative? Should our declaratory SSBN deployment policy include positioning our sea-based strategic nuclear reserve well out of missile firing range to complicate Soviet ASW and ensure survivability?

The logic of tying up the Soviet Navy in bastions is sound strategy. The need to conserve U.S. aircraft carriers for the post-war era and for mid-ocean wartime SLOC duty conflicts with the pre-war need to reassure flank allies that they will not be abandoned. Perhaps when accuracies and ordnance are sufficiently developed to allow conventional warheads, we can substitute land- or sea-based theater missiles for the planned use of carrier aircraft to strike vital Soviet flank positions in support of our allies.

The need to deliver strikes against the actual territory of one's prime opponent will remain a high strategic priority. The U.S. Navy has exploited its advantage in this area for years with threats of conventional aircraft carrier strikes on the Kola Peninsula and elsewhere. We should expect a quid pro quo manipulation of the threat to conduct conventional strikes on the U.S. from the Soviets once their conventional land-attack SLCMs deploy.

Methodology

Content Analysis

Content analysis is not the ultimate tool for analysis, but when properly used and cross checked, it can assist. Criticism of selective citation extraction can be circumvented and time series analyses by author can demonstrate the continuity of thought, changes, and initiation of themes.

In doing a post-research validity test, the author demonstrated the worth of the extra steps of the more academically correct content analysis method. The various Politburo leaders, Defense Ministers, and Admiral Gorshkov authored a number of new articles, speeches, in 1984 and 1985 which contain themes used in this study.

In these additional articles, there was only a limited amount of new data, i.e., most themes had been used before. Of interest was Gorshkov's February 17, 1984 use of the triad of strategic nuclear forces (SRF, Navy, and Strategic Aviation). The Navy Chief credited this triad with being the "main component part of the combat might of the Soviet Armed Forces," and "the main factor of containing the aggressor." Up until then, Gorshkov had played down the role of Strategic Aviation and not mentioned it at all in the context of deterrence.

A June 1984 article by Gorshkov, in the English language journal Soviet Union, contains two new items of interest. One is the theme of Western aircraft carriers as a threat to Soviet and other socialist countries territory. As was pointed out in the content analysis, the Soviet declaratory perception of threats from aircraft carriers was heretofore listed as a threat to the Soviet fleet, not shore. Is this a reorientation in thinking or the use of Western capability as a surrogate for a future Soviet threat?

The second item of interest is a boast by the Soviet Navy Chief that the Soviet Navy is now able " . . . in the event of war, to confront the enemy in strategic parts of the world ocean of our own choosing." He continues that the Soviet fleet can pose to an aggressor the problems which he poses to the USSR. Since the nuclear attack threat is not new, does this refer to a conventional strike capability?

Having the benefit of tracking themes over time, it is possible to isolate what is new and what is not. By also considering the method of communication, additional information is gleaned. For example, the above two items of interest from Gorshkov's article in June 1984 appear specifically for foreign consumption. Virtually the same text appeared in his internally distributed Sotsialisticheskaya Industriya article of May 9 without these additional comments on aircraft carriers and confronting the enemy.

In 1984 Defense Minister Ustinov repeated earlier statements which: (1) rejected the possibility of a limited nuclear war, (2) made threats to the territories where new NATO missiles are deployed as well as from where orders are issued, and, (3) stated that increasing the number of Soviet submarines off the U.S. coast was a direct counterbalance to new U.S. systems in Europe. In a June 27 speech to the graduates of the military academies, the Defense Minister emphasized the need to "seek tactical methods which the enemy does not expect." None of Ustinov's comments were new.

In a March 1985 article in Bulgaria, Admiral Gorshkov repeated his renewed emphasis on the strategic nuclear triad as the basis of combat power of the Soviet armed forces and the basic factor for stopping aggressors. In his April Morskoy Sbornik article directed at a more naval audience, the Navy Chief boasted that contemporary conditions allowed the fleet to perform missions well-beyond that permissable in 1941 and that previously belonged only to other services.

Gorshkov's April 1985 Voyenno-Istoricheskiy Zhurnal article contains lengthy discussions of joint operations and SLOC campaigns in the Great Patriotic War and apparent reference to the use of submarine groups employed in combat operations. His July article in the same journal made a few new claims: (1) defense of the Motherland's borders takes place in remote ocean regions, (2) the response to a nuclear strike from the sea will be an instant response, and, (3) the basic goal of the navy is to deter.

A November 1985 Pravda article by the new Defense Minister, Marshal of the Soviet Union, S. L. Sokolov, re-emphasized the Soviet use of the term "strategic" with respect to weapons: "every U.S. medium-range weapon stationed near the Soviet border is essentially a strategic weapon as far as the USSR is concerned. Party Secretary Mikhail Gorbachev told the Supreme Soviet this same month that he was upset by the appearance of the U.S. battleship IOWA, carrying long-range cruise missiles, in the Baltic.

The new Chief of the General Staff, Marshal of the Soviet Union S. Akhromeyev, wrote in the journal Kommunist in February 1985, that the USSR would respond inevitably and immediately to aggression by the United States. He repeated that a future world war would be global.

Why do the Soviets continue openly to print their declaratory doctrine? In the deterrence of war, messages must be sent to the opposition as signals of intention and resolve. Communication must take place. Yet the extent and detail of declaratory policies is often surprising, since it contradicts Western spokesmen who are still arguing for MAD.

By inference, this means that the Soviets are not as sophisticated in their manipulation of the West as they are often credited with being. Their own literature undermines those Western spokesmen and leaders who would make unilateral reductions in military preparedness and maximize arms control concessions to the USSR. Fortunately for the Soviets, there are few in the West who read or evaluate the available foreign literature.

A few comments must be made about the translation materials used in the research. By and large, meaningful analysis can be done by the non-Russian speaker as long as it is subjected to a critical evaluation by others conversant in Russian. Since the author tracked themes in English, he discovered a surprising lack of standardization of terms which might be solved by stricter editorial supervision and/or the publishing of a guide for translators.

Some other more modest problems include the incompleteness of the PASKEY data base and duplicate entries. Only 66% of all Gorshkov documents from 1965 - 1983 were found in PASKEY. The occasional multiple translations encountered are understandable due to the lack of centralization over translations and afford the analyst the opportunity to cross-check words and themes.

The content analysis methodology used by this author allows him to comment on the man, Sergei Gorshkov, as well as analyze his writings. From reading hundreds of Gorshkov speeches, articles, books, etc., this author was struck with Gorshkov's manipulation of material to stroke Party leaders and ministers, reinforce good decisions, and to find subtle ways to criticize poor ones. This should not be surprising considering anyone who rose to command of the Soviet Navy in a time of turmoil and survived from 1957 - 1985.

By tracking themes over time and by analysis of Politburo and Defense Minister statements, the pattern emerges that Gorshkov has said very little that was new regarding nuclear war. At best, he was allowed to publicize targeting for SLBMs and the at-sea SLOC mission. The key conclusion in this area is that Gorshkov announces or follows the established party line to a great extent. It is difficult to demonstrate Gorshkov as an advocate with regard to nuclear war issues.

By knowing what his seniors said first and then reading Gorshkov, one can observe how the party line is followed and whether subtle additions or deletions are made. A great deal of what has been taken as evidence of a debate should be viewed instead as statements of policy. One cannot, however, make the same claim about other naval issues, especially naval diplomacy and the manipulative use of a fleet in time of peace, unless a similar systematic ayalysis of those themes has been undertaken. It would be interesting to see what a similar investigation of U.S. naval policies reveals.

Hardware Analysis

The hardware analysis used in this research is not necessarily innovative. Rather, it makes use of techniques developed previously. After modest improvements, what surprised the author was the lack of calculations and sensitivity analysis in earlier analyses of Soviet Navy strategic nuclear issues. "Number crunching" is simply necessary in order to measure the varying threat scenarios.

For those who are still searching for the causal reasons for key decisions made in earlier years, aggregation of forces, best and worst-case measurements, scenario variation, and sensitivity analysis might serve to generate acceptable explanations. A time series would be helpful but would be a major undertaking. Trends are often more revealing than the snapshot.

Use of real numbers and not artificial SALT numbers is a basic requirement when dealing with strategic nuclear forces. The multiplicity of naval force missions for the same units must be accounted for by varying assumptions. Findings of capability are obviously limited by assumptions, but too many previous analyses have not listed their assumptions. Once identified, problems can easily be reworked by simply changing the assumptions which will help determine what is it that appears to drive the problem.

General Comments

One can approach problems from the particular evidence and induce theories. On the other hand, one can have the theory and look for the evidence. This research effort has attempted to blend both methods but did have a theoretical framework for analysis prior to the start. The theory for investigation came first.

Most of the previous published studies on the Soviet Navy have been by traditional area specialists, well qualified to understand the operational aspects of the techniques and hardware of naval warfare. Quantitative or behaviorist methodology has been used sparingly in current Soviet Navy analyses. The current group of world class analysts doing Soviet Navy can only improve their product by including more empirical methods. Such academic rigor will not result in replacement of the area specialist, but rather it will enhance his already finely tuned awareness.

Perhaps the best advice is to not research one decision tree or scenario but rather gather the evidence for all possible explanations, present it, and then argue for one. The willingness to test new ideas and methods should not be viewed as a threat.

To a large degree, one can find the conclusions, findings, and implications stated herein in previous work by a variety of authors, many outside the Soviet Navy field. By using more rigorous methods, however, the level of uncertainty over those conclusions, findings, etc. has been reduced. The assumptions and evidence are carefully laid out and available for scrutiny. Admiral Gorshkov was replaced in 1985. The time is now to develop the methodologies for how to analyze the Soviet Navy into the 21st Century.

Appendix

MATERIAL USED FOR CONTENT ANALYSIS

I.   Pre-Study Period (1956 - 1964)

1956

Gorshkov   Navy Day Speech in Leningrad, July 26, 1956, carried by Moscow Soviet Home Service at 1720 GMT.

1957

Khruschev   Message of November 8, 1957 sent to President Eisenhower contained in TASS news release reported by Reuters and printed in New York Times, November 9, 1957, p. 12.

Interview with Henry Shapiro of United Press in Moscow reported in New York Times, November 16, 1957, pp. 1 and 3.

1958

Malinovskiy   Soviet Army and Navy 40th Anniversary Speech at Sports Palace, Central Stadium on February 22, 1958, carried live by Moscow, Soviet Home Service at 1405 GMT.

Gorshkov	<u>Pravda</u> article of July 27, 1958 excerpts reported by TASS, Radioteletype in Russian to Europe at 0802 GMT.
	"Faithful Defender of Our Sea Frontiers," <u>Agitator</u>, July 1958.

<u>1959</u>

Gorshkov	"Mounting Guard Over The Achievements of Socialism," <u>Sovetskiy Flot</u>, February 23, 1959 including excerpts reported by Moscow, TASS Radioteletype in Russian to Europe at 0715 GMT.
	"The Navy of the Land of Soviets," <u>Pravda</u>, July 26, 1959, excerpts reported by Moscow, Soviet Home Service at 0600 GMT.
Khruschev	Comments to reporters in San Francisco reported by William J. Jorden in <u>New York Times</u>, September 22, 1959, p. 22.

<u>1960</u>

Khruschev	"Disarmament Is The Path Toward Consolidating Peace and Safeguarding Friendship Among Peoples," Speech to 4th Session of Supreme Soviet, January 14, 1960, carried live by Moscow, Soviet Home Service at 0800 GMT.
Malinovskiy	Speech to 4th Session of Supreme Soviet, January 15, 1960, reported by Moscow, Soviet Home Service, at 1125 GMT.
	"On Guard Over Peace," <u>Pravda</u>, February 23, 1960 as reported by Moscow, Soviet Home Service at 0600 GMT.
Gorshkov	"A Reliable Guard for the Motherland's Security," <u>Sovetskiy Flot</u>, February 23, 1960.

Malinovskiy	Order of the Day of the USSR Minister of Defense, No. 177, Moscow, July 31, 1960 as reported by Moscow, Soviet Home Service, 2130 GMT, July 30, 1960.
Gorshkov	"True Sons of Their Motherland," Pravda, July 31, 1960 as reported by Moscow, Soviet Home Service at 1200 GMT.

1961

Malinovskiy	"Mounting Guard Over the Labor of the Builders of Communism," Pravda, February 23, 1961, including report of this article broadcast by Moscow in English to South and Southeast Asia at 1130 GMT.
Gorshkov	"Mounting Guard Over the Soviet State's Naval Borders," Pravda, July 29, 1961 including radio reports of this article carried by Moscow Domestic Service in Russian at 0400 GMT and Moscow TASS in Russian at 0756 GMT and an East Berlin ADN report in German to East Germany at 0929 GMT on July 30, 1961.
	Gorshkov Radio Address, July 29, 1961, carried by Moscow Domestic Service in Russian at 1445 GMT.
Khrushchev	Report of The Central Committee to 22nd Congress of The Communist Party of the Soviet Union, October 17, 1961, reported by Moscow Domestic Service in Russian at 0600 GMT October 18, 1961.
Malinovskiy	Speech to 22nd Congress of The Communist Party of the Soviet Union, October 23, 1961, read by Moscow Domestic Service announcer in Russian at 1030 GMT October 24, 1961.

1962

Gorshkov	Pravda Interview February 2, 1962 including report by Moscow TASS in English to Europe at 0633 GMT.

Malinovskiy	Soviet Army and Navy Day Speech in Moscow of February 22, 1962, excerpts carried by Moscow in English to Eastern North America at 2320 GMT.
	"Standing Guard Over the Peaceful Toil of the Builders of Communism," Pravda, as reported by Moscow Domestic Service in Russian at 0600 GMT February 23, 1962.
Gorshkov	"The Navy of the Soviet State," Narodna Armiya (Sofia), July 27, 1962. Navy Day Speech reported by Moscow in Polish to Poland at 2100 GMT on July 28, 1962 and by Moscow TASS in Russian to Europe at 1736 GMT on July 29, 1962.
	"Loyal Sons of the Motherland," Pravda, July 29, 1962 including report by Moscow Domestic Service in Russian at 0100 GMT.
	Krasnaya Zvezda Interview, October 31, 1962 reported by Moscow TASS in English to Europe at 0640 GMT.

1963

Gorshkov	"The Great Tasks of the Soviet Navy" Krasnaya Zvezda, February 5, 1963 including report by Moscow TASS in English to Europe at 0830 GMT.
Malinovskiy	Soviet Army and Navy 45th Anniversary Speech at Kremlin Palace of February 22, 1963, carried by Moscow Domestic Service in Russian at 1415 GMT.
Gorshkov	"Short-sighted Strategy," Izvestiya, May 19, 1963 (condensed text).
	Pravda article July 28, 1963 reported by Moscow TASS in English to Europe at 1109 GMT.

Navy Day Speech in Vladivostok, July 28, 1963 carried by Vladivostok Domestic Service in Russian at 1130 GMT.

"Defender of Our Sea Frontiers," *Agitator* No. 7, July 1963, pp. 24-26.

"The Party's Concern for the Navy," *Morskoy Sbornik*, No. 7, July 1963, pp. 9-18.

1964

Malinovskiy — Soviet Army and Navy 46th Anniversary Speech at Moscow Central Theater in Moscow of February 22, 1964, reported by Moscow TASS International Service in Russian at 1510 GMT.

"A Faithful Guardian of Peace," *Pravda*, February 23, 1964 including report by Moscow TASS International Service in English at 1021 GMT.

Gorshkov — "Navy on a Distant Cruise," *Krasnaya Zvezda*, March 21, 1964, excerpts reported by Moscow TASS International Service in Russian at 0012 GMT.

Khrushchev — Speech at Kremlin Reception for Graduates of Military Academies, July 8, 1964 reported by Moscow TASS International Service in English at 1543 GMT.

Gorshkov — Navy Day Speech in Moscow at the House of the Unions, July 25, 1964, excerpts carried by Moscow Domestic Service in Russian at 1550 GMT.

"Guarding the Sea Borders," *Pravda*, July 26, 1964.

"Participation of Soviet Sailors in Battles to Liberate the Danube Countries," *Morskoy Sbornik*, No. 8, August 1964, pp. 3-13.

II. Research Period (1964 – 1983)

1965

Gorshkov — "The Nuclear Fleet: Goals and Miscalculations," Za Rubezhom, No. 5, January 29 – February 4, 1965, p. 10 including report of this article broadcast by Moscow in English to the United Kingdom at 2000 GMT January 30, 1965.

Malinovskiy — Soviet Army and Navy Day Speech at Central Theater in Moscow of February 22, 1965 carried live by Moscow Domestic Service in Russian at 1430 GMT.

"The Reliable Guard of the Homeland," Pravda, February 23, 1965 including summary report of article broadcast by Moscow in German to Germany at 1600 GMT.

Gorshkov — Interview "To Improve Combat Training of the Navy on Sea and Ocean Expanses," Kommunist Vooruzhennykh Sil, No. 4, February 1965, pp. 18-23.

Izvestiya article reported by Moscow TASS International Service in English at 1615 GMT May 5, 1965.

Interview with N. Mar, "Battle on the Sea," Literaturnaya Gazeta, May 6, 1965 (excerpts).

Malinovskiy — "May 14 — The 10th Anniversary of the Warsaw Pact: A Mighty Guard of the Peoples Security," Krasnaya Zvezda, May 13, 1965.

Gorshkov — Victory Day Statement of May 20, 1965 carried by Moscow in Serbo-Croation to Yugoslavia at 1830 GMT.

Malinovskiy — "Historical Exploits of the Soviet People and Their Armed Forces in the Great

	Patriotic War," <u>Voyennaya Mysl'</u>, No. 5, May 1965.
Gorshkov	"The Soviet Navy in the Great Patriotic War," <u>Voyennaya Mysl'</u>, No. 5, May 1965.
	"The Homeland's Honored Decorations Carry Obligations," <u>Morskoy Sbornik</u>, No. 6, June 1965, pp. 3-4.
Brezhnev	Speech at Kremlin Reception for Graduates of Military Academy, July 3, 1965 reported by Moscow Domestic Service in Russian at 1530 GMT.
Kosygin	Speech at Baltiysk Presentation of the Red Banner Order to the Baltic Fleet, July 24, 1965 carried by Moscow Domestic Service in Russian at 1730 GMT.
Gorshkov	"Loyal Sons of the Motherland," <u>Pravda</u>, July 24, 1965.
	Navy Day Talk read by announcer, Moscow in English to South Asia on July 25, 1965 at 1100 GMT.
Malinovskiy	Radio article of July 28, 1965 broadcast in Albanian to Albania at 1700 GMT.
Gorshkov	"Naval Might of Soviet Power," <u>Soviet Military Review</u>, No. 7, July 1965, pp. 3-6.

1966

Gorshkov	"The Watch on the Sea" <u>Sovetskaya Rossiya</u>, February 1, 1966.
Malinovskiy	"Indestructible Shield of Peace and Socialism," <u>Narodna Armiya</u> (Sofia), February 22, 1966.
	Speech to 23rd Congress of the Communist Party of the Soviet Union, April 2, 1966 reported by Moscow Domestic Service in

Russian at 1300 GMT, <u>Krasnaya Zvezda</u>, April 2, 1966, and <u>Neues Deutschland</u> (East Berlin) April 3, 1966.

Gorshkov   <u>Krasnaya Zvezda</u> statement of April 3, 1966 including report by Moscow TASS International Service in English at 1000 GMT.

"The XXIIIrd Congress of the KPSS and the Tasks of Navymen," <u>Morskoy Sbornik</u>, No. 5, May 1966, pp. 3-13.

Malinovskiy   "Terrible Lesson of History," <u>Voyennaya Mysl'</u>, No. 6, June 1966.

Gorshkov   Navy Day Speech at Central Theater on July 30, 1966 carried by Moscow Domestic Service in Russian at 1730 GMT and excerpts reported by Moscow TASS International Service in English at 1528 GMT.

<u>Pravda</u> interview of July 31, 1966 reported by Moscow TASS International Service in English at 2145 GMT July 30, 1966.

1967

Malinovskiy   "On Guard Over the Gains of the Great October," <u>Pravda</u>, February 23, 1967, reported by Moscow Domestic Service in Russian at 0840 GMT.

Gorshkov   "A Glorious Battle Road," <u>Sel'skaya Zhizn'</u>, February 23, 1967, (excerpts).

"The Development of Soviet Naval Science," <u>Morskoy Sbornik</u>, No. 2, February 1967, pp. 9-21, including abridged form which appears as "Soviet Naval Art," in <u>Soviet Military Review</u>, No. 7, July 1967, pp. 2-7.

Brezhnev   Karlovy Vary (Czechoslovakia) speech of April 24, 1967, at Conference of Communist

	Workers Parties of Europe reported by Moscow TASS International Service in Russian at 2130 GMT.
Gorshkov	*Komsomol'skaya Pravda* interview, May 8, 1967, p.1.
	Victory Day Statement of May 9, 1967 broadcast by Moscow in Macedonian to Yugoslavia at 1830 GMT.
	Izvestiya interview reported by Moscow TASS International Service in English at 1459 GMT May 17, 1967 and Moscow in English to South Asia at 1600 GMT on May 18, 1967.
	"Battle Training on the High Seas," *Kommunist Vooruzhennykh Sil*, No. 12, June 1967, pp. 16-22, extracts.
	Agitator article, June 1967, pp. 21-23.
	"Our Mighty Ocean Fleet," *Pravda*, July 30, 1967, p. 2, including reports by Moscow TASS International Service in Russian at 0402 GMT and Moscow Domestic Service in Russian at 0400 GMT.
	Navy Day Speech in Leningrad, July 30, 1967, reported by Vladimir Umanskiy on Moscow Domestic Service in Russian at 1330 GMT.
Grechko	Speech before Supreme Soviet regarding bill on Universal Military Service, reported by Moscow Domestic Service in Russian at 1230 GMT October 12, 1967.
	"The Solemnity of Lenin's Ideas on the Defense of the Socialist Fatherland," *Kommunist Vooruzhennykh Sil*, No. 20, October 1967, pp. 31-39.
Gorshkov	"Guarding the Conquests of the Great October," *Morskoy Sbornik*, No. 10, October 1967, pp. 3-15.

Grechko	"The Army of October," <u>Krasnaya Zvezda</u>, November 3, 1967, p. 3.
	Order of the Day of the USSR Minister of Defense, No. 297, Moscow November 19, 1967, as reported by Moscow, Domestic Service in Russian at 2130 GMT November 18, 1967.
Gorshkov	Interview "The Fleet of Oceanic Spaces," <u>Sovetskiy Voin</u>, No. 24, December 1967, pp. 2-3.

1968

Gorshkov	"The Navy of the Socialist State," <u>Voyennaya Mysl'</u> No. 1, January 1968.
	"The Navy of Our Motherland," <u>Krasnaya Zvezda</u>, February 11, 1968, p. 2.
Grechko	50th Anniversary of the Soviet Armed Forces speech at Military-Scientific Conference in Moscow of February 14, 1968 reported in <u>Krasnaya Zvezda</u> on February 16, 1968, p. 1.
Gorshkov	Interview "On the High Seas and the Oceans," <u>Pravda</u>, February 14, 1968, p. 3.
	Interview with Lieutenent Colonel Guenter Engmann of February 15, 1968 broadcast by East Berlin Domestic Television Service in German at 1202 GMT.
Grechko	Speech "Fifty Years Guarding the Gains of Great October," February 23, 1968 at Kremlin Meeting Devoted to the 50th Jubilee of the Soviet Armed Forces carried live by Moscow Domestic Service in Russian at 1429 GMT.
Gorshkov	"The Country's Armed Forces," <u>Trud</u>, February 23, 1968, p. 2.

Grechko "The Fiftieth Anniversary of the Soviet Armed Forces, "Voyenno-Istoricheskiy Zhurnal No. 2, February 1968, pp. 3-14.

"Born Under Fire," Sovetskiy Voin, No. 3, February 1968, pp. 2-5.

Gorshkov Interview "The Navy is on the Alert," Ogonek No. 6, February 1968, pp. 6-8 including report by Moscow TASS International Service in English at 1349 GMT on February 2, 1968. Extracts of this interview appeared as articles; "A Fleet Mounting a Military Guard: Fifty Years of the Soviet Army and Navy," Narodna Armiya (Sofia), February 20, 1968, p. 1 and 2; and "An Interview With Soviet Navy Chief," Navy Magazine, Vol. II No. 6, June 1968, pp. 20-23.

"A Half Century on Combat Watch," Tekhnika i Vooruzheniye, No. 2, February 1968, pp. 12-13.

"Victory Day," Ekonomicheskaya Gazeta, May 6, 1968, p. 9.

Trud statement, June 6, 1968, p. 3.

Izvestiya statement reported by Moscow TASS International Service in English at 1006 GMT on July 12, 1968.

Izvestiya article summarized by Moscow Domestic Service in Russian at 1600 GMT on July 20, 1968.

Krasnaya Zvezda comments reported by Moscow Domestic Service in Russian at 0600 GMT July 21, 1968.

Navy Day statement of July 27, 1968 broadcast by Moscow Domestic Service in Russian at 1430 and 1600 GMT.

Navy Day comments of July 27, 1968 reported in <u>Krasnaya Zvezda</u>, July 28, 1968, p. 1.

<u>Pravda</u>, statement of July 28, 1968, p. 2.

<u>Neues Deutschland</u> (East Berlin) article of August 3, 1968, p. 5.

<u>1969</u>

Grechko "Ever on Guard," <u>Pravda</u>, February 23, 1969, p. 3.

"V.I. Lenin and The Building of The Soviet Armed Forces," <u>Kommunist</u>, No. 3, 1969, pp. 15-26.

Gorshkov <u>Izvestiya</u> interview with V. Goltsev April 5, 1969 including report by Moscow TASS International Service in English at 1418 GMT on April 4, 1969.

Grechko "The Great Victory," <u>Pravda</u>, May 9, 1969, p. 2.

Gorshkov "The People's Great Achievement," <u>Sel'skaya Zhizn'</u>, May 9, 1969, p. 1.

<u>Agitator</u> article in issue No. 13, June 1969, pp. 24-27.

Navy Day Speech in Moscow July 25, 1969 reported by Moscow Domestic Service in Russian at 2000 GMT.

Navy Day Politechnic Museum Speech July 26, 1969 reported by Moscow Domestic Service in Russian at 0300 GMT.

Grechko Order of the Day of the USSR Minister of Defense, No. 177, Moscow, July 27, 1969 as reported in <u>Krasnaya Zvezda</u>, July 27, 1969, p. 1 and Moscow TASS International Service in Russian at 2230 GMT on July 26, 1969.

Gorshkov	Interview "The Ocean Watch of the Fatherland," Pravda, July 27, 1969, p. 2, including report by Moscow Domestic Service in Russian at 0600 GMT.
	Interview with A. Denisovich "The Ocean Fleet of the Soviet Country," Sovetskaya Litva (Vil'nyus), July 27, 1969, p. 3.
	"The Navy Has Put Out to Sea," Starshina Serzhant, No. 7, July 1969, p. 1-2.
	Novosti interview "The Ocean Guard of the Soviet Union," Rabotnichesko Delo (Sofia), September 19, 1969, p. 4.
Gorshkov	Romanian Army Day Speech, October 23, 1969 reported by Moscow in Romanian to Romania at 1600 GMT on October 24, 1969.
	"On the Subject of Naval Defense," La Revue Maritime, No. 269, October 1969, pp. 1139-1143.
Grechko	Speech "The Growth of the Young Officers' Role, Tasks, and Responsibility at the Present Stage of Development of the Soviet Armed Forces," at All-Army Conference of Young Officers of November 26, 1969, reported in Krasnaya Zvezda, November 27, 1969, pp. 1,3.

1970

Grechko	"Born in Battles," Pravda, February 23, 1970, p.2.
Gorshkov	"Battles on the Seas," Izvestiya, February 27, 1970, Morning Edition, p. 3.
Grechko	"On Guard of Peace and Socialism," Kommunist No. 3, 1970 pp. 51-64, including report by Moscow TASS International Service in English at 1204 GMT on February 21, 1970.

Gorshkov	Comments in *Ogonek*, article by Anatoliy Yelkiv, issue No. 9, February 1970, p. 5.
Grechko	"Loyalty to the Leninist Behests on the Defense of the Motherland," *Kommunist Vooruzhennykh Sil*, No. 7, 1970, pp. 19-26.
Gorshkov	Interview with V. Goltsev "A Great Review," *Izvestiya*, April 15, 1970, Morning Edition, p. 3.
	"Long Voyages Are a School for Naval Training," *Krasnaya Zvezda*, April 16, 1970, p. 2, including report by Moscow TASS International Service in English at 1017 GMT.
Grechko	"The Triumph of the Leninist Doctrine on the Defense of the Achievements of Socialism," *Krasnaya Zvezda*, April 18, 1970, p. 2.
Gorshkov	"Over the Seas and Oceans," *Narodna Armiya* (Sofia), May 5, 1970, pp. 1,3 (excerpt).
Grechko	Victory Day Speech in Kremlin, May 8, 1970 carried live by Moscow Domestic Service in Russian at 1409 GMT.
Gorshkov	Navy Day Speech at Central Theater in Moscow July 24, 1970 excerpts reported by Moscow Domestic Service in Russian at 1900 GMT and Moscow TASS International Service in English at 2008 GMT.
Grechko	Order of the Day of the USSR Minister of Defense as reported in *Pravda* July 26, 1970, p. 1 and Moscow TASS International Service in English at 2145 GMT on July 25, 1970.
Gorshkov	"The Motherland's Ocean Guard," *Pravda*, July 29, 1970, p. 2 including report by Moscow TASS International Service in English at 2316 GMT on July 25, 1970.

"The Fleet on a Great Cruise," <u>Tekhnika i Vooruzheniye</u>, No. 7, June 1970, pp. 1-3.

"Navy" <u>Great Soviet Encyclopedia</u>, a translation of the 3rd Ed. (New York: MacMillan, 1974), Vol. 5, pp. 295-300.

1971

Grechko — "The Unconquerable Shield of the Motherland," <u>Pravda</u>, February 23, 1971, p. 2 including report by Moscow TASS International Service in English at 0115 GMT and radio report by Moscow in English to South Asia at 1000 GMT.

Gorshkov — "Engendered by Great October," <u>Sovetskaya Moldaviya</u> (Kishinev), February 23, 1971, pp. 1 and 4.

"Born by the Great October," <u>Vecherni Novini</u> (Sofia), February 23, 1971, pp. 1-2.

Grechko — "The Mighty Guard of Peace and Socialism," <u>Krasnaya Zvezda</u>, March 27, 1971, p. 2.

"The CPSU and the Armed Forces," <u>Kommunist</u>, No. 4, March 1971, pp. 38-48.

Grechko — "The Great Victory," <u>Pravda</u>, May 9, 1971, p. 2 including report by Moscow TASS International Service in English at 2200 GMT on May 8, 1971.

Brezhnev — Election Speech of 11 June 1971 reported in <u>Pravda</u>, June 12, 1971, pp. 1,2.

Grechko — <u>On Guard for Peace and the Building of Communism: Implementing the Decisions of the 24th Party Congress</u>, Moscow: Military Publishing House, signed to press June 14, 1971, 112 pp.

"Destruction of the Assault Forces of Imperialism (In Honor of the 30th

	Anniversary of the Beginning of the Great Patriotic War)," <u>Voyennaya Mysl'</u>, No. 6, June 1971.
Gorshkov	Navy Day Speech at Central Soviet Army Club in Moscow, July 23, 1971, excerpts reported by Mikhail Levchinskiy on Moscow Domestic Service in Russian at 1800 GMT and summary by Moscow in English to South Asia at 1000 GMT on July 24, 1971.
Grechko	Order of the Day of the USSR Minister of Defense, No. 151, Moscow, July 25, 1971 as reported by <u>Krasnaya Zvezda</u>, July 25, 1971, p. 1 and Moscow TASS International Service in English at 2138 GMT July 24, 1971.
Gorshkov	Interview "An Ocean, Nuclear and Missile Fleet," <u>Pravda</u>, July 25, 1971, p. 2 including report by Moscow TASS International Service in English at 2352 GMT on July 24, 1971.
	"Soviet Sailors Defend the Interests of Socialism," <u>Sovetskaya Litva</u> (Vil'nyus), July 25, 1971, p. 2.
Grechko	"The Fleet of Our Homeland," <u>Morskoy Sbornik,</u> No. 7, July 1971, pp. 3-9.

1972

	"A Trusty Guard for Socialism" <u>Pravda</u>, February 23, 1972, p. 2 including report by Moscow TASS International Service in English at 0613 GMT.
Gorshkov	"Navies in War and Peace," <u>Morskoy Sbornik</u>, No. 2, February 1972, pp. 20-29.
	"The Navy: Past and Present," <u>Voyennaya Mysl'</u>, No. 3, March 1972.

"Russia's Road to the Sea, Peter I to Napoleon," *Morskoy Sbornik*, No. 3, March 1972.

"The Post-Napoleonic Period to Russo-Japanese War," *Morskoy Sbornik*, No. 4, April 1972.

"The Soviet People's Great Victory," *Sotsialisticheskaya Industriya*, May 9, 1972, p. 1.

"The First World War," *Morskoy Sbornik*, No. 5, May 1972.

"The Soviet Navy in the Revolution," *Morskoy Sbornik*, No. 6, June 1972.

Interview with V. Goltsev "For Security of Navigation on the High Seas," *Izvestiya*, July 8, 1972, Morning Edition, p. 4.

Novosti interview, "Guarding the Peace," *Zolnierz Wolnosci* (Warsaw), July 28, 1972, pp. 1,2.

Novosti interview, "An Oceanic Guardian of Socialism and Peace," *Narodna Armiya* (Sofia), July 29, 1972, pp. 1,3.

Interview, "Ruggedness of Naval Life," *Ogonek*, No. 31, July 29, 1972, pp. 4-5.

Grechko — Order of the Day of the USSR Minister of Defense, No. 146, Moscow, July 30, 1972 as reported by *Krasnaya Zvezda*, July 30, 1972, p. 1 and Moscow Domestic Service in Russian at 2130 GMT on July 29, 1972.

Gorshkov — Interview "On the Seas and Oceans," *Pravda*, July 30, 1972, p. 2 including report by Moscow TASS International Service in English at 2140 GMT on July 29, 1972.

"The Commanding Officer of a Ship -- The Leading Figure in the Fleet," *Morskoy Sbornik*, No. 7, July 1972, pp. 3-8.

"The Soviet Navy Rebuilds, 1928-41," *Morskoy Sbornik*, No. 8, August 1972.

"The Second World War," *Morskoy Sbornik*, No. 9, September 1972.

Interview "The Komsomol's Naval Watch," *Pravda*, October 16, 1972, p. 2.

"The Soviet Navy in the Great Patriotic War," *Morskoy Sbornik*, No. 10 October 1972.

"Analysis of Navies in the Second World War," *Morskoy Sbornik*, No. 11, November 1972.

Grechko   "The Formation of the USSR and the Soviet Armed Forces," *Novaya i Noveishaya Istoriya,* No. 6 November - December 1972, pp. 9-26.

"A Socialist, Multinational Army," *Krasnaya Zvezda* December 17, 1972, pp. 1-2.

Gorshkov   "Navies as Instruments of Peacetime Imperialism," *Morskoy Sbornik*, No. 12, December 1972.

1973

Grechko   "Guardians of the Revolution and Socialism," provided by Novosti to *Rabotnichesko Delo* (Sofia), February 22, 1973, pp. 1 and 5.

"On Guard Over the Motherland," *Pravda*, February 23, 1973, p. 2.

Gorshkov   Army Navy Day Speech of February 24, 1973 as reported by Moscow Domestic Service in Russian at 1530 GMT.

"Some Problems in Mastering the World Ocean," *Morskoy Sbornik*, No. 2, February 1973.

"Ship's Commanding Officer," *Soviet Military Review*, No. 3, March 1973, pp. 2-5.

Bloknot Agitatora article, No. 8, April 1973, pp. 3-6.

Grechko   "On Guard Over Peace and Socialism," *Kommunist*, No. 7, May 1973, pp. 12-16.

Gorshkov   Interview "On Ocean Watch," *Pravda*, July 29, 1973, p. 2 including report by Moscow TASS in English at 0710 GMT.

Interview "We Always Remember the Order of the Homeland," *Sovetskiy Voin*, No. 13, July 1973, pp. 2-3.

1974

Grechko   Speech in Kazan at awarding Tatar ASSR with Order of the Friendship of the Peoples, January 8, 1974, reported by *Komsomolets Tatarii* (Kazan), January 9, 1974, pp. 3-4.

Gorshkov   "Foreword," in *Combat Path of the Soviet Navy*, 3rd Ed. supplemented, V. I. Achkasov, et al., Moscow: Military Publishing House, signed to press February 13, 1974, pp. 3-7.

"The Reliable Guard of the Fatherland," *Sovetskiy Patriot*, February 20, 1974, p. 1, excerpts.

Grechko   "On Guard of Peace and Socialism," *Pravda*, February 23, 1974, p. 2.

Gorshkov   Armed Forces Day Speech at Central Theater in Moscow, excerpts reported in *Krasnaya Zvezda*, February 23, 1974, p. 1.

Grechko	"V.I. Lenin and the Soviet State's Armed Forces," *Kommunist* No. 3, 1974, pp. 12-24, including report by Moscow TASS International Service in Russian at 0947 GMT on February 25, 1974.
	The Armed Forces of the Soviet State, Moscow: Military Press of the Ministry of Defense, signed to press April 9, 1974.
Gorshkov	"The Heroic Exploit of the People," *Trud*, May 9, 1974, p. 1.
Grechko	"The Leading Role of the CPSU in Building the Army of a Developed Socialist Society," *Voprosy Istorii KPSS*, No. 5, May 1974, pp. 30-47.
Brezhnev	Sejm speech carried live by Moscow Domestic Service in Russian at 1015 GMT July 21, 1974.
Gorshkov	Navy Day Speech at Central Theater in Moscow, July 26, 1974, excerpts reported by Moscow Domestic Service in Russian at 1900 GMT.
Grechko	Order of the Day of the USSR Minister of Defense, No. 165, Moscow, July 28, 1974 as reported by *Krasnaya Zvezda*, July 28, 1974, p. 1.
Gorshkov	Interview "The Maritime Might of the Land of the Soviets," *Pravda*, July 28, 1974, p. 2 including report by Moscow TASS in English at 2234 GMT.
	"The Oceanic Guard of the Homeland," *Agitator*, No. 13, July 1974, pp. 30-33.
	"Certain Questions Concerning the Development of the Naval Art," *Morskoy Sbornik*, No. 12, December 1974, pp. 24-32.

1975

Grechko · The Armed Forces of the Soviet State, 2nd Ed. Moscow: Military Press of the Minister of Defense, signed to press March 26, 1975.

Gorshkov · "The USSR's Decisive Contribution to Victory Over Fascism," Prace (Prague), April 5, 1975, pp. 1,2.

"The Sailors' Feat," Trud, April 11, 1975, p. 4.

Interview "The Battle Pennants of the Motherland," Izvestiya, April 29, 1975, p. 1,5.

"Navy in Great Patriotic War," Voyenno-Istoricheskiy Zhurnal, No. 4, April 1975, pp. 35-42.

"The Navy Did Its Duty for the Motherland Right to the End," Morskoy Sbornik, No. 5, May 1975, pp. 8-15.

"Historical Experience and the Present Day," Voprosy Filosofii, No. 5, May 1975, pp. 26-38.

Interview "The Navy of the Soviet Union," Soviet Military Review, No. 6 June 1975, pp. 2-5.

Navy Day Speech at Central Theater in Moscow, excerpts reported in Krasnaya Zvezda, July 26, 1975, p. 1 and carried by Moscow Domestic Service in Russian at 1530 GMT on July 27, 1975.

Grechko · Order of the Day of the USSR Minister of Defense, No. 175, Moscow July 27, 1975, as reported by Krasnaya Zvezda, July 27, 1975, p. 1 and Moscow Domestic Service in Russian at 2100 GMT July 26, 1975 and 0200 GMT July 27, 1975.

Gorshkov	Address broadcast by Moscow Domestic Television Service in Russian at 1335 GMT on July 27, 1975.
	Interview "Flying the Motherland's Flag," Pravda, July 27, 1975, p. 2 including report by Moscow TASS in English at 2200 GMT on July 26, 1975.
	"The Oceanic Shield of the Homeland," Kommunist Vooruzhennykh Sil, No. 14, July 1975, pp. 9-17.
	The Sea Power of the State, Oxford: Pergamon Press, 1979, authorized translation of Russian original signed to press November 27, 1975, 290 pp.

1976

Gorshkov	"On Ocean Watch," Krasnaya Zvezda, February 11, 1976, p. 2 including report by Moscow TASS in English at 0953 GMT.
Brezhnev	"The Report of the CPSU Central Committee and the Party's Immediate Tasks in the Fields of Domestic and Foreign Policy," Report to 25th Congress of Communist Party of the Soviet Union, February 24, 1976 reported by Pravda and Izvestiya, February 25, 1976, pp. 2-9.
Gorshkov	"Greeting the 25th Congress of the CPSU," Morskoy Sbornik, No. 2, February 1976, pp. 8-13.
	"The Naval Art," Sovetskaya Voyennaya Entsiklopediya, Vol. 2, signed to press July 20, 1976, pp. 231-234.
	"Navy" Sovetskaya Voyennaya Entsiklopedia, Vol. 2, signed to press July 20, 1976, pp. 235-243.

Excerpts of Navy Day Speech in Moscow reported by "Ceremonial Meeting in Moscow," <u>Krasnaya Zvezda</u>, July 24, 1976, p. 1.

Navy Day Speech July 24, 1976 carried by Moscow Domestic Service in Russian at 0840 GMT.

Interview "The Homeland's Naval Might," <u>Pravda</u>, July 25, 1976, p. 2.

"A Most Important Factor of the Navy's Combat Readiness and Combat Efficency," <u>Tyl i Snabzheniye Sovetskikh Vooruzhennykh Sil</u>, No. 7, July 1976, pp. 3-9 (extracts).

<u>World Ocean Atlas</u>, S. G. Gorshkov, Ed. Oxford: Pergamon Press, 1979, authorized translation of Russian original published in 1976.

1977

Gorshkov
<u>Narodna Armiya</u> (Sofia) interview with Stepan Fedoseyev, Novosti military observer, February 23, 1977, pp. 1,4, including report by Moscow in Serbo-Croatian to Yugoslavia at 1730 GMT on February 22, 1977 containing additional information.

Ustinov
"The Guard of Peaceful Labor and the Bulwark of Universal Peace," <u>Kommunist</u>, No. 3, February 1977, pp. 11-22; including reports by Moscow TASS in English at 0819 and 0917 GMT February 17, 1977.

Gorshkov
<u>Krasnaya Zvezda</u> comments contained in article "Friendly Meeting in Tunis," by Novosti correspondent V. Bolshakov and TASS correspondent I. Myakishev, March 31, 1977, p.3.

Interview with Stepan Fedoseyev, Novosti military commentator "We Shall Never Raise the Sword," <u>Bratislava Pravda</u>

Slovak Weekend Supplement, April 1, 1977, p. 16 (excerpts).

Interview "On Sea Boundaries," Pravda, July 31, 1977, p. 2.

Message reported by Juventud Rebelde (Havana), August 3, 1977, p. 1.

The Navy, Knowledge Press, signed to press September 22, 1977, 64 pp.

Komsomol Central Committee speech October 20, 1977 reported by Moscow Domestic Service in Russian at 1100 GMT, October 22, 1977.

"The Navy," Voyenno-Istoricheskiy Zhurnal, No. 10, October 1977, pp. 44-51.

"Guarding the Accomplishments of the Great October," Morskoy Sbornik, No. 11 November 1977, pp. 6-12.

Speech at Cuban Naval Academy, summarized and reported by Havana Domestic Service in Spanish at 1100 GMT on December 22, 1977.

1978

Gorshkov
"Always on Guard," Krasnaya Zvezda, February 7, 1978, p. 2.

Pravda comments contained in article, "Soverigns of the Deep," by Timur Gaydar, February 9, 1978, p. 6.

Soviet Army and Navy 60th Anniversary Speech of February 23, 1978 carried by Moscow Domestic Service at 0545 GMT.

"Sixty Years of the USSR Armed Forces," Sudostroyeniye, No. 2 February, 1978, pp. 3-5.

"The Motherland's Naval Might," Kommunist Vooruzhennykh Sil, No. 3, February 1978, pp. 9-16.

Interview "Sentries of the Maritime Borders," Voyennyy Vestnik, No. 2, February 1978, pp. 23-25.

"Foreword to the English Edition," and changes which appear in authorized translation of The Sea Power of the State, Oxford: Pergamon Press, 1979, Foreword dated March 31, 1978, pp. vii-viii.

Brezhnev   Speech to Personnel of the Pacific Fleet in Vladivostok reported in Kommunist, No. 6, April 1978, pp. 23-26.

Vorwaerts interview appearing in Pravda and Izvestiya, May 4, 1978, p. 1 (condensed text).

Gorshkov   "The Light of a Great Feat," Nedelya No. 18, signed to press May 4, 1978, pp. 4-5.

Ustinov   "Victory in the Name of Peace," Pravda, May 9, 1978, p. 2.

Gorshkov   "Navy Shipboard Regulations -- Basis of a Navyman's Service," Morskoy Sbornik, No. 5, May 1978, pp. 3-7.

Interview, "Ocean Watch," Soviet Military Review, No. 6, June 1978, pp. 2-7.

Navy Day Speech July 29, 1978 carried by Moscow Domestic Service in Russian at 1330 GMT.

Ustinov   Order of the Day of the USSR Minister of Defense, No. 182, Moscow, July 30, 1978, as reported by Krasnaya Zvezda, July 30, 1978, p. 1.

Gorshkov   Interview "Our Power's Ocean Might," Pravda, July 30, 1978, p. 2.

"The Great Patriotic War and the Postwar Period: Cooperation of the Navy with the Ground Forces," <u>Voyenno-Istoricheskiy Zhurnal</u>, No. 11, November 1978, pp. 18-25.

1979

Gorshkov — "The CO and Combat Readiness," <u>Morskoy Sbornik</u>, No. 1, January 1979, pp. 3-7.

Ustinov — Order of the Day of the USSR Minister of Defense, No. 175, Moscow, July 29, 1979, as reported by <u>Krasnaya Zvezda</u>, July 29, 1979, p. 1 and Moscow Domestic Service in Russian at 0000 GMT.

Gorshkov — Interview "On the Eve of Navy Day: On The Ocean Borders," <u>Pravda</u>, July 29, 1979, p. 3, including report by Moscow TASS in English at 2225 GMT on July 28, 1979.

"The Navy's Ocean Watches," <u>Morskoy Sbornik</u>, No. 7, July 1979, pp. 3-7.

<u>Znamenosets</u> comments contained in article "The Initiators Report" by Captain 2nd Rank V. Nikolayev, No. 7, July 1979, p. 9.

<u>The Sea Power of the State</u>, 2nd Ed., Moscow: Military Publishing House, signed to press August 6, 1979, 411 pp.

Comments at Fifth Military Region reported by Hanoi VNA in English at 1544 GMT and Hanoi Domestic Service in Vietnamese at 1430 GMT on December 25, 1979.

Comments at Seventh Military Region reported by Hanoi VNA in English at 1543 GMT on December 25, 1979.

"Naval Tactics," <u>Sovetskaya Voyennaya Entsiklopedia</u>, Vol. 7, 1979, pp. 631-632.

1980

Ustinov	"A Source of Great Strength," *Pravda*, February 22, 1980, pp. 2-3.
Gorshkov	"Tomorrow is Soviet Army and Navy Day: Guarding Peace and Socialism" *Sovetskaya Rossiya,* February 22, 1980, p. 1.
	"Glorious Offspring of the Soviet People," *Kommunist*, No. 3, February 1980, pp. 43-56.
	Article in *Vodnyy Transport*, May 9, 1980, p. 1 (extract).
	"Problems with Respect to Control of Naval Forces," *Morskoy Sbornik*, No. 5, May 1980, pp. 7-12.
	"Problems With Respect to Control of Naval Forces," *Morskoy Sbornik*, No. 6 June 1980, pp. 3-11.
	Comments in Addis Ababa reported by Moscow TASS International Service in Russian at 1106 GMT on July 9, 1980.
	Comments in Addis Ababa reported by Moscow TASS in English at 1100 GMT on July 10, 1980.
Ustinov	Order of the Day of the USSR Minister of Defense, Moscow, July 27, 1980 as reported by *Krasnaya Zvezda*, July 27, 1980, p. 1.
Gorshkov	Interview "Today is USSR Navy Day: On the Ocean Watch," *Pravda*, July 27, 1980, p. 2.
Brezhnev	India Parliament Speech of December 10, 1980 broadcast by Moscow TASS in English at 1458 GMT.

1981

Gorshkov
"The Navy — The 26th Party Congress," Morskoy Sbornik, No. 1, January 1981, pp. 3-8.

"The Ocean Watch of the Sailors," Kommunist Vooruzhennykh Sil, No. 2 January 1981, pp. 26-33.

"From Congress to Congress: From Positions of Combat Readiness," Krasnaya Zvezda, February 13, 1981, p. 2.

Ustinov
"Loyal to the Cause of the Party" Pravda, February 21, 1981, p. 2.

Brezhnev
"Report of the Central Committee of the CPSU to the 26th Congress of the Communist Party of the Soviet Union and the Immediate Tasks of the Party in Home and Foreign Policy," February 23, 1981 including report carried by Moscow Domestic Service in Russian at 0720 GMT on February 23, 1981.

Gorshkov
"Today is Soviet Army and Navy Day," Sotsialisticheskaya Industriya, February 23, 1981, p. 4.

"Feat of All the People," Ekonomicheskaya Gazeta, No. 19 signed to press May 4, 1981, p. 5.

Ustinov
"Against the Arms Race and the Threat of War," Pravda, July 25, 1981 as reported by Moscow TASS International Service in Russian at 2100 GMT on July 24, 1981.

Order of the Day of the USSR Minister of Defense, No. 190, Moscow, July 26, 1981 as reported by Krasnaya Zvezda, July 26, 1981, p. 1.

Gorshkov	Interview "The Ocean Watch: Today is USSR Navy Day," Pravda, July 26, 1981, p. 2, excerpts.
	"For Sea Cruises -- Excellent Rear Services Support," Tyl I Snabzheniye Sovetskikh Vooruzhennykh Sil, No. 7, July 1981, pp. 3-8.
	"Strategic Operations in the Pacific Theater of Military Operations in World War II (Based on the Experience of the Japanese Armed Forces)," Voyenno-Istoricheskiy Zhurnal, No. 8, August 1981, pp. 58-65.
	Interview with Vasilij Morozov "Myths and Reality About Naval Military Threat," provided by Novosti to Military Science and Technology, Vol. 1, No. 4 (August) 1981, pp. 18-20.
Brezhnev	Der Spiegel interview reported by Moscow TASS in English at 0530 GMT on November 2, 1981 and published in Pravda November 3, 1981, pp. 1-2.
Gorshkov	Speech Honoring 40th Anniversary of Yugoslav People's Army in Moscow on December 21, 1981, excerpts broadcast by Moscow in Serbo-Croatian to Yugoslavia at 1700 GMT on December 22, 1981.

1982

	"The Commanding Officer's Personal Example," Morskoy Sbornik, No. 1, January 1982, pp. 3-8.
Ustinov	"The Army of the People's Friendship," Pravda, February 23, 1982, p. 2 including report by Moscow World Service in English at 2100 GMT on February 22, 1982.
Brezhnev	Letter to Australian disarmament organization reported by Moscow TASS in

English at 1815 GMT on February 24, 1982.

Speech "Put Concern for the Working People, Concern for Production at the Center of Attention of the Trade Unions," at Congress of Soviet Trade Unions reported by Moscow TASS in English at 1000 GMT on March 16, 1982.

Gorshkov — Interview "Great Victory: Its Importance, Its Lessons," Moscow APN Daily Review, in English, April 29, 1982, pp. 1-5.

Ustinov — "For Averting the Threat of Nuclear War," Pravda, July 12, 1982 as reported by Moscow TASS in English at 1110 GMT and a press release from the Embassy of the USSR including another TASS release at 2138 GMT.

Gorshkov — Navy Day Speech at Moscow Garrison of July 23, 1982 carried by the Vremya newscast on Moscow Domestic Television Service in Russian at 1700 GMT.

Interview with Aleksandr Abramov "On Guard of the Homeland," broadcast by Moscow Domestic Service in Russian at 1000 GMT on July 24, 1982.

Navy Day Address broadcast by Moscow Domestic Service in Russian at 0710 GMT on July 25, 1982.

Interview "Ocean Vigil," Pravda, July 25, 1982, p. 2 (excerpts) including report by Moscow TASS in English at 2039 GMT on July 24. 1982.

"Soviet Art of Warfare in the Great Patriotic War - The Development of the Art of Warfare," Voyenno-Istoricheskiy Zhurnal, No. 7, July 1982, pp. 10-18.

	Novosti interview dated September 9, 1982 and distributed by press release from the Embassy of the USSR also appearing as "Whence Comes the Threat; Adm. S. Gorshkov on the true correlation of USSR and U.S. Naval Forces," <u>Rude Pravo</u> (Prague), September 13, 1982, p. 6, and in reworded form as APN interview with Vasiliy Morozov, <u>Morning Star</u> (London), November 30, 1982, p. 2.
Ustinov	Interview "Answers of USSR Defense Minister Marshal of the Soviet Union Dmitriy Ustinov to Questions of TASS Correspondent," Moscow TASS in English at 1755 GMT on December 6, 1982 including press release from Embassy of the USSR December 7, 1982.
Gorshkov	"Contemporary Problems in Studying and Exploiting the Oceans of the World," <u>Morskoy Sbornik</u>, No. 12, December 1982, pp. 16-26.
	Foreword "The Ocean Shield of The Soviet Power," in <u>The Navy of the USSR</u>, Admiral A. I. Sorokin, Ed. Moscow: Planet Publishing, 1982, p. 14-15.

1983

Gorshkov	"Strong Naval Forces - An Important Factor of the USSR's Security," <u>Naval Forces</u>, Vol. IV No. II/1983, pp. 34-39 appearing in slightly different form as "Die Starke der Seestreitkrafte des Sowjetstaates - ein Wichtiger Faktor der Sicherheit der UdSSR," <u>Marine Rundschau</u>, Vol. 80, No. 1, 1983, pp. 5-7.
	Soviet Army and Navy 65th Anniversary Speech of February 22, 1983 carried by Moscow Domestic Service in Russian at 0715 GMT.
Ustinov	<u>Krasnaya Zvezda</u> comments to Northern Fleet contained in correspondent's

	report "Meeting with Seamen", March 13, 1983, 1st Ed., p. 1.
Andropov	"Yu. V. Andropov Answer to a Pravda Correspondent's Questions," Pravda March 27, 1983, p. 1, also reported by Moscow Radio in English to North America at 2300 GMT on March 26, 1983, and report of TASS release contained in press release from the Embassy of the USSR (undated).
Gorshkov	Comments following visit to Peoples Democratic Republic of Yemen reported by Aden Domestic Service in Arabic at 1230 GMT on March 29, 1983. "Bases of Aggression," Pravda April 15, 1985, pp. 4-5.
Andropov	Interview with Rudolf Augstein of April 19, 1983 for Der Spiegel reported by Moscow TASS in English at 1515 GMT on April 24, 1983 and press release from the Embassy of the USSR on April 25, 1983.
Gorshkov	Account "The First Salvos at Sevastopol," told to V. Goltsev Izvestiya April 27, 1983, Morning Edition, p. 3.
Ustinov	"The Immortal Feat," Pravda May 9, 1983, p. 2.
Gorshkov	Interview with Dimitur Kostov "Parity — Guarantee for Peace," BTA Round the World, (Sofia) in English at 1325 GMT on May 12, 1983. "An Example for Posterity" Sovetskiy Voin, No. 9, May 1983, pp. 1-3. "Soviet People's Great Victory," Ekonomicheskaya Gazeta, No. 19, May 1983, p. 9.

Andropov	Kremlin Speech Honoring President of Finland Mouno Koivisto reported by Moscow TASS on June 6, 1983, in a press release from the Embassy of the USSR June 7, 1983, and in <u>Krasnaya Zvezda</u> June 7, 1983, 2nd. Ed., pp. 1,3.
Ustinov	<u>Pravda</u> interview July 31, 1983, p. 4.
Gorshkov	Interview "Under the Motherland's Flag," <u>Pravda</u>, July 31, 1983, p. 2.
	Navy Day Address carried by Moscow Domestic Television Service in Russian at 0650 GMT on July 31, 1983.
	"Questions of the Theory of the Navy," <u>Morskoy Sbornik</u>, No. 7, July 1983, pp. 27-38.
	"U.S. Aircraft Carriers -- An Instrument of Expansion," <u>Krasnaya Zvezda</u>, October 14, 1983, 2nd Ed., p.3.
Andropov	Statement in <u>Pravda</u>, November 25, 1983, p. 1 also reported by Moscow Domestic Service and Television Service in Russian at 1800 and Moscow TASS in English at 1832 GMT on November 24, 1983 and distributed by a press release from the Embassy of the USSR on November 28, 1983.

III. Post-Study Period (1984-1985)

1984

Gorshkov	Interview reported by TASS in English at 1205 GMT on February 7, 1984.
	"The People's Great Feat," <u>Sotsialisticheskaya Industriya</u>, May 9, 1984. p. 1.
Ustinov	Answers to questions of TASS correspondent reported by Moscow TASS in English at 1339 GMT on May 20, 1984 and distributed by a press release from the Embassy of the USSR on May 21, 1984, carried in a slightly

different version in Krasnaya Zvezda on May 22, 1984 on pp. 1, 3, and distributred as "Marshal Ustinov's Missiles Deployment in Europe Does Not Strengthen Security of U.S. and Other NATO Countries," by Novosti Press Agency Publishing House, in English in 1984.

Gorshkov "Remember the War," Morskoy Sbornik, No. 5, May 1984, pp. 5-11.

"June 1941 Shall Not Be Repeated," Izvestiya, June 22, 1984, Morning Ed., p. 3.

Ustinov Speech at Kremlin Reception for Graduates of Military Academies, July 27, 1984, reported by Moscow TASS in English at 1018 GMT and appearing in Krasnaya Zvezda, June 28, 1984, 2nd Ed., pp. 1, 3.

Gorshkov "Ocean Shield: A Talk with Admiral S. Gorshkov, Commander-in-Chief, USSR Navy," report by V. Zubkov and A. Khrupov in English, Soviet Union, No. 6, June 1984, pp. 16-17.

Interview "On the Ocean Watch; Today is USSR Navy Day." Pravda, July 29, 1984, 1st Ed., p. 2.

Navy Day Speech carried by Moscow Television Service in Russian at 1215 GMT on July 29, 1984.

"His Whole Life Devoted to Serving The Motherland," Krasnaya Zvezda, December 23, 1984, 2nd Ed., p. 2.

1985

Gorshkov "The Motherland's Ocean Guard," Krasnaya Zvezda, 2nd Ed., March 5, 1985; p. 2.

"The Defense of Socialism is an Objective Necessity," provided by Novosti to Narodna Armiya (Sofia), March 28, 1985, pp. 1, 4.

"The Experience of The Great Patriotic War and The Present Stage in The Development of Naval Art," Morskoy Sbornik, No. 4, April 1985, pp. 13-22.

"The Operational-Strategic Employment of the Navy in The Great Patriotic War," Voyenno-Istoricheskiy Zhurnal, No. 4, April 1985, pp. 73-81.

Interview with N. Mara in Literaturnaya Gazeta, May 1, 1985, p. 10.

"The Army and Literature: Allies in the Exploit," Soverskiy Voin, No. 10, May 1985, pp. 2-3.

Ogonek interview carried by Moscow TASS International Service at 1300 GMT, July 16, 1985, and Moscow APN Daily Review in English, Vol. XXI, No. 139, July 17, 1985.

"To Increase Combat Readiness is to Knowledgeably Use Accumulated Experience," Voyenno-Istoricheskiy Zhurnal, No. 7, July 1985.

Sokolov   "To Preserve What Has Been Achieved in The Sphere of Strategic Arms Limitation," Pravda, 1st Ed., November 6, 1985, p. 4.

Gorbachev   Live speech to Joint Session of USSR Supreme Soviet of November 27, 1985 in the Great Kremlin Palace broadcast by Moscow Television Service in Russian at 0842 GMT.

Index

ABM. See Anti-ballistic missiles
Aircraft carriers, 54-56, 59, 61,66, 66(n4), 71, 85, 88, 91, 92, 97, 99, 145-146, 159, 182, 184, 186, 188, 194(n27), 207-210, 218, 221, 224, 227, 232-234
Air Force, Soviet, 29, 58, 60, 76, 173, 183, 207, 226
  See also Long Range Aviation; Strategic Aviation
Akhromeyev, Sergey, 76, 235
Amphibious warfare, 42, 56, 63, 66(n4), 85-89, 175, 178, 180-181, 183, 192(n9), 207-208, 227
Andropov, Yuri, 14, 16, 20-21, 161(n1)
  See also Politburo
Anti-ballistic missiles (ABM), 59, 64, 75, 145, 166, 210, 222-223, 229
Antisubmarine warfare (ASW), 13, 18, 33, 41-42, 56-61, 66, 67(n6), 70, 82, 84-85, 87-88, 92, 97, 99-100, 153, 157, 159-160, 161(n2), 171, 176-178, 180-185, 203-204, 207, 209-210, 212, 220-221, 224-225, 227-230, 232
Arctic Ocean, 19, 54, 58-59, 69, 126-127, 158, 186, 191, 221, 225.
  See also Bastions
Armed conflict, 25-26, 28-32, 70, 72, 77, 81, 91, 99, 156, 186, 190, 205
  See also War
Arms Control, 8, 21, 55, 66(n3), 91-92, 157, 159, 166, 172, 221-222, 225, 229-230, 232, 235
  See also SALT I Interim Agreement
Army, Soviet. See Ground forces, Soviet
Assured destruction, 99, 120, 149, 155, 166, 169, 170, 203, 211-212, 217-218
  See also Mutual assured destruction
ASW. See Antisubmarine warfare
Atlantic Ocean, 48-49, 54, 81, 86, 88, 126, 129, 130(n6, n10, n11), 133, 135, 137-138, 140-141, 153-154, 163-164, 170-

173, 177–179, 182, 184–191, 199–200, 209–213, 220–221, 224–226, 230–233
Aviation, Soviet naval. See Naval Aviation, Soviet

Balanced fleet, 79, 85, 87–88, 90–91, 223
Baltic Fleet, Soviet. See Baltic Sea
Baltic Sea, 46, 49, 87, 95(n22), 97, 126, 128, 130(n7), 135–138, 140–141, 178, 187, 189, 191, 235
Barents Sea. See Bastions
Bastions, 18, 61, 64–66, 90, 92(n3), 97–98, 100, 107, 126, 128, 130(n7), 135–143, 148, 153–156, 165, 169–171, 173, 175, 177–179, 182–186, 188, 191, 193(n15), 200–204, 207–208, 212, 219, 224, 227, 229–230, 232
  See also Arctic Ocean; Blue belt of defense; Reserve, strategic nuclear; Withholding
Battle, concept of, 34, 65, 79
  See also Strike, concept of
Bering Sea. See Bastions
Blue belt of defense, 64–65
  See also Bastions
Bolt from the blue. See Scenarios, bolt from the blue
Brezhnev, Leonid, 16, 27, 54, 71, 91–92, 98, 161(n1), 174(n5)
  See also Politburo

CEP. See Circular error of probability

Circular error or probability (CEP), 121–125
CMP. See Counter military potential
Command and control, naval, 75–78, 84, 86, 88, 101, 172, 198–199, 202, 209, 220, 225, 227
Communist Party of the Soviet Union (CPSU), 8, 14–15, 58, 63–64, 83, 218–220, 223, 225, 227–229
Content analysis. See Methodology, content analysis
Conventional war. See War, conventional
Counter military potential (CMP), 123–125
Course of a war. See War, course of
CPSU. See Communist Party of the Soviet Union

Decisiveness in war. See War, decisiveness in
Declaratory policy, concept of, 7–8, 11, 18, 25, 34, 90–91, 97, 105, 107, 110, 146–147, 235
Deployment analysis. See Methodology, deployment analysis
Deterrence, 4, 6–7, 17, 58, 69, 71–74, 78, 93(n8), 98–100, 149, 165, 204, 211–213, 215, 217–218, 220, 222, 228, 230, 232–233, 235
Doctrine. See Military doctrine
Dyad. See Strategic nuclear forces, dyad

Electromagnetic pulse (EMP), 123, 142–143, 150(n4), 168

EMP. See Electromagnetic pulse
EMT. See Megatons, equivalent
Escalation, 70, 75, 81, 88, 98, 136, 154, 184, 230
Exercises, 7-8, 71, 97, 105, 136, 156-157, 178-179, 180, 183-185, 187, 193(n14, n15), 206, 231

Fleet versus fleet, 31-32, 36, 42, 53-66, 76, 91, 97, 99, 107, 109
Fleet versus shore, 29-31, 35-36, 41-50, 53, 57, 59, 65-66, 91, 107, 109
France, 54, 193(n16)
  See also North Atlantic Treaty Organization

General purpose naval forces, 4-6, 108-110, 173, 175-192, 198, 207-212, 221
  See also Submarines; Surface ships
Germany, Federal Republic of, 54
  See also North Atlantic Treaty Organization
Gorbachev, Mikhail, 235
  See also Politburo
Gorshkov, Sergei, 12-21, 26-36, 41-49, 53-65, 70-92, 99, 100-101, 188, 201-202, 204, 210, 224, 233-237
Great Patriotic War. See History, Great Patriotic War
Grechko, Andrey, 16, 20-21, 27-28, 30, 43, 46-48, 58, 62, 70, 72, 75-76, 78, 80, 82, 85-86, 89, 100, 204

See also Minister of Defense
Ground forces, Soviet, 29, 42, 80, 86-87, 183, 220

Hardware analysis. See Methodology, hardware analysis
History, 7, 21, 49, 58, 63, 79-80, 90-91, 100, 202
  Czarist, 80-81, 90, 223
  Great Patriotic War, 76, 79-80, 84-91, 97, 99, 179, 186, 234. See also History, World War II
  inter-war years, 82-86, 90
  post-war era, 87, 88-89, 90, 204
  World War I, 81-82, 97, 187, 189
  World War II, 63, 87-88, 91, 97, 187, 189-190. See also History, Great Patriotic War

ICBM (intercontinental ballistic missile). See Strategic Rocket Forces
Initial period of a war. See War, initial period of a
Inter-war years. See History, inter-war years

Khrushchev, Nikita, 14, 17-18, 21, 46, 62, 69, 73-74, 88
  See also Politburo
Kosygin, Aleksey, 16, 43
  See also Politburo

Leninist principles of war, 80, 82, 90
Limited nuclear war. See War, limited nuclear

Long Range Aviation (LRA),
    27, 57, 58, 60
  See also Air Force, Soviet;
    Strategic Aviation;
    Strategic nuclear forces
LRA. See Long Range Aviation

MAD. See Mutual assured
    destruction
Malinovskiy, Rodion, 16-19,
    27, 33, 43, 46-47, 57,
    62, 64, 72, 76
  See also Minister of
    Defense
Mediterranean Sea, 46, 54,
    131(n11), 187-188, 191,
    193(n20),
Megatons (MT), 118-121,
    123-125, 128, 142-145,
    147-149, 167-169, 171
  equivalent (EMT), 119-124,
    134-142, 147-149, 154-
    155, 164-167, 169-171
Methodology, 5-8, 105-110,
    197, 231, 237
  content analysis, 5, 7-8,
    11-21, 25-26, 69, 74,
    78, 80-81, 83, 90-91,
    97, 101, 105, 153, 163,
    197-213, 233-236
  development analysis, 7-8,
    78, 97, 100, 105, 107,
    125-129, 133-146, 148-
    150, 153-160, 163-173,
    177-179, 182-192, 197-
    204, 207-209, 213
  hardware analysis, 5-8, 47,
    78, 97, 100-101, 105-
    110, 113-129, 130(n5,
    n9, n10, n11), 133-150,
    150(n1), 153-160, 163-
    173, 175-192, 197-213,
    236-237
  sensitivity analysis, 7,
    108, 134, 150(n1), 163-
    173, 197, 203-204, 236-
    237

Military art, 63
Military doctrine, 7, 18,
    70-73, 84, 88-89,
    93(n8), 98-101, 209,
    211, 215-222, 224, 226,
    229, 234-236
Military-economic potential,
    31-36, 39(n12), 41-43,
    45, 47, 48-49, 53, 87-
    88, 91, 100, 198, 201,
    207
Military strategy, 4, 7, 18,
    29, 36, 41, 59, 63, 65,
    76-79, 84, 86-88, 90-
    91, 94(n16), 101, 107-
    108, 188, 191, 199-213,
    222-236
Mine warfare, 61-62, 187, 192,
    211, 226
Minister of Defense (MOD), 5,
    14-16, 18, 20-21, 26,
    28, 36, 43, 54, 58, 61,
    74, 78, 84, 92, 233,
    236
  See also Grechko, Andrey;
    Malinovskiy, Rodion;
    Sokolov, Sergey;
    Ustinov, Dmitry
Missiles. See Anti-ballistic
    missiles; sea launched
    cruise missiles;
    Strategic Rocket
    Forces; Submarne
    launched ballistic
    missiles
Mobilization. See Scenarios,
    mobilization
MOD. See Minister of Defense
MT. See Megatons
Mutual assured detruction
    (MAD), 7, 212-213, 217-
    218, 226, 228-229, 235
  See also Assured destruc-
    tion

NATO. See North Atlantic
    Treaty Organization

Naval art, 18, 31, 74-79
Naval Aviation, Soviet (SNA), 18, 33, 35, 41-42, 44-45, 48-49, 54, 58, 60-61, 64, 84-85, 86-88, 173, 175-187, 189-192, 207, 209-211
Naval diplomacy, 7, 18, 72, 74, 172, 180, 188, 202, 208, 216, 218-219, 224, 228, 230, 236
Naval forces, stratetgic. See Strategic forces, naval
Naval operational art. See Naval art
Naval strategy. See Military strategy
Navy roles, Western theories. See Role of Soviet Navy, Western theories
North Atlantic Treaty Organization (NATO), 54, 56, 70, 75, 101, 107, 185, 187-188, 190-191, 205, 216, 218, 223-226, 230, 232, 234
Northern Fleet, Soviet. See Arctic Ocean; Atlantic Ocean
North Sea, 46, 187
Norwegian Sea. See Bastions
Nuclear forces. See Strategic nuclear forces
Nuclear reserve. See Reserve, strategic nuclear
Nuclear War. See War; War, limited nuclear
Nuclear Weapons, 34, 49, 57, 62, 75, 78-79, 88-89, 99-101, 109, 159, 183-184, 190, 198, 206, 211, 223, 227

Ogarkov, Nikolay, 36-37(n3), 71, 73, 76, 91, 93(n8), 174(n5)

Operational art, naval. See Naval art
Outcome of a war. See War, outcome of a

Pacific Fleet, Soviet. See Pacific Ocean
Pacific Ocean, 49, 54, 88, 126, 129, 130(n10, n11), 133, 135, 137-138, 140-141, 153-154, 163-164, 170-173, 178, 182, 185-186, 189-191, 199-200, 209-213, 220-221, 224-226, 229-233
Politburo, 14, 16, 20-21, 28-29, 43, 54, 58, 61, 74, 92, 198, 233, 236. See also Andropov, Yuri; Brezhnev, Leonid; Gorbachev, Mikhail; Khrushchev, Nikita; Kosygin, Aleksey
Post-war era. See History, post-war era

Reserve, strategic nuclear, 55, 69, 74, 82-83, 90, 94(n12), 99, 143, 153-158, 164, 169, 175, 201, 203, 207, 210, 212, 217, 227, 232
See also Bastions; Withholding
Roles of Soviet Navy, Western theories, 3-4, 6, 55, 69, 153-154, 156-157
Russia. See History, Czarist

SALT I Interim Agreement, 113-115, 218, 229, 237
See also Arms control
Scenarios
 bolt from the blue, 107, 133-136, 139, 143-145, 148-149, 164-165, 167-171, 216, 231

mobilization, 136–139,
142–144, 148–149, 163,
165, 169–171, 177–179,
182, 185, 189
surge, 139–144, 165–166,
168–171, 177–178, 182,
185
Sea launched cruise missiles
(SLCM), 42, 45, 50(n2),
54–55, 59, 61–62, 66,
67(n8), 92, 97, 158,
188, 192, 198, 211,
225–226, 232–233,
235
See also Submarines,
cruise missile
Sea lines of communication
(SLOC), 42–43, 48–49,
50, 51(n11), 53, 60–61,
63, 66, 81–82, 86–88,
91, 100–101, 108, 184,
186, 188–192, 201, 208,
226, 231–232, 234, 236
Sea, nuclear war at. See
War, limited nuclear
Sea of Japan, 49, 128,
130(n7)
Sea of Okhotsk. See
Bastions
Sensitivity analysis. See
Methodology, sensitivity
analysis
SLBM. See Submarine launched
ballistic missiles
SLCM. See Sea launched
cruise missiles
SLOC. See Sea lines of communication
SNA. See Naval Aviation,
Soviet
Sokolov, Sergey, 235
See also Minister of
Defense
Sokolovsky, Vasily, 27–29,
47–48, 54, 57–58, 62
SRF. See Strategic Rocket
Forces

SSB (conventional powered
ballistic missile
submarine). See
Submarines, ballistic
missile
SSBN (nuclear powered ballistic missile submarine).
See Submarines, ballistic
missile
SSG (conventional powered
cruise missile submarine).
See Submarines, cruise
missile
SSGN (nuclear powered cruise
missile submarine).
See Submarines, cruise
missile
Stability, strategic, 212,
230, 232
Strategic Arms Limitation
Talks (SALT). See SALT
I Interim Agreement
Strategic Aviation, 58, 60,
148, 165–166, 169–170,
173(n3), 198, 233
See also Air Force, Soviet;
Long Range Aviation;
Strategic nuclear
forces
Strategic forces, naval, 30,
41, 73, 198, 212,
227–228
See also Strategic nuclear
forces
Strategic goals, 4, 25–26,
32–34, 41, 46, 49, 53,
57, 100, 198, 210,
207.
See also Strategic missions/operations; War,
decisiveness in; War,
outcome of; War,
victory
Strategic missions/operations,
4, 25–26, 32–35, 41–42,
48, 54, 57, 65, 73, 77,
86, 101, 163, 191, 198,

207, 223-224, 226, 228
  See also Strategic goals
Strategic nuclear forces,
  4-5 32, 36, 56, 98,
  107, 109, 113, 146,
  155, 170, 172, 197-198
  dyad, 27-28, 37(n3), 72
  triad, 27-30, 37(n3, n6),
    44, 47, 57, 60, 197-
    198, 233-234
  See also Long Range
    Aviation; Strategic
    Aviation; Strategic
    Rocket Forces; Sub-
    marines, ballistic
    missile
Strategic reserve, nuclear.
  See Reserve, strategic
  nuclear
Strategic Rocket Forces (SRF),
  27-29, 37(n6), 38(n9),
  43-44, 46-47, 58-59, 66,
  72, 76, 89, 99-100, 123,
  143, 145-146, 148, 154,
  165-166, 169-170, 174(n4,
  n5), 190, 198, 200-205,
  209-211, 220, 224-225,
  229, 233
  See also Strategic nuclear
    forces
"Strategic", Soviet view of,
  4, 11, 33, 56, 154, 198,
  207, 235
Strategic stability. See
  Stability, strategic
Strategy, military. See
  Military Strategy
Strike, concept of, 32-35,
  46, 50, 53, 57, 61,
  66, 101, 107
Submarine launched
  ballistic missiles, 21,
  33, 35, 42, 44-48, 50,
  50(n2), 54, 58-59, 62-63,
  65-66, 67(n8, n12), 72,
  74-75, 78, 92, 99-100,
  114-128, 130(n4), 133-
  150, 150(n1), 154-159,
  164-172, 173(n2, n3, n4),
  174(n6), 185, 191-192,
  197-205, 210, 221, 225,
  227, 229
  See also Submarines, bal-
    listic missile
Submarines, 19, 33, 35, 43-44,
  48-49, 54, 56-59, 61-64,
  84, 87, 89, 97, 99-100,
  160, 175-187, 189-192,
  209-211, 220, 226-227,
  234
  ballistic missile (SSB/SSBN),
    13, 27-29, 31-33, 36,
    38(n7), 41, 43, 45-46,
    55-59, 63-64, 72-75, 77,
    85, 91-92, 97, 99, 107,
    113-115, 118, 125-129,
    130(n5, n6, n7, n10,
    n11), 133-150, 153-160,
    163-173, 173(n4), 175,
    179, 182-183, 185-186,
    188-189, 193(n15,
    n16), 197-205, 207-210,
    212, 217-221, 224-227,
    229-230, 232. See also
    Strategic nuclear forces;
    Submarine launched
    ballistic missiles
  cruise missile (SSG/SSGN),
    33, 35, 41, 45, 157-158,
    176-179, 181, 188, 211,
    226. See also Sea
    launched cruise missiles
Surface ships, 18, 33, 42, 45,
  48-49, 56, 60-63, 66, 85,
  87-89, 101, 159, 175-188,
  207-209, 219, 230, 235
  See also Aircraft carriers;
    amphibious warfare
Surge. See Scenarios, surge

Tactics, 18, 63, 75, 78-80,
  90-91, 99, 101, 167,
  227, 234

Targeting, 18, 27, 31-35, 41-47, 49-50, 58, 62-63, 69, 78, 88-89, 92(n1), 99-101, 108, 118-125, 127-128, 129(n4), 134, 136, 142-150, 150(n7), 151(n8), 153-154, 157, 163-172, 199-205, 209-212, 220, 224-225, 236
Threats to the USSR, 18, 35-36, 54-57, 64-65, 73, 79, 92, 208, 233
Translations, 12, 15-17, 235-236
Triad. See Strategic nuclear forces, triad

United Kingdom, 54, 88, 185, 193(n16)
Ustinov, Dmitry, 14, 16, 56, 71, 76, 98, 101, 161(n1), 234
See also Minister of Defense

Victory in war. See War, victory

War, 4, 8, 11, 13-14, 17, 25-26, 29, 31, 36, 57, 69-71, 73-74, 75-78, 80, 90-91, 101, 107, 163, 175, 184, 189-192, 197-213, 215-218, 223-228, 232, 234-236. See also Armed conflict
  conventional, 5-9, 69-71, 73, 75, 98, 100-101, 184, 189-190, 205, 209-210, 217-219, 223-224, 226, 229, 232, 234
  course of, 25, 28, 30-32, 34-35, 37-38(n7), 77, 81, 86
  decisiveness in, 27-29, 37(n3, n6) 38(n7), 47, 70, 71. See also Strategic goals; War, out-

  comes of; War, victory
  initial period of a, 71, 86-87, 91, 99, 184, 191, 199, 216, 232, 235
  Leninist principles of. See Leninist principles of war
  limited nuclear, 55, 69-71, 73-75, 79, 89, 98, 101, 184, 190-191, 205-207, 209-210, 216, 230, 234
  limited nuclear at sea. See War, limited nuclear
  nuclear. See War; War, limited nuclear
  outcome of, 8, 25, 27-32, 34-35, 37(n3, n6), 41, 46-50, 53, 80, 81, 86-87, 89, 99, 101, 163, 198, 201-202, 205, 211, 215-217. See also Strategic goals; War, decisiveness in; War, victory
  victory, 17, 25-26, 28-29, 80, 83, 86, 98-99, 155, 201, 203, 205, 211, 215-216. See also Strategic goals; War, decisiveness in; War, outcome of

Withholding, 58, 69, 73-75, 90, 98-99, 136, 138-140, 149, 153-156, 163, 175, 201, 207, 210, 212. See also Bastions; Reserve, strategic nuclear
World War I. See History, World War I
World War II. See History, World War II